Frontispiece: The rococo as applied to the davenport desk. See Colour Plate 4, page 23.

Victorian and Edwardian Furniture

PRICE GUIDE AND
REASONS FOR VALUES

John Andrews

ANTIQUE COLLECTORS' CLUB

British Library Cataloguing-in-Publication Data
A catalogue record for this book is
available from the British Library

Printed in England on Consort Royal Supreme Matt from Donside Mills, Aberdeen, by
the Antique Collectors' Club Ltd., 5 Church Street, Woodbridge, Suffolk IP12 1DS

THE
ANTIQUE COLLECTORS' CLUB

The Antique Collectors' Club was formed in 1966 and now has a five figure membership spread throughout the world. It publishes the only independently run monthly antiques magazine *Antique Collecting* which caters for those collectors who are interested in widening their knowledge of antiques, both by greater awareness of quality and by discussion of the factors which influence the price that is likely to be asked. The Antique Collectors' Club pioneered the provision of information on prices for collectors and the magazine still leads in the provision of detailed articles on a variety of subjects.

It was in response to enormous demand for information on 'what to pay' that the price guide series was introduced in 1968 with the first edition of *The Price Guide to Antique Furniture* (completely revised, 1978 and 1989), and a book which broke new ground by illustrating the more common types of antique furniture, the sort that collectors could buy in shops and at auctions rather than the rare museum pieces which had previously been used (and still to a large extend are used) to make up the limited amount of illustrations in books published by commercial publishers. Many other price guides have followed, all copiously illustrated, and greatly appreciated by collectors for the valuable information they contain, quite apart from prices. The Antique Collectors' Club also publishes other books on antiques, including horology and art reference works, and a full book list is available.

Club membership, which is open to all collectors, costs little. Members receive free of charge *Antique Collecting*, the Club's magazine (published ten times a year), which contains well-illustrated articles dealing with the practical aspects of collecting not normally dealt with by magazines. Prices, features of value, investment potential, fakes and forgeries are all given prominence in the magazine.

Among other facilities available to members are private buying and selling facilities, the longest list of 'For Sales' of any antiques magazine, an annual ceramics conference and the opportunity to meet other collectors at their local antique collectors' clubs. There are over eighty in Britain and more than a dozen overseas. Members may also buy the Club's publications at special pre-publication prices.

As its motto implies, the Club is an amateur organisation designed to help collectors get the most out of their hobby: it is informal and friendly and gives enormous enjoyment to all concerned.

For Collectors – By Collectors – About Collecting

The Antique Collectors' Club, 5 Church Street, Woodbridge, Suffolk

PRICE REVISION LISTS

The usefulness of a book containing prices rapidly diminishes as market values change.

In order to keep the prices in this book updated, a price revision list will be issued annually. This will record the major price changes in the values of the items covered under the various headings in the book.

To ensure you receive the price revision list complete the pro forma invoice inserted in this book and send it to the address below:

Antique Collectors' Club
5 Church Street, Woodbridge, Suffolk, IP12 1DS

CONTENTS

ACKNOWLEDGEMENTS

In producing a new volume such as this, I have leant on many newly-recruited sources of assistance in addition to the original stalwarts of the 1980 edition. My grateful thanks go to:

My wife Geraldine, my son Sam, Sallie Scott, Christopher Payne of Sotheby's London, Samantha Georgeson of Sotheby's Sussex, Christie's South Kensington, Christie's Nine Elms, Pauline Agius, Michael Whiteway, Tom Crispin, John Steel, Diana Steel, Primrose Elliott, Cherry Lewis, Dianne Whinney, Sandra Pond, Susan Wilson, Peter Ling, David Smith of Smith and Smith Designs, Driffield, Richard Kimbell of Market Harborough, John and Susan Bonner, Peter Greenhalf, and many antique dealers and enthusiasts who have helped generously and unstintingly.

PHOTOGRAPHIC ACKNOWLEDGEMENTS

The photographs which appear in this book are derived from a large number of sources over a long period. I should particularly like to thank the following auctioneers, dealers and private individuals who allowed photographs to be used or specially taken for use in this book:

The Antique Furniture Warehouse, Woodbridge
Bonhams, London
John and Susan Bonner, Hastings
Christie's Nine Elms, London
Christie's, South Kensington, London
Jeremy Cooper, London
Tom Crispin, Chesfield
The Fine Art Society, London
Peter Greenhalf, Rye
The High Wycombe Chair Museum
Richard Kimbell, Market Harborough
Ann Lingard, Rye
The Old Mint House, Pevensey
John Phelps of Phelps Ltd., Twickenham
The Pine Mine, London
Alan Shead, Staplehurst
Silvester's of Warwick
Smith and Smith Designs, Driffield
Sotheby's South Kensington, London
Sotheby's Sussex, Billingshurst
The Victoria and Albert Museum, London
Michael Whiteway, London

I am particularly grateful to Sotheby's in London and Sussex for the use of colour transparencies taken from their sales catalogues over the last two or three years.

If by accident I have included photographs without having made proper acknowledgement I apologise most sincerely; some labels are missing or may have become detached from the back of the photographs.

PREFACE

It was in 1968 that the *Price Guide to Antique Furniture* was first published. At that time it was an innovation, greeted sceptically in some quarters, but soon well established and imitated. The *Price Guide to Victorian Furniture* followed, as a separate publication, in 1973, for while the antique furniture publication had some Victorian furniture in it, the post-1837 period was already demanding specific consideration. A new edition of the Victorian furniture book, entitled *The Price Guide to Victorian, Edwardian and 1920s Furniture,* was produced in 1980 and, at the time, caused considerable and widespread comment. It is hard to remember that so short a time ago it was considered debatable whether the great furniture designers and craftsmen of the period deserved the praise or recognition they were awarded in the 1980 book. Now, it is almost universally accepted. The Victorian and Edwardian periods have become a major part of the antique dealer's repertoire.

In producing this new book, which deals exclusively with Victorian and Edwardian furniture, the material from the previous editions has been incorporated in improved form and, to enrich and clarify the range of styles, much additional furniture appears. The book has nearly double the number of illustrations of its predecessor. Colour has been added. The need to replace the earlier volumes has arisen from the greater importance which the period has now assumed in the collecting world and from the availability of so much more information and illustrations which were not accessible before. As a companion volume to *British Antique Furniture: Price Guide and Reasons for Values* (the 1989 edition of the original *Price Guide to Antique Furniture*), this new book stands very much on its own, as a quite separate work with an appeal which may be even wider than its distinguished fellow-guide to mainly earlier pieces. The decision to remove the 1920s furniture from this book is due to the need to deal with the 20th century quite separately; while there is a certain integration between the Victorian and Edwardian periods — it will soon become apparent to the reader that much so-called 'Edwardian' furniture is in fact Victorian — the post-1900 era now needs a volume of its own, and will get one soon.

Collectors of all periods of antique furniture now recognise the fine quality and original concept of the best of the Victorian and Edwardian pieces. To replicate such pieces would be very expensive and the craftsmen available but scarcely. It is a period of great variety, highly rewarding to study, and exciting to pursue, for there is still much to discover. For over twenty years in these books the point has been laboured that, although information is invaluable, nothing can replace the training of the eye by seeing furniture, like sculpture, in real form and, preferably, by handling it. Catalogue descriptions and flattering photographs are not enough. To acquire a sound knowledge of Victorian and Edwardian furniture is a serious undertaking which needs involvement with it, living with it, and the risk of disappointment. It is, however, a study well worth pursuing. I hope these pages will not only assist in making a start but will prove a rich source of reference material and clarification for those enthusiasts already long familiar with the pleasures of collecting period furniture.

John Andrews

PRICES -
<u>THE LAST TWENTY YEARS</u>

Although the first, specialised *Price Guide to Victorian Furniture* was not published until 1973, our records for antique and Victorian furniture prices go back five years further, to 1968 when the first *Price Guide to Antique Furniture* was published. This was entirely new material in those days. It was some time afterwards that Lyle, followed by Millers, produced their mass-market handbooks based, then, on a single stated price, often derived from auctions, which gave rise to great scepticism about the validity of price-related publications. From the start the Antique Collectors' Club, however, gained the confidence of those sceptics and has retained it by using a retail price range into which pieces would mostly fall, usually defining the reasons why a given piece would tend to be at one end of the scale or another. Great care has always been taken to explain points of value which, in frequent cases, may be due to subjective opinion but which nevertheless are mostly the same points which the antique furniture trade, including the auctioneers, use to make their value judgements. Each piece is also put into the context of its period and related to the development of styles and qualities which influence both collectors and investors. Good examples, where possible, are compared with those of lesser quality. The ACC guides are thus much more explanatory and informative than any single-piece, single-price guide could ever be.

Every year since their publication the ACC has produced a price revision list for its two famous furniture guides. This has led to a unique record of price movements. When in 1988 we published the first-ever twenty-year assessment of antique furniture prices, calculating detailed indices of seven separate categories based on these revision lists, considerable publicity came from the fact that antique furniture had proved a better investment than houses in the South-East of England over the same period, because the housing boom was then nearing its height. Chart 1 illustrates this feature. An 'average' piece of antique furniture had increased by over 100 per cent per year on its original investment and had proved much more than a hedge against inflation. There is of course no such thing as an 'average' piece of furniture any more than there is an 'average' share or house or investment trust, but nearly all the different categories of furniture we detailed, including Victorian furniture, had done extremely well.

The way in which furniture prices behaved was encouraging but seemed slightly erratic. We had had economic downturns in 1971, 1975 and 1980/81 which appeared to affect the upward movement of prices. In 1981 there was a fall in certain categories. It seemed then — and it still does — that the index was more influenced by confidence or by general optimism than by specific market demands, although fashion came into consideration when certain styles were examined. We published graphs in the new edition of *British Antique Furniture* of 1988, showing how furniture price indices followed a readily available public statistic, the CBI Business Confidence survey. At the current time of publication — late 1992 — this confidence is again low and the indices have been likewise affected. Antique, Victorian and Edwardian furniture, however, is not bought as a short-term investment by most enthusiasts or even simple furnishers. It is liked, valued and even loved as an emotional, stylistic, nostalgic and egocentric expression of connoisseurship, in which the skills of craftsmen and the lines of designers are appreciated in themselves, quite apart from scarcity and market values. Other than dealers and auctioneers, few people buy and sell their furniture readily week on week, month on month, or even year on year. Very often, however, they buy when changing houses and a slowdown is a reflection of the housing market as much as other influences on confidence. The ACC has always advised a long-term view of collecting and this is particularly advisable in the case of furniture.

The following tables are therefore based on five-year periods up to 1988 for ease of reading and as longer-term indications. After 1988, i.e. for the last five years, they are detailed for each individual year. The two tables are different because, as mentioned above, for the first table we are lucky to have records for the Early Victorian period back to 1968 (from *British Antique Furniture*). The second table, which is a new one, covers a representative range of high quality and plain furniture of the later Victorian and Edwardian period taken from the first *Price Guide to Victorian Furniture* of 1973 and continued from the *Price Guide to Victorian, Edwardian and 1920s Furniture* first published in 1980. The pieces are representative ones for which in one or two cases the actual illustration was changed between editions, but they are for all practical purposes the same representative items.

What is interesting is that over the period from 1973 the two tables provide very close parallels in terms of the movement of indices. Taking the first table and using its index figure of 245 in 1973 as a base equal to 100, the following comparison can be made:

Year	Table 1 Early Victorian	Table 2 Victorian and Edwardian	All antique furniture
1973	100	100	100
1978	280	238	267
1983	366	337	434
1988	775	886	932
1989	916	993	1051
1990	1033	1102	1125
1991	1117	1201	1132
1992	1120	1241	1083

Indices based on 1973 = 100

From the above table it can be seen that the Victorian and Edwardian periods, early and late, have closely correlated with each other and held up well compared with antique furniture as a whole, where the index dropped in 1992 mainly due to falls in the Oak, Walnut, Country and Late Mahogany sectors of the seven separate categories from which the index is taken. Indeed, Victorian furniture has not only caught up with the general antique furniture index but has actually passed it, with the later Victorian and Edwardian table gaining the most. In a sense, this is not surprising; at a time when money is tight, collectors turn to lower-priced items, pushing up demand. In some cases the pieces have picked up from a very low level and this affects their index very strongly. Fashion is also an important factor; the boom in 'William IV' furniture of the last five years has affected the Early Victorian sector and the current strength of the 'Edwardian Sheraton' style has affected the later period.

The economic depressions of 1975, 1980/81 and 1991/92 have affected the rise in the index of antique and Victorian furniture from 1973 quite adversely in comparison with a scale from 1968 (see Chart 1). Between 1968 and 1988, for instance, the Victorian index rose from 100 to 1898. By 1992 it had reached 2745 despite the vicissitudes of the last few years and low percentage gains which can be seen in the 1983 and 1991/92 columns. Thus the Victorian furniture collector starting in 1968 would have fared much better over his or her first twenty years (and extremely well over twenty-five years) than the collector starting in 1973, whose index would have risen to only 1120 or 1241 in the same length of time. Much the same applies to an 'antique' furniture collector starting in 1968, whose index rose to 2172 as compared with an enthusiast who started in 1973, from when the index has risen to a mere 1083 in twenty years.

To obtain an increase of eleven times in the value of a collection made over the last twenty years is not bad going, especially when that increase has occurred during times which include two severe economic depressions. An average gain of over 50 per cent per year more than compensates for inflation and compares well with housing and Stock Exchange. Chart 1 graphically illustrates these comparisons; over the whole period both the general ACC antique furniture index and the particular Victorian one have outperformed the FT 500 Index and house prices by a substantial margin. Were the 'Victorian and Edwardian' index from Table 2 to be available over the same period it would exceed these performances.

It is undeniable that trading levels have fallen dramatically in the last three years and that therefore the prices, which appear to have held up well considering the depression, relate to a much smaller volume of business, but the same is undoubtedly true of house prices, which would have to drop much further also were the same unit levels of trading as the boom years to be achieved.

The Victorian and Edwardian eras have long been ones with considerable potential and much furniture from the period still has it, even though it may be stylistically confusing for the collector. It is hoped that the following two illustrated tables will help to put the potential in perspective whilst the succeeding pages of this book will clarify much of the stylistic confusion.

CHART 1
COMPARISON OF DIFFERENT FORMS OF INVESTMENT

KEY

——— Antique Furniture Prices based on ACC Index.

– – – Victorian Furniture Prices based on ACC Index.

— — House prices in the South East (figures supplied by the Council of Mortgage Lenders).

.... F.T. 500 Share Index.

➤ Highest point of F.T. Index after adjustment for cumulative 4% dividend.

TABLE 1 Victorian (Mainly Early) from *British Antique Furniture* (starts 1968)

		1968	1973	1978	1983	1988	1989	1990	1991	1992
VICTORIAN										
Dining Chair	£	70	135	420	550	900	900	900	1,100	1,100
(No. 193)	**Index**	100	193	600	786	1,286	1,286	1,286	1,570	1,570
Dining Chair	£	105	300	600	900	1,600	1,750	2,100	2,100	2,100
(No. 197)	**Index**	100	286	571	857	1,524	1,667	2,000	2,000	2,000
Button Back Chair	£	35	105	325	363	1,200	1,250	1,450	1,450	1,450
(No. 293)	**Index**	100	300	929	1,037	3,429	3,571	4,142	4,142	4,142
Settee	£	80	200	550	650	1,200	1,500	1,600	1,600	1,600
(No. 612)	**Index**	100	250	688	813	1,500	1,875	2,000	2,000	2,000
Canterbury	£	35	85	213	350	700	850	950	1,250	1,250
(No. 102)	**Index**	100	243	603	1,000	2,000	2,429	2,714	3,571	3,571
Wellington Chest	£	35	125	500	575	1,050	1,200	1,200	1,200	1,200
(No. 397)	**Index**	100	357	1,429	1,643	3,000	3,429	3,429	3,429	3,429
Davenport Desk	£	55	140	725	600	1,600	1,750	2,000	2,000	2,000
(No. 455)	**Index**	100	255	1,318	1,091	2,909	3,182	3,636	3,636	3,636
Desk	£	110	275	575	1,250	2,750	4,000	5,000	5,750	5,750
(No. 462)	**Index**	100	250	523	1,136	2,500	3,636	4,545	5,227	5,227
Chiffonier	£	28	85	200	300	500	700	700	700	750
(No. 403)	**Index**	100	304	714	1,071	1,786	2,500	2,500	2,500	2,678
Work Table	£	50	60	140	125	350	350	350	425	425
(No. 925)	**Index**	100	120	280	250	700	700	700	850	850
Whatnot	£	55	125	250	350	800	800	800	900	900
(No. 1001)	**Index**	100	227	455	636	1,455	1,455	1,455	1,636	1,636
Teapoy	£	35	60	250	200	500	500	500	500	500
(No. 970)	**Index**	100	171	714	571	1,429	1,429	1,429	1,429	1,429
TOTAL VICTORIAN	£	693	1,695	4,748	6,213	13,150	15,550	17,550	18,975	19,025
Group Index	**Index**	100	246	736	908	1,960	2,263	2,486	2,665	2,680
Group Ave. Value (12 items)	£	57.75	141.3	395.7	517.8	1095.8	1,296	1,462	1,581	1,585
VICTORIAN INDEX		100	245	685	897	1,898	2,244	2,532	2,738	2,745
Victorian % change			145%	180%	31%	111%	18%	13%	11%	1%

The numbers in brackets refer to illustrations in *British Antique Furniture*

(No.193)

(No.197)

(No.293)

(No.925)

(No.970)

(No.612)

(No.102)

(No.397)

(No.455)

(No.462)

(No.403)

(No.1001)

15

(No.2)

(No.86)

TABLE 2 Victorian and Edwardian (starts 1973)

		1973	1978	1983	1988	1989	1990	1991	1992
VICTORIAN AND EDWARDIAN									
Bookcase 1840-1880	£	70	300	400	1,250	1,700	1,875	1,875	2,050
(No. 2)	Index	100	428	571	1,786	2,428	2,678	2,678	2,928
Bureau — Cylinder	£	100	375	700	2,125	2,500	3,000	3,250	3,250
(No. 86)	Index	100	375	700	2,125	2,500	3,000	3,250	3,250
Bureau Bookcase	£	300	575	800	2,500	3,000	3,250	3,750	4,250
(No. 51)	Index	100	191	266	833	1,000	1,083	1,250	1,416
Chair — Inlaid Arm	£	70	375	312	550	725	850	1,050	1,250
(No.403)	Index	100	535	445	786	1,036	1,214	1,500	1,786
Chair — Smoker's Bow	£	10	80	200	210	250	287	350	350
(No. 267)	Index	100	800	2,000	2,100	2,500	2,870	3,500	3,500
Cabinet — Credenza	£	550	1,050	1,400	3,000	3,000	3,250	3,500	3,500
(No.142)	Index	100	191	254	545	545	591	636	636
Sideboard — Art Nouveau	£	14	75	215	375	500	850	850	850
(No. 806)	Index	100	535	1,536	2,678	3,571	6,071	6,071	6,071
Table — Carlton House 1890	£	800	1,300	1,875	6,250	6,250	6,250	6,250	6,250
(No. 1015)	Index	100	162	234	781	781	781	781	781
Table — Centre, Rococo	£	215	600	900	1,750	2,500	2,875	3,500	3,500
(No. 912)	Index	100	279	418	814	1,163	1,337	1,628	1,628
Table — Dressing	£	87	275	400	1,000	1,000	1,450	1,750	1,750
(No. 938)	Index	100	314	457	1,143	1,143	1,657	2,000	2,000
Table — Sutherland, Walnut	£	30	200	350	825	825	825	900	900
(No. 975)	Index	100	666	1,166	2,750	2,750	2,750	3,000	3,000
Table — Work/Sewing, Walnut	£	50	250	185	500	550	550	550	600
(No. 999)	Index	100	500	370	1,000	1,100	1,100	1,100	1,200
TOTAL	£	2,296	5,455	7,737	20,335	22,800	25,312	27,575	28,500
Group Index	Index	100	414	701	1,445	1,709	2,094	2,283	2,349
Group Average Value (12 items)	£	191	455	645	1,695	1,900	2,109	2,298	2,375
VIC. AND EDW. INDEX		100	238	337	886	993	1,102	1,201	1,241
Vic. and Edw. % change			138%	42%	163%	11%	11%	9%	3%

The numbers in brackets refer to illustrations in this book

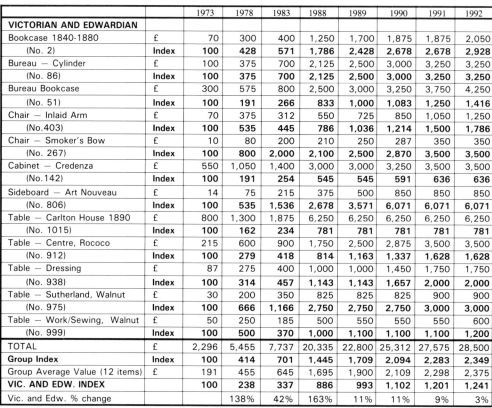

(No.142)

(No.806)

(No.267)

(No.938)

(No.51)

(No.1015)

(No.912)

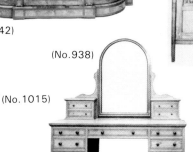

(No.999)

(No.403)

(No.975)

BRITISH FURNITURE STYLES
1837-1911

At the time of the accession to the throne of Queen Victoria in 1837 the design of interior furnishings, as much as that of exterior architecture, was in a state of considerable turmoil. The reign of the Hanovers from the early 18th century onwards had come to an end with the contempt of the British people. It is hard, now, to imagine British monarchs being pelted with stones and rubbish in the streets of London, or loudly jeered at theatre attendances, but the always robust character of the Kings' and the Prince Regent's subjects frequently made itself evident in such demonstrations. It was Victoria, in the first decade of her long reign, who calmed the irritated nerves of the people with her combination of pious domestic morality and obstinate political singlemindedness. The results, translated into effects on style, are very interesting: from a turbulent, reactionary rejection of the previous century the nation reverted, over a period of thirty years, to a more restrained, traditional taste enlivened by occasional bursts of natural, exuberant vulgarity based on wealth or manufacturing capability. This change in attitude and its interpretation into the tastes of an increasing population, which had to reconcile the stifling conformity of its monarch's example with its own natural iconoclasm, gives the furniture of the period its varied and versatile character as well as its confusing stylistic range. The Victorians were careless with their historical definitions and eclectic in the composition of their designs. So-called purists were far from pure; tradition conflicted with reform; mass-production threatened to swamp craftsmanship. It was the first time that furniture of quality was not just made to order for a particular patron. Large retail stores dictated what their stock should be and what their customers probably wanted; to order a special piece was highly expensive and was the privilege of the rich. In this situation the enormous number of furniture-making establishments worked under the thumb of these large furniture stores, who tried to follow and to assess the demand for pieces of a particular style or fashion.

In this section of the book the major movements are briefly summarised and illustrated. Separate compartmentalism of this kind is misleading because there was considerable overlap between some movements and in much decoration. However, a basic definition is intended to assist with identification and to explain brief descriptions in the captions throughout the book. The styles follow a more or less chronological sequence to provide an idea of dating but it will be seen that some styles persisted throughout the whole era. The chart below may help to clarify the style chronology.

	1840	1850	1860	1870	1880	1890	1900	1910
Sub-Classical								
Elizabethan/Medieval								
Victorian Rococo								
Gothic & Reformed Gothic								
Aesthetic								
Anglo-Japanese								
Arts & Crafts								
Art Nouveau								
'Queen Anne'								
Georgian Revival								
Edwardian Sheraton								

SUB-CLASSICAL MAHOGANY 1830-1850

At the accession of Queen Victoria the heavy Sub-Classicism of the Regency and William IV period did not suddenly vanish like water at the closing of a tap. It was a stylistic basis which served many furniture producers for a considerable time. The pattern books published from 1800 onwards, including those of Ackermann, Thomas Hope and George Smith, culminating with Loudon's *Encyclopedia of Cottage, Farm and Villa Architecture and Furniture* in 1833, provided a neo-classical, French, Greek, Egyptian and Rustic set of examples which pervaded much general furniture production. The Gothic and Medieval (Elizabethan) tastes (dealt with separately), which also coincided with this Sub-Classical taste, were perhaps a reaction to its dully ponderous approach, which had a particular emphasis on the Grecian of Thomas Hope with occasional Gothic arching in the panels or glazing of doors.

This design of sofa — extolled by Loudon in a convertible bed form — leans heavily on French Empire neo-classicism for its origins but is popularly associated with William IV's reign, which ended in 1837. Designers' and manufacturers' catalogues show it unchanged up to 1850.

A bookcase in the 'Grecian' style from Loudon's 1833 Encyclopedia. The rather heavy severity of this style employed an almost universal curled-leaf carving, added to emphasise mouldings and pediments, which is the usual decoration. In this case a scrolled pediment above the central section helps what would otherwise be a gravely ponderous piece.

A 'Loudon' sub-classical form in the flesh. This secretaire bookcase is of 'Grecian' characteristics with the usual applied scroll carvings like brackets under projections but not on the plain pedimented base.

The use of a gadrooned obelisk-shaped panel, particularly on sideboards, can be seen in Ackermann's Repository of Arts in 1822 and clearly goes back to Classical Greece. In fact catalogues of 1850 still show it and this form of sideboard of late Regency or William IV date is emulated by early Victorian examples.

Colour Plate 1. An 'Elizabethan' walnut cabinet by Seddon of London c.1840 which includes applied diamond-lozenge and strapwork decoration typical of the style which can be found in Whitaker (q.v.), especially in the drawer-knob embellishments. The upper, fall-front drawers enclose sliding trays whereas the lower drawer is a straightforward long one. The piece is only 6ft.7ins. (200cm) high, 4ft.6ins. (136cm) wide and 1ft.6½ins. (47cm) deep and was probably designed as a special display cabinet for a collection.

ELIZABETHAN (including Jacobean and Stuart) 1830-1890

One of the popular styles of the late Regency — possibly inspired by Walter Scott's novels — which continued well into the Victorian period. Scott's house, Abbotsford, enlarged after 1819, became a famous example of the Scottish Baronial style and certain pieces of furniture have acquired the Abbotsford adjective as typical of the genre.

In fact, Victorian Elizabethan furniture leans upon Tudor, Jacobean and Stuart styles. It is not averse to leaning upon a few others, either. The twist-turned, or barley-sugar column, leg, upright and stretcher is a feature of this 'Elizabethan' furniture, but not always. Sometimes cabriole legs borrowed from the rococo might also be included.

Carolean chairs of the caned type and Restoration Stuart furniture seem to have had a very popular vogue towards the end of the century, particularly the 1890s, when antique collecting and reproductions of 18th century styles also were in fashion. These Stuart chairs must have been turned out in large numbers, since there are plenty of them still in evidence, and must have gone well with the 'Jacobean' and 'early English oak' dining rooms that were by then so popular.

Three prie-dieu chairs with Berl'n woolwork coverings from Cheval & Pole Screens, Ottomans etc., *by Henry Wood, published c.1850. All three show the influence of the 'Elizabethan' style, but particularly the left two chairs with their twist-turned uprights and finials.*

A first-class example of a mixture of styles. The back of this mahogany low chair is in what the Victorians called the 'Elizabethan' manner, with twist-turned uprights — actually belonging to the Restoration (1660) rather than the Elizabethan (1558-1603) period. The legs, however, owe nothing to the style of the back and are typical early Victorian cabrioles following the Louis XV or French Rococo (misnamed Louis XIV by the Victorians) style then popular.

Another example of the Victorian 'Elizabethan' style in a rosewood chair with woolwork upholstery. The twist-turning of the back uprights is capped by the very typical turned finials of the 1850s and 1860s and there are 'C' scrolls embellishing the centre splat. The legs and stretchers are turned in a later Stuart baluster style.

An oak dining carver chair typical of the late 19th century 'Jacobean' type, harking back to the 'Elizabethan' taste of the early part of the century. Twist-turning is used more consistently but the style leans more on Restoration Stuart forms than anything else.

VICTORIAN ROCOCO 1830-1890

One of the most prolifically produced styles of the Victorian period was the rococo furniture which Victorians referred to as Louis XIV, but which was, in fact, more correctly Louis XV. It first appeared as a reaction to the rather severe sub-classical designs of the Regency and William IV periods — those Greek, Gothic, French Empire-Egyptian, Elizabethan and other rather historic styles that possibly invoked a feeling of duty to taste rather than pleasure in their beholders.

Rococo can be traced back as far as the early 1820s but it probably was in full swing in the 1840s and through the 1850s. What made it so enduringly popular was its highly decorative nature. Trade catalogues of the 1880s and even the 1890s still illustrated it, although by then its vogue was over. The later rococo furniture of the 19th century — perhaps from the 1860s onwards — tends to lose the flowing, assured lines of the earlier period. The odd cusp or point suddenly cranks a curve and there is, quite often, a dot-dash grooving to interrupt the surface. Despite the destruction of much of it, large quantities have survived. Handley-Read points out that it was frivolous and hence a decorator's style, whereas architects frowned upon it. This is perhaps one of the key points to bear in mind about the period, since architects' furniture is scarce.

The rococo, as applied to chairs, generally affected the legs and arms but in this bergère chair of the 1850s-1860s has also gone into the scrolling of the top rail. Such chairs were still made and shown in manufacturers' catalogues of the 1880s, although the style was out of date by then.

A walnut centre table of c.1860, showing how the scrolls and swerves of the rococo 'Louis XIV' style were applied to the rather decorative and exuberant mid-Victorian period.

The rococo as applied to a fire screen with needlework tapestry. Note the extensively scrolled rosewood frame and the use of the acanthus leaf in carving — a classic Victorian decoration.

An arm and a single chair in the 'Rococo' style referred to by Victorians as 'Louis XIV' showing its French character, which was more correctly Louis XV. The scrolling is strongly emphasised and the use of naturalistic carving, so deplored by purists concerned with the 'honest' use of raw materials, is a characteristic feature.

Colour Plate 2. An 'Elizabethan' oak buffet c.1840 with twist-turned column supports ending in carved dragons and chimera at the top. The central top cresting is, however, more rococo than medieval, showing how the Victorian interpretation of style was quite unrestrained in application.

Colour Plate 3. An example of the Victorian rococo in combination with colourful needlework upholstery. In this chair the French origins of the style are clearly evident; the scrolling is restrained and follows the example of its 18th century forebears in a manner reminiscent of French Hepplewhite.

Colour Plate 4. The rococo as applied to the davenport desk. This popular piece was severely square in its original Regency form, but by the 1850s had acquired supports which were no longer simulated pillars but had become scrolled and carved in the manner seen here. The use of walnut — burr or figured veneers included — was also a popular feature. The piano-top design is a later, but, to the collector, desirable variation on the normal desk slope.

Colour Plate 6. Eastlake's Hints on Household Taste also illustrated work by other designers including this oak chiffonier by the architect A.W. Blomfield (in whose office the young Thomas Hardy trained). The use of the sunflower motif was to become universal in Gothic, Aesthetic, Arts and Crafts and 'Queen Anne' movements. The hinges are made in the forms of fish, flesh and fowls.

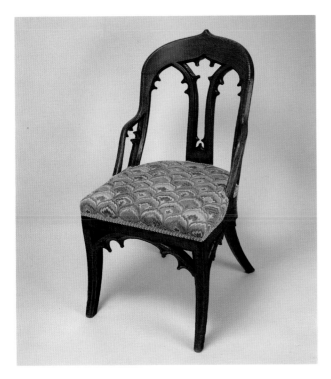

Colour Plate 5. A practical illustration of oak 'Gothic' in a chair which is a blend of Regency sabre-leg, a degree of Reform, and a pinch of Loudon in concept. 1835-1840.

GOTHIC AND THE REFORMERS — Revivalist Gothic 1860-1890

W. Burges   W. Morris & Co.   R. Norman Shaw
E. Burne-Jones   A.W.N. Pugin   B. Talbert
C.L. Eastlake   J.P. Seddon   P. Webb

A corner cupboard in the Gothic Revival manner, showing the pointed arches typical of the style. It also has carved decoration which includes the whorls, suns, 'pies', sunflowers and other motifs of the 1860s Revivalist designers.

The origins of the Gothic style are said to be Islamic, since the pointed arch is a feature of that culture. The Normans are said to have found it in Sicily and hence brought it to England where, from about the year 1200, an indigenous version was developed and used for several centuries. Chippendale used the style in the 18th century and so did the designers of the Regency period in rather decorated form. It is A.W.N. Pugin who, in 1835, published his *Gothic Furniture* and set off the reform in design away from the sub-classical sources used in the 1830s and 1840s. In all senses, he marked the watershed between the 'Gothick' used by the Regency designers, the early Victorian Gothic of the '40s and '50s, and the reformed or revivalist Gothic of the '60s and onwards, since he provided examples of all three types.

After the Great Exhibition of 1851, at which Pugin's Medieval Court caused wide discussion, Ruskin in 1853 published his *Stones of Venice* in which a chapter 'The Nature of Gothic' was a source of inspiration to the reformers. William Morris, using the designers Webb and Seddon, exhibited at the 1862 London International Exhibition, at which Norman Shaw and William Burges also showed Gothic furniture. All of them were supposedly reacting aginst the over-ornamental furniture of their time but their exhibition pieces were conceived on a rather massive scale, inflated to vastly out-of-domestic proportions. What is more, these exhibition pieces were highly decorated — the Morris cabinets were extensively painted by Morris himself, Madox Brown, Rossetti and Burne-Jones, so that in one sense they were no different from the commercial and popular pieces with which they were exhibited. Indeed, in these pieces of Morris's, in which the plain wood surface is hardly allowed to appear, it is difficult to conceive of the furniture with which one associates the company and which was subsequently made by them.

Norman Shaw's subsequent work used Aesthetic (q.v.) and Queen Anne (q.v.) inspiration. Burges continued to design furniture in the Gothic style, much of it quite elaborate, until his death in 1881. Seddon produced books of drawings of Gothic furniture but only the 1862 exhibition pieces are known of his work. Webb continued with William Morris & Co.

A Puginian type of centre table showing characteristics of the earlier type of Gothic Revival furniture — architectural in concept and decoration and superbly made. 1850-1860.

A table by Pugin in the Gothic Revival style c.1851 in which ogee curves are used extensively in the very structural base.

A much simpler table showing a version of Pugin forms but far straighter in style as might be expected from later derivations. Possibly 1860s.

A.W.N. Pugin, 1812-1852

All the early reformers or 'progressive' designers acknowledged their debt to Pugin. His theoretical version of Gothic (not the picturesque, decorative 'Gothick' of the Regency, which his father had illustrated in 1820 and which Loudon showed in 1833) was concerned with revealed construction and lack of sham decoration, a sort of solid, simple version with plain arched construction. In practice, he had designed the decorative kind as a young man for Windsor Castle and his work includes some very unreformed Gothic examples. None the less, his simpler designs were probably popular and were copied by commercial producers.

The William Morris-Seddon version of 1862 Gothic, exhibited at the London Exhibition. In oak, with panels painted by Madox Brown, Burne-Jones, Rossetti and Morris on a design of cabinet by the architect J.P. Seddon. Never intended as domestic furniture and made to make statements about design.

William Morris & Co.

As we have said earlier, Morris himself was not greatly interested in furniture — his early attempts were over heavy, structurally unsound and disastrously large — so that the firm's furniture tended to be left to the chief designers. Among these were Philip Webb, George Jack and William Lethaby, who designed furniture that was not necessarily always different from that of other good commercial producers. They often used simple traditional designs; the rush-seated Sussex chairs are an example. They made reproduction-inspired satinwood furniture in the 1890s and 1900s; they made both cheap and expensive furniture; they made green stained bedroom furniture from a jollop introduced

Colour Plate 8. A fall-front oak writing desk of c.1885 in the form of an upright piano. Although designated 'Arts and Crafts' by auctioneers, this mixed style exhibits the 'honest' plank construction inherited from Reformed Gothic and Eastlake whilst employing circular sunflower-style and foliage carving nearer to the Aesthetic Movement. Inside there are three leather-lined writing surfaces and a fitted pigeon-hole rack. Due to the size — about 5ft. (152cm) wide — and ponderous weight, this is not a very popular collector's item so far.

Colour Plate 7. An ebonised Aesthetic Movement bureau bookcase with painted panels depicting ladies in classical dress reclining on yet more spindled furniture. The pierced gallery at the top, the revealed constructional nature of the upper door panel, the turned front supports with ringed grooving and the consciously Pre-Raphaelite nature of the painted panels are all typical of Aesthetic Movement furniture.

Colour Plate 9. A plainer variant of the 'Arts and Crafts' fall-front oak writing desk above. In this case the diagonal planking serves as virtually the only decorative treatment of the surfaces apart from the ebony inlays. Such pieces have yet to find an enthusiastic following, even though the residual spirit of Reformed Gothic construction lingers on.

Colour Plate 10. A further progression of the 'Queen Anne' style was to inlay the surfaces with marquetry whilst retaining many of the other, rectilinear characteristics of this architectural style although not, in this case, a broken pediment. The square fluted columns of the lower section are, however, true to the original concept.

27

Three views of an exceptional roll-top desk by J.P. Seddon made of oak and inlaid with marquetry of various woods. Shown at the 1862 International Exhibition and rather owing something to Burges in the exuberance of the decoration (the drawer handles were ornamented with turquoise cameos, cabochon-cut malachite and ruby glass). By any standards a unique and expensive piece of furniture, like Shaw's bookcase, probably designed for his own use.

Photo: Courtesy Michael Whiteway and the Fine Art Society

by Ford Madox Brown in the 1860s. In other words, Morris & Co. were a good-quality commercial firm whose furniture is often difficult to date and who moved with the times.

William Morris & Co. are referred to again under Arts and Crafts Movement (q.v.).

John Pollard Seddon, 1827-1906

Designed furniture for Morris & Co. at the 1862 Exhibition. A roll-top desk with much decoration designed by him and made by Thomas Seddon is shown here. J.P. Seddon left several books of designs for Gothic furniture (now in the Victoria and Albert Museum). Little has been identified of his work apart from the 'King René's Honeymoon Cabinet' also shown at the 1862 Exhibition.

Philip Webb, 1831-1915

Architect, met William Morris in the office of the architect G.E. Street (1824-1881), who was a productive High Victorian Gothic enthusiast. (Norman Shaw was Street's assistant from 1859 to 1863.) Webb became one of the founder members of the William Morris firm and was responsible for early furniture design, since Morris was interested in other things. Webb designed Gothic, medieval-style oak tables, painted furniture and even leather panels and gesso decoration. He was responsible for a good deal of the William Morris & Co. furniture in the 1860s and onwards until others took over in the 1890s. None the less his designs remained in the company's catalogues until much later.

Bruce Talbert, 1838-1881

In 1867 Talbert published *Gothic Forms Applied to Furniture.* One of the objections to Victorian Gothic furniture is that it has a rather ecclesiastical flavour, redolent of vicarages and the headmaster's study — both perhaps

A characteristic oak refectory table designed by Philip Webb for Morris and Co. Note the heavy 'revealed' construction and simplicity of line to which Webb, always a purist, adhered. The type was probably designed in the 1860s but was still advertised by the firm much later.

A Gothic cabinet of the Revival period, made by Gillows & Co. possibly to a design of Talbert's (q.v.).

'Pet' sideboard by Talbert, made by Gillows in 1873 in oak, with carved creatures, foliage and a quotation in Latin of an improving nature across the back. (Arts and Crafts Movement designers became fond of doing the same quotational features on sideboards.)

A wardrobe in the Eastlake manner of the 1870s showing in simple measure the features characteristic of the genre: diagonal tongued-and-grooved planking to the doors, inlaid decoration, inset pillars, architectural mouldings and long strap hinges.

uncomfortable images for a domestic interior. In a generation or so this imagery will doubtless have disappeared, but one of the advantages of Talbert's designs at the time was that they were less ecclesiastical and a bit more domesticated. His designs were influential and he had a grasp of construction as well as an understanding of decoration, although he was rather fond of turned spindles and, again, had a tendency to enormously large scale. Pauline Agius has summarised the characteristics of the Talbertian or 'progressive' revolution of the 1870s as follows:

— straight lines, long strap hinges and ring handles
— the enrichment of mouldings with dentils and other architecturally inspired ornaments
— tongue and groove planking sometimes set diagonally (Handley Read has

(Left) A roofed cupboard and secretaire designed by William Burges for the 1862 International Exhibition and made by Harland and Fisher. This highly-decorated and very colourful expression of the Gothic Revival is almost unique to Burges but he had followers and assistants in H.W. Lonsdale, E.J. Turner, W. Gualbert Saunders (q.v) and Henry Stacy Marks.

(Below left) Washstand designed by William Burges in 1879-80 and known as the Vita Nuova, in which the 'Jennings Patent' tip-up basin was used. The tap is of Chinese bronze and there were inlays of gold and silver fishes. Again, the decoration is highly colourful and the piece was for his own use.

(Right) A painted cabinet by Gualbert Saunders, follower of William Burges, whose approach in this case, though battlemented like Burges, is perhaps closer to the William Morris form of medievalism in terms of decoration and cabinet work.

pointed out that Seddon used this on the Morris cabinet of 1862, although this is not evident to anyone inspecting the piece externally in the Victoria and Albert Museum. Richard Charles and Eastlake also display it in their designs)
— cut through work and rows of spindles
— applied enamelled plates and painted panels
— inlay and occasional appropriate low relief carving in place of 'unmeaning scrolls'
— revealed construction showing dovetail and tenons (for some reason, Pugin and his followers thought this to be more 'honest' than concealed joints. Roll over, Chippendale!)
— the inset panel
— unstained oak merely oiled (sometimes resulting in a rather livid orange colour)

Charles Lock Eastlake, 1836-1906
Published the book *Hints on Household Taste* of 1868, a down-to-earth sound-fellow approach with the influence of Webb, Burges and Talbert in his designs. Unlike the other reformers he was more in tune with domestic realities and his designs moderate the scale, which the others — including Talbert — were apt to use. It was as if, in Talbert's case, he were sometimes still working on the drawings of the Albert Memorial for Sir Giles Gilbert Scott. Eastlake, on the other hand, puts forward simple, honest construction, rational forms and less complex decoration, although he was capable of using the inlays, stained glass panels, bespindled galleries, diagonal tongued planking, inset panels, carved grooving and architectural mouldings that were features of the period — all on one piece!
Eastlake's book was very influential in England and America (where 'Eastlake' furniture was widely produced, not very accurately), yet he remains a designer, not a maker, and few pieces made exactly to his designs have been identified.

William Burges
Architect famous for his decorative designs and furniture, mainly his French Gothic work of the 1860s, in which pieces of furniture aped little houses and castles. The sloping house-type roof with imitation tiles is a hallmark of Burges, who used the armoires of Northern France, with their iron bindings and painted decoration, as a model. His scholarship in Gothic was considerable but he was

willing to use decoration of a classical, Renaissance or Japanese derivation on Gothic structures. He was well into Japanese ornament before the 1862 Exhibition and the flamboyant pieces painted with scenes from Chaucer or Malory reflect the medieval enthusiasms of this rich influential character who had a strong effect on the Morris firm in figurative techniques and on E.W. Godwin in terms of Anglo-Japanese taste. Burges furniture now fetches enormous sums of money.

Richard Norman Shaw, 1831-1912

Celebrated architect, mostly domestic, but also of churches and public buildings. Started off using Gothic-ecclesiological styles, but soon moved to 'Old English' based on Kentish-Sussex Wealden houses of tile-hung and half-timbered types. In the 1870s moved to 'Queen Anne' styles for mainly town houses and ended up using classical-baroque revival styles for public buildings. The famous Gothic bookcase of 1860 in the Victoria and Albert Museum is of great stylistic interest but not typical (see below). His furniture designs included Queen Anne-style rush-seated corner chairs for Willesley, Cranbrook, Kent, stained green, in 1865; large plain Gothic-reformed settles, sideboards and beds à la Webb-Burges; and flimsier ebonised bespindled chairs and furniture, Japanese and traditional in design. Little survives and no design can be dated after 1880. Knew Webb, Morris, Burges, Godwin, Voysey and many other famous architects, artists and designers. His pupils — Lethaby, Sydney Barnsley, Prior, Newton and Horsley jnr. — became great forces in the Arts and Crafts Movement (q.v.) but Shaw, although encouraging them, did not belong nor did he admire that stylistic trend. Was united with Philip Webb in disliking the art nouveau work of the Century Guild and the Glasgow School (Mackintosh).

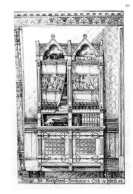

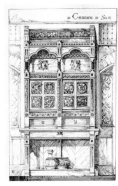

Two designs from Talbert's Gothic Forms *of 1867, showing (above) a Scriptural bookcase in oak and (below) a cabinet. The bookcase has a considerable similarity to the Richard Norman Shaw piece exhibited in 1862. Both pieces illustrate Talbert's use of inlays, complicated locks and hinges, 'joined' construction and large size.*

Bookcase by Richard Norman Shaw now in the Victoria and Albert Museum. Shown in 1861 and again in the Medieval Court at the London International Exhibition of 1862. Produced at a time when Shaw was working for the great architect G.E. Street, and of a Gothic flamboyance not normally associated with Shaw. Made to Shaw's design by the carver James Forsyth to a standard of craftsmanship far higher than many of the Burges and Morris pieces but still an architectural structure, more allied to stone than wood, imitating a building rather than a piece of furniture. The style and embellishments are, however, fascinating, for the piece incorporates, within its oak structure, surfaces of rosewood, satinwood and bird's-eye maple. Much so-called 'honest' construction, with exposed dowels, joints and tenons; marquetry and ornamental motifs abound, with overlapping suns, flowers, peacock tails and part circles or 'pies' derived partly from guilloche carving on medieval church chests, partly from the whorls on Rossetti's picture frames. The piece was intended for Shaw's own use and is interesting in the early integration of Japanese motifs with Gothic forms. It has been suggested by Andrew Saint that the top gables were intended for the display of Shaw's few precious blue-and-white Nanking porcelain pots which he collected, again following Rossetti and Whistler and perhaps bought from his friend Arthur Liberty who was the first regular importer, or Murray Marks, another friend in that trade. It contained Shaw's pots, his books, secret possessions, correspondence and, underneath in the thin cupboard, his rolls of drawings. Not a piece of domestic furniture but a working architect's piece of self-indulgence. Shaw tired of the piece and gave it to his daughter's convent, where it was rediscovered in 1962.

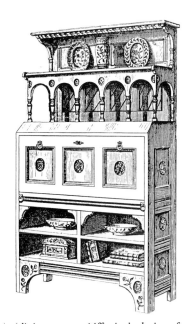

A 'dining-room chiffonier' design from Eastlake's Hints on Household Taste *which leans towards a blend of medievalism combined with arcaded spindling and dentillation in the top moulding.*

ART FURNITURE — The Aesthetic Movement 1865-1890

The term 'art furniture' tends nowadays to be superseded in auctioneers' jargon by 'Aesthetic Movement' or even 'art aesthetic' furniture so as to avoid confusion with art nouveau, or arts and crafts or, even, art deco. Art furniture was a term used in the late 1860s and on into the 1880s as a trendy name by firms considering themselves apart from ordinary manufacturers. It came, perhaps, as a result of the Aesthetic Movement, a term generally describing the middle class enthusiasm of the 1870s and 1880s for artistic matters, when art magazines, art pottery and art clothes were the 'in thing'.

The key piece which is always cited as highly influential in this type of furniture is a cabinet designed by T.E. Collcutt, made by a firm called Collinson & Lock, and exhibited at the London International Exhibition of 1871. It has many of the features of the black, ebonised furniture which became characteristic of the Art or Aesthetic Movement, namely painted and coved panels, bevelled-edged mirrors, rows of turned spindles and many straight lines in the design. Sometimes, instead of ebonising, dark woods such as black walnut were used or even wood stained green, as with William Morris whose green stain is said to have been discovered by Ford Madox Brown.

There is no doubt that this type of ebonised furniture, influenced by France, where the relevant cabinet makers were not called *ébénistes* for nothing, was very popular for about twenty years. Gillows and Shoolbred, reputable commercial firms, produced much ebonised furniture. Eventually, the fussily bracketed, bespindled, shelved and mirrored furniture fell out of fashion and the ebonised appearance, particularly when dusty and secondhand, is disliked by the modern antique trade so much that large quantities must have been broken up and lost for ever.

The celebrated cabinet designed by T.E. Collcutt, made by Collinson & Lock and exhibited at the International Exhibition of 1871. In ebonised wood with painted panels. This type of furniture was illustrated by Yapp (see Pictorial Dictionary of British 19th Century Furniture Design) *and Shoolbred, Gillows and other manufacturers. It was much copied and must have been popular.*

An Aesthetic Movement sideboard of good quality exhibiting many of the major characteristics of the type. Note that it is of ebonised wood with mahogany panels and incorporates a coved top à la Collcutt; a spindled ebonised gallery; bevelled panels and mirrors; many straight lines in the design.

Photo: Courtesy Michael Whiteway

ANGLO-JAPANESE — E.W. Godwin and Art Furniture 1865-1890

The London International Exhibition of 1862 had on view the collection of Japanese artefacts of the first British consul, Sir Rutherford Alcock. It has been suggested by Pauline Agius that this collection had a strong influence on visitors but E.W. Godwin, who is associated inextricably with the style, was a friend of Burges (q.v.) who also had a large Japanese collection. Indeed the Gothic reformers were attracted to the ideals of Japanese society in the Pre-Raphaelite terms in which they conceived them. In addition to design characteristics, it was like the Gothic medieval society they admired — knights in armour bashing evil doers, artist-craftsmen treadling away, maidens sighing, a royalist structure with attendant priests, etc. etc. (It would be interesting now to get the reformers' reactions to the current return to our society of Japanese influence in its electro-mechanical, rather than medieval, form.)

Godwin is credited with the great originality of using Japanese answers to western furniture problems of design. He produced his celebrated sideboard (in the Victoria and Albert Museum) around 1867, showing how purely western pieces of furniture might benefit from Japanese concepts. Other versions of this sideboard and pieces of writing furniture were also produced by him in the 1860s and 1870s. Later, in 1877, a catalogue of Godwin's designs was produced by

A chair designed by E.W. Godwin for the Art Furniture Co. in 1867. Note the use of the stamped decoration on the leather-covered panel in the back — very similar to that on upholstered chair 389 in the Price Guide section. The back spacing and uprights are somewhat 'Japanese' but the turned ringing in the uprights is similar to that used by Shaw and Morris contemporaneously and, later, by Arts and Crafts designers.

Celebrated sideboard designed by Godwin c.1867 now in the Victoria and Albert Museum. Made by the firm of Watt who published a catalogue entitled Art Furniture *in 1877. The whole attraction of this design is its relationship and place as a milestone in the progression of designs towards the Modern Movement of the 20th century.*

ANGLO-JAPANESE

Chair designed by Godwin c.1885 showing his design influences. The craze for Anglo-Japanese furniture became debased in the 1890s.

William Watt, a furniture producer, entitled *Art Furniture,* which was a sell-out, being reprinted in 1878. A lot of the furniture was ebonised and subsequent commercial producers of Anglo-Japanese or 'Art' furniture over the next fifteen years used ebonising as well as the painted and coved panels, bevelled-edged mirrors and rows of turned spindles characteristic of the Aesthetic Movement (q.v.).

A more detailed study is due on the influence of Japanese styles in British furniture. In his early days, around 1896, Charles Rennie Mackintosh (q.v.) hung up reproductions of Japanese prints in his basement room. It is said that the houses depicted in them would have had a strong effect on him, particularly in the relationship of space, line and form. It is not enough, therefore, simply to sniff at Japanese influences as a passing fad for a few fashion-conscious dandies. Burges, Godwin and Mackintosh are major figures in British furniture design of the period. The pity is that commercial copyists leapt on to the Godwin-inspired bandwagon and produced half-baked versions of 'Japanese' styles which eventually debased the whole art furniture movement. This is a pity because Godwin's original designs are quite delightful and now highly prized.

A tantalising piece of ebonised furniture — a secretaire bookcase showing the influence of both Burges and Godwin, both of them Japanese enthusiasts. Burges' influence is in the sloping, roofed top; the Japanese arrangement of the mirrors reflects(!) Godwin. Yet the three-panelled fall concealing the fitted writing interior and the rather square 'Chippendale' legs are derived from English origins. The sides are panelled in sloping tongued-and-grooved planking à la Eastlake; the open compartments like drawers between the legs may have been for rolls of small drawings or plans, for the piece is very architectural. It is almost as though Burges, Godwin, Eastlake and possibly Norman Shaw sat down together one rainy afternoon and designed a bureau for fun, then got James Forsyth to make it, for the cabinet work is of high quality.
Photo: Courtesy Michael Whiteway

THE ARTS AND CRAFTS MOVEMENT

C.R. Ashbee
M.H. Baillie Scott
Ernest and Sidney
  Barnsley
Ernest Gimson
Heal & Co.

William Lethaby
Liberty & Co.
Charles Rennie
  Mackintosh
A.H. Mackmurdo
George Walton

William Morris & Co.
W.A.S. Benson
George Jack
Philip Webb
C.F.A. Voysey

In the 1880s a number of architects and craftsmen formed guilds and associations in an attempt to get away from the prevailing mass-produced debased styles or reproductions of the commercial furniture trade. They were inspired by William Morris and Ruskin. These guilds and societies sprang up in various parts of the country, Mackmurdo having founded the Century Guild in 1882. The Arts and Crafts Exhibition Society held its first exhibition in 1888 (with very little furniture) and followed this up in 1889, 1890, 1893, 1896 and 1899. Some of the progressive designers, like Mackintosh and Voysey, merit separate treatment as independent spirits, but from many followers of the movement there was a far too slavish adherence to the hatred of all machinery and to the condemnation of the whole commercial furniture world as being run by tasteless tradesmen, which was ridiculous. In some cases this culminated in a withdrawal to rustic workshops in such places as the Cotswolds to live and work out an idealised life which ignored the age of machinery.

It is perhaps too easy to deride the Cotswold and other rural handicraft makers as ostriches now. It was not so much their preoccupation with the avoidance of machines that we should remember. Gimson and his followers were not the equivalent of the modern back-to-craftwork brigade, retiring to subsistence living in the country, throwing pots, weaving ponchos and rushing seats in competition with India, Korea or Taiwan. They were unique designers and craftsmen who wished to be different. Gimson made pieces that are not always successful and pieces which are clearly 18th century-inspired but they are individual and his example was beneficial to many people. Certainly none of the Cotswold craftsmen were prolific; the comparative rarity of pieces by Gimson and the Barnsleys has perhaps established a high value for them, although it is hard to say yet what kind of market exists for their work outside museums.

The ironic thing is that while those who followed Morris were evolving their curious attitudes towards production methods, the firm of William Morris & Co. was turning out the sort of furniture which met the contemporary demands of the trade, as the catalogues show. It was, of course, perfectly possible to turn out commercial furniture that was both well-designed and well-constructed, which is why Heal & Co., in addition to Morris, are usually included in the category of progressive producers. Liberty is more often associated with art nouveau furniture, with 'quaint' associations.

The various names lumped together in this broad category cover a variety of architects and designer-craftsmen who form a loosely-related group in terms of ideals or personal relationships. There are many inconsistencies, and the movement's relationship with art nouveau is liable to confuse the layman. It is odd that Mackmurdo is often associated with the origination of art nouveau designs, because the Arts and Crafts Exhibition Society considered art nouveau to be degenerate, a sinuous, plastic Continental form that had no place in their scheme of things. What is more, Mackmurdo's designs are mainly quite severe and only one chair gives rise to his association with art nouveau. Voysey's designs were influential on Continental art nouveau but he disliked the foreign version intensely. Mackintosh exhibited with the Arts and Crafts Exhibition Society twice, in 1896 and 1899, but his designs were disapproved of as being too art nouveau in manner. There are, clearly, many similarities between the British and the probably precedent Continental forms but in essence the main difference is that the British is more rectilinear and less plastic than the Continental. The reader is recommended to look at the comparison in *British Furniture 1880-1915* by Pauline Agius (pp.92-3) to get a visual impression of the major differences.

Chairs by A.H. Mackmurdo, founder of the Century Guild in 1882. The tall chair below is said to have influenced many later designers, while the sinuous forms in the back of the chair above were said to be influential on the art nouveau movement.

A cabinet with floral inlay designed by George Jack, who took over at William Morris & Co. from Philip Webb. Jack was a very decorative carver and inlayer and many of his pieces are much more sophisticated than one associates with the Arts and Crafts Movement c.1895.

A.H. Mackmurdo, 1851-1942

Founder of the Century Guild in 1882 and virulently opposed to the prevailing commercial productions. Credited with the 'tall chair' movement's origination by virtue of his chair exhibited in 1886 (see illustration on previous page) which was not well received by contemporary critics. It was, however, a very clean and simple design when compared with the turned spindled galleries of commercial art furniture and he was very influential in textiles and wallpapers on European art nouveau. His furniture designs are not, however, particularly consistent with each other and reflect a variety of approaches. The sinuous design in the back of his other, famous, chair (see illustration) is partly derived from Blake, partly from the Pre-Raphaelites and partly from plant designs such as the tulip. The fretwork is ornamental, not part of the structure which is severe in style.

William Morris & Co.

Morris himself was not particularly interested in furniture but he and his associates, George Jack, William Lethaby, Philip Webb and W.A.S. Benson, all sent work to the Arts and Crafts Society's Exhibitions. George Jack designed furniture for Morris & Co. for many years and is associated with marquetry inlays and carving, on which he published a book. Webb and Benson designed for Morris before Jack, with Webb being the most influential. The output of Morris & Co. seems to have been either inexpensive, good commercial stuff like the Sussex rush-seated chairs and general furniture; or very, very expensive elaborate cabinets, etc. The point about Morris' difficulties with handicrafts has been well made by Charlotte Gere: because he was committed to hand weaving his 'Hammersmith' carpets, their cost dictated a selling price at the end of the 19th century of £4 a square yard — a modern equivalent would be at least £200 a square yard.

Table by George Walton.

Bureau by the architect C.F.A. Voysey c.1896. Voysey designed very restful rooms in which plain oak furniture of original lines contributed to the lightness of design. Now thought of as art nouveau in manner but in fact nothing like the Continental version.

William Lethaby, 1857-1931
Included because of his associations with Morris and Gimson (qq.v.). One of the founders of Kenton & Co. (see Gimson) and not primarily a furniture designer, but was Principal of the Central School of Arts and Crafts.

C.R. Ashbee, 1863-1942
Founder of another Guild, in 1888. Worked in the East End, teaching young people. Liked the idea of several craftsmen combining their skills on one piece. Little of his furniture has been identified.

C.F.A. Voysey, 1857-1941
An important figure. Rather an austere purist in character but very influential in domestic architectural design. Often designed houses complete with furnishings and made a good living from textile pattern design as well. Nearly always used oak in plain surfaces but with complex hinge or metalwork decoration in a style now generally thought of as art nouveau (which he hated).

M.H. Baillie Scott, 1865-1945
Another architect, now famous for the 'Manxman' piano design. Lived in Bedford and was associated, in 1902, with the publication of *A Book of Furniture* by the firm J.P. White, a high class joinery producer.

George Walton, 1867-1933
Another architect, from Glasgow, who was, like Mackintosh, commissioned to do work for Miss Cranston's Tea Rooms. Designed quite a lot of furniture as well as other work.

Charles Rennie Mackintosh, 1868-1923
Now almost notorious in antique trade circles following the sale of one of his cabinets for £90,000 to the Glasgow authorities who, between them, have the largest collection of his work. Generally acknowledged to be brilliant as a designer of furniture that falls into the category of Fine Art rather than furniture. Mackintosh was a designer who was, if anything, inhibited by the use of wood as a material and did not follow those principles of construction and craftsmanship which the Gothic reformers and most progressives would have

Chair by Charles Rennie Mackintosh.

A cabinet by Mackintosh shown closed and open. Furniture by Mackintosh is now a rich man's possession, due to the fervour of the Glasgow authorities and other museums (the Louvre was the underbidder for the £90,000 cabinet) to purchase his work. For an appreciation of Mackintosh's furniture, a read of the book Charles Rennie Mackintosh, The Complete Furniture etc., *by Roger Billcliffe is essential.*

Colour Plate 11. A Georgian style corner cupboard made in the late 19th century. It contains some elegant influences of Hepplewhite whilst presaging the popularity of much reproduction furniture of the 20th century.

Colour Plate 12. A 'Sheraton' style sideboard of the late 19th century. The original late 18th century form and construction have been decorated by the use of inlays and marquetry to produce a much fancier piece of furniture.

Colour Plate 13. A painted satinwood wardrobe, part of a suite c.1900, showing the 'Angelica Kauffman' style of painted decoration beloved of high-Edwardian 'Sheraton' fashion. Cherubs, ribbon-tied baskets of flowers, swags and neo-classical foliage cheer the light surface of one of the most expensive woods available to the cabinet maker. Sold at the time as 'Adam' furniture.

insisted upon. In this sense his designs sometimes are mildly 'wrong' when seen out of the context for which they were designed despite their brilliance and originality. Some were even badly made and some chairs could fall apart if sat upon for long.

His furniture is often decorated with motifs such as the weeping rose or shapes which puzzle the viewer. Handley-Read has made the point that 'there is also the evidence among his decorations of a curious neuroticism — the ''spook school'' element evoked by weeping spirits, disconcerting eyes and tall figures caged among roses' — a marvellously accurate description.

Mackintosh has merited many studies and there are excellent books available about him. In some ways he has been almost too much written up. Yet he is a major figure, of European influence, and there is no doubt his pieces will be coveted by museums. See illustrations.

Ernest and Sidney Barnsley, 1863-1926 and 1865-1926
Both were founders, with Gimson, of Kenton & Co. Ernest made furniture for himself, but Sidney, with whom he moved to the Cotswolds — with Gimson — in 1895, was an archetypal artist-craftsman and worked at his bench until 1924. Sidney made robust, bow-fronted planked pieces which were dubbed the 'butter tub and carpenter's bench style'.

Heal & Co.
Inspired by Ambrose Heal, Jnr., who was not trained as an architect, but as a craftsman, the well-known Tottenham Court Road firm showed how good design could be allied to commercial production. Pieces from 1895 onwards are now somewhat sought after and merit attention, particularly if involved in any of the well-received exhibitions that the firm staged.

Pieces by the Barnsleys showing a walnut desk by Ernest Barnsley, with characteristic inlay and in a style much associated now with Gimson and Gordon Russell, and a dresser by Sidney Barnsley, again somewhat after Gimson but with modifications. Exhibited in 1903 and not admired by the critic of the Cabinet Maker.

Cupboard chest in holly green with chamfers picked out in bright red, by Ambrose Heal 1899.

Liberty & Co.
Very much associated with high quality art nouveau furniture. Had earlier imported Moorish styles, but the art nouveau furniture was often designed by George Walton.

Ernest Gimson, 1864-1919
Doyen of the Cotswold craftsmen and capable of superb designs. One of the founders of a firm called Kenton & Co. in 1890, with the Barnsleys, Lethaby, etc. It folded in 1892, and he subsequently moved to Gloucestershire. He was not so much a craftsman himself, like Barnsley, but was very familiar with all the processes, having worked with J.D. Sedding next door to Morris & Co. By 1903 he was established at Sapperton, where his Daneway workshops turned out the pieces with distinctive fielded panels and through joints in the 'revealed construction' manner beloved of the reformers. This is not entirely representative, however; some of his work is very light and elegant, and he inspired many followers.

Postscript
It is interesting to note that in Germany the work of Gimson inspired a movement of architects and craftsmen to set up the Werkbund in 1907. The Germans were less worried about the use of machinery than the socialist-inspired followers of Morris, who were so obsessed with the social and craftsmanship effects of the Industrial Revolution. In 1914, inspired by the Deutsche Werkbund, a group in Britain formed the Design and Industries Association to bring the artist and the manufacturer together. Ambrose Heal, William Lethaby and others were involved from the start. Exhibitions were held in the 1930s and the association was still influential on Joel when he wrote in 1953.

Plate rack and dresser by Ambrose Heal c.1906. Designed for production in quantity and of good clean lines.

Wardrobe by Ambrose Heal c.1900. Characteristic Arts and Crafts Movement design, mainly oak inlaid with box and holly in chequered patterns.

Colour Plates 14, 15 and 16. Three examples of the 'Edwardian Sheraton' approach to display cabinets showing (left and centre) the Georgian Revival approach, formal on top in the late 18th century manner, if a little curvaceous below, and (right) a more curvilinear, sinuous interpretation based loosely on the French vitrine style of showcase. Whereas the left-hand example sticks to a very undecorated, almost severe surface treatment with a crossband to the drawers, the other two examples exhibit painted decoration in the 'Adam' manner which became fashionable in the 1870s.

Cabinet by Ernest Gimson and table designed by him c.1908 but actually a version executed in the 1930s by his successor, Peter Waals. Gimson was quite fond of tightly-drawered cabinets of Renaissance inspiration as well as his more celebrated fielded oak panelling on more bucolic pieces.
Cabinet courtesy Michael Whiteway
Table courtesy Sotheby's Belgravia

Oak sideboard by Ernest Gimson shown at the 1900 Paris Exhibition. A characteristic fielded-panel design also influential on other modern designers.

Cabinet designed by W.A.S. Benson for William Morris & Co. c.1899. Benson used a style based on traditional forms but with elaborate embellishments, in this case in the glazing of the doors. Satinwood panels and inlays define strong panel designs and the hinges display the extension and 'naturalism' of the style even though the bulbous balusters of the short pillar supports hark back to the bun feet of the 17th century.

ART NOUVEAU

In the British Isles, Charles Rennie Mackintosh and M.H. Baillie Scott are considered to be the leaders of the art nouveau movement. In fact — both are dealt with in the Arts and Crafts section — this sinuous, plastic style is essentially French Continental and the British versions preserve a rectilinear form which is absent from genuine art nouveau. Nearly all British critics and designers reviled the style, even though Mackintosh was celebrated on the Continent, as was Baillie Scott.

The overlap between art nouveau and the British Arts and Crafts movement caused by these designers has led to much confusion. A.H. Mackmurdo, founder of the Century Guild in 1882, is often credited with the introduction of art nouveau design but this was mainly due to his work in textiles and wallpapers. The sinuous design of his chair, illustrated in the Arts and Crafts section, coupled with his incorporation of Japanese influences, is used to attribute the art nouveau label to him. The English art nouveau, including Liberty's, was a restrained version of the style whereas the Scots, particularly the Glasgow School — Charles Rennie Mackintosh, Herbert McNair, and Margaret and Frances Macdonald — were more influential on the Continent, particularly in Vienna.

In some respects the art nouveau style can be traced back to the rococo, whose scrolls and elimination of verticals and horizontals serve as an early model to be embellished with Japanese naturalistic forms — plants, birds, even animals — and the refined asymmetry which was not traditional in Europe.

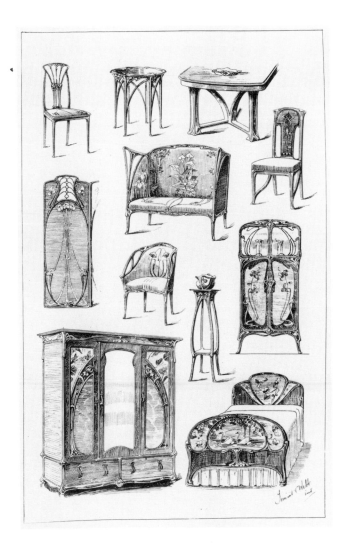

A sideboard by Voysey of c.1900, showing the flat-capped uprights and extended heart-shaped hinging associated with art nouveau but none of the sinuous curving of the structure itself.

Plate 'L'Art Nouveau' from Timms and Webb, Thirty Five Styles of Furniture, *1904. These exhibits at the Paris Exhibition of 1900 show how sinuous the Continental form was.*

45

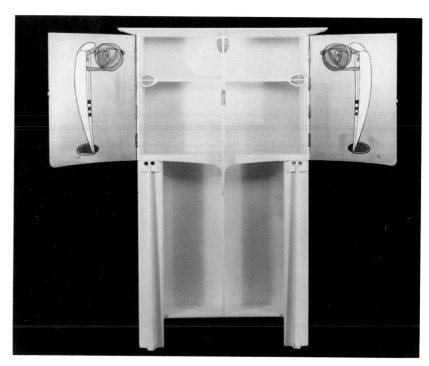

A white-painted oak cabinet by Mackintosh, the inside doors silvered and inlaid with white and coloured glass. Much nearer in spirit to Continental forms and far from the 'honest' or 'natural' treatment of wood surfaces essential to Arts and Crafts thinking.

An almost aggressively art nouveau oak sideboard, more on the Continental lines of the style than the British. The sides of the lower half, with their protruding tapering stiles in the 'Eastlake' manner, are broken by the sinuous curves of carved floral decoration. The bronze hinges, handles and applied tulips are over-decorative and there is a good deal of ostentation about the amount of carving used all over. Notice the flat capped finials along the top — a feature used by Voysey but emulated in a way he disliked intensely.

A 'Lochleven' dresser or buffet made by Liberty & Co. c.1890 which it is interesting to compare with the art nouveau sideboard opposite. The Liberty treatment still hints at the extended stiles and hinges of art nouveau but is much more rectilinear, almost severe, in treatment. The pillared supports and arched spaces are more in sympathy with the Arts and Crafts Movement, as is the 'bottle' glass decoration of the upper door.

An art nouveau settle which exhibits the naturalistic carving in heart-shaped forms which is characteristic of the style. The way in which the front legs swell into gadrooned 'feet' is also typical, as is the shaping of the balustered railings below the arms and panelled back.

An art nouveau hanging cupboard with beaten copper elongated hinges which show the typical heart shapes associated with the style. The inlays are of naturalistic forms which, in the upper panels, frame matched peacocks of stylised and elongated-baluster shaping. On the sides there are umbrella stands, bracketed glove shelves and hooks for, presumably, caps or hats. The upper gallery with its pierced railings (again using heart shapes) was perhaps for more delicate, brimmed headgear.

An elaborate art nouveau display cabinet exhibiting the floral and naturalistic motifs so frequently associated with the style. These are incorporated into the leaded and stained glass panels in the doors. Note also the flat reverse capping of the feet which Voysey used on his uprights.

An art nouveau chair showing the flat-capping applied to uprights in modified form in both this and the Arts and Crafts styles. The back is inlaid with flowers and the pierced centre splat incorporates a variant on the heart shape.

'QUEEN ANNE'

The style referred to as 'Queen Anne' by the Victorians was an architectural approach based on early 18th century classicism. It had little to do, in furniture, with real Queen Anne design, although Richard Norman Shaw produced, for the farmhouse at Willesley, Cranbrook, Kent, green-stained corner chairs (see illustration) in what was genuinely a Queen Anne period style.

Collinson & Lock presented a design at the Paris Exhibition in 1878 which has most of the characteristics of the style although it was executed in rosewood. Broken pediments, dentils, urns, and fluted columns were major features, which led to the description 'bracket and overmantel' school for the rather large pieces with which it is associated.

A Collinson and Lock rosewood cabinet shown at the 1878 Paris Exhibition. It has the broken pediment, dentils and pilasters characteristic of Queen Anne architecture.

A late Victorian side cabinet-cum-sideboard in what has been called the 'Victorian Queen Anne' style — the Victorians thought that William Kent was a Queen Anne designer. Also known as the 'bracket and overmantel' school. It has many characteristics of the style associated with William Kent in 1720-1730 — broken pediment, reeded flat columns, classical bits, dentil frieze or mouldings, etc. Note, however, that it is made in satinwood and inlaid with swags and floral decoration in box or ivory and harewood, etc., a style associated with really expensive Edwardian Sheraton furniture.

This satinwood cabinet in the Adam style, made by Wright & Mansfield and exhibited at the Paris Exhibition of 1867, is said to be an early example of the reversion of the Victorians' horror of 18th century design, which accompanied the 'Queen Anne' revival.

Green-stained rush-seated chair designed by Richard Norman Shaw in 1865 for Willesley, Cranbrook, Kent, a farmhouse extended by Shaw in the 'Wealden' or 'Old English' manner although peacocks, pies, sunbursts and features of the Aesthetic Movement were also used. This chair is more genuinely Queen Anne in design than the 'Victorian Queen Anne' style used by Collinson & Lock, and perhaps presages Shaw's move towards the Queen Anne style of architecture which he and his partner Nesfield subsequently employed.

GEORGIAN REVIVAL

To anyone engaged in collecting 18th century furniture in the 1990s, the furniture made from the late 1860s onwards is a frightening prospect. Until the 1860s, the Victorians wished to forget 18th century styles but, almost as a logical result of their 'education' by Morris and the reformers, they were bound to come round, or back, to these styles as their appreciation of cleaner lines and purer original tastes was developed. In some senses, the early Victorians, despite their prejudices, had not deserted some of the 18th century sources anyway. Adam is a classical style; rococo was used by Chippendale; Hepplewhite and Sheraton are French-influenced. But in the 1870s and 1880s it appears to have become increasingly acceptable to go back to the 18th century in a purely copying sense and to attempt, not a Victorian 'version' of the other styles they had developed, but a real copy of the original.

Many of these copies are, quite clearly, wrong in proportion, design or execution, or all three. There were, however, firms of excellent craftsmen who produced versions of 18th century furniture that were remarkable in spirit, interpretation and skill, using materials of the highest quality. The firm of Wright & Mansfield is often cited as the instigator of the revival and, in particular, their neo-classical Adam-style cabinet exhibited at the 1867 Exhibition in Paris, although they also exhibited neo-classical 18th century detail in 1862 in London. But the Wright & Mansfield cabinet of 1867 is not likely to disturb very much the modern-day collector of antiques. It is the pieces made from the 1870s onwards by them and by superb firms like Edwards & Roberts (usually identifiable from makers' labels) which are now so difficult to distinguish from the originals. Many faithful copies must have been made for country and town house owners to replace damaged items, to increase the numbers in sets of chairs, or simply to duplicate for a variety of reasons. There was also, however, a thriving trade in fakes and in the 'improvement' of workaday furniture of earlier periods, by carving or by adding decorative inlays and crossbandings to plain surfaces. Sometimes these activities are evident from the character of the piece, but some of the less forthright cabinet makers and firms were in the business of making 'antiques' and had no scruples about passing off their work as something much older. It is highly probable that many pieces now sold as 18th century antiques originated in this way.

The Victorians were rather vague themselves about stylistic attribution and used the term Queen Anne, or Chippendale and other 18th century names, to describe pieces which were only vaguely related to the original style. We have not bothered here to plot the course of such mistaken appellations, preferring to deal with the pieces on the basis of present-day knowledge.

A late Victorian 'Chippendale' chair in mahogany, on cabriole legs ending in ball-and-claw feet. The back uses a Gothic design form in the splat but the wavy uprights are not to period and the ankles of the cabrioles show typical Victorian weakness.

A pedestal desk of c.1870 showing how some pieces of furniture hardly needed reviving. This essentially late 18th/early 19th century design probably continued in favour throughout the period but seems to have had a resurgence at the time of Shoolbred's catalogue of 1876 and onwards.

Another Victorian 'Chippendale' chair of simpler form using a 'country Chippendale' back and rather shortened arms. The square tapering legs belong more to Sheraton style and look weak in balance with the back; the original straight square legs of the 18th century would have looked better.

EDWARDIAN SHERATON

A sub-division of the Georgian Revival, the term Edwardian Sheraton has come to mean a particular type of furniture, much of it actually pre-1902, made of mahogany or satinwood and copiously inlaid with marquetry, or painted, in an Adam manner. The essential style is late 18th century but the rather dull, dark mahogany of the original has been replaced by a lighter variety or by satinwood. This rather cheerful, sometimes gaudy furniture has long had its adherents. It is often of high quality and when associated with such firms as Edwards & Roberts is highly valued. Catalogues of the 1870s and 1880s show so-called 'Adam' furniture which would now fall into this category.

The 'Edwardian Sheraton' treatment applied to a fall-front bracket-foot bureau of 18th century characteristics, possibly even a period bureau to which the painted 'Adam' decoration has been applied c.1890-1910. The cheerful colour of such pieces has ensured a special followership for this style, known in the trade as 'girlie' furniture.

A typical example of Edwardian Sheraton applied to the bureau bookcase of classic late 18th century form but here inlaid boldly with 'Adam' decoration on the fall and crossbanded in satinwood throughout. In fact it is a revival type not confined to the Edwardian period and was made from about 1880 onwards.

LIBRARY FURNITURE.

No. 937. MAHOGANY CABINET, 6FT. 5IN. HIGH.
£12 0 0.

No. 470. FIGURED MAHOGANY SECRETAIRE CABINET,
(AFTER AN ANTIQUE MODEL.)
£35 0 0.

No. 664. INLAID MAHOGANY DWARF BOOKCASE,
EXTRA HIGH FINISH.
£9 15 0.

No. 664. INLAID MAHOGANY DWARF CHEST OF
DRAWERS, 2FT. 9IN. HIGH.
£5 15 0.

7

BOOKCASES

At the opening of the Victorian period bookcases, particularly the high library type, seem to have been made essentially in the sub-classical 'Grecian' or 'Gothic' manner illustrated by Loudon in 1839 and of ponderous appearance. The rococo does not seem to have been considered a suitable style for the earnest storage of writing or literature and it is not until the mid-19th century that the influence of other styles, such as Reformed Gothic, becomes apparent. By the last quarter of the century the Georgian Revival affected bookcases more than any other single style and the faithful reproductions of Georgian breakfront types made from the 1880s onwards are now much prized. William Morris & Co. illustrated several in their catalogue.

Low bookcases of three or more shelves were embellished with fashionable uprights of Classical, Elizabethan or Gothic design. By the 1880s a much simpler form had emerged, much closer to the spare lines of the modern bookcase. This vied with cabinets which were in part intended for display and in part for books. Morris & Co. illustrated a wide variety in their catalogue.

The revolving bookcase first made its appearance some time in the 18th century as a tripod-based type rather like a dumb waiter. Other inventions followed, including a cylindrical one at the 1851 Exhibition, but the square type now so popular appeared in the 1870s or 1880s, perhaps inspired by the tall roofed version of 'Queen Anne' characteristics made in selected numbers for the Tabard Inn Library associated with Bedford Park aestheticism. Again, William Morris & Co. made several versions of the normal commercial type.

1 Bookcases from the William Morris catalogue of c.1900 showing how the Georgian Revival had brought stylistic popularity round in a full circle — these are essentially 18th century types.

2 The 'Grecian' design of mahogany bookcase with arched panels below and applied scroll brackets for decoration, characteristic of the 1830s and 1840s. The moulded drawer fronts are typical of William IV and early Victorian sub-classical design.
1830-1840   *£1,800-£2,350*

3 A three-panel mahogany bookcase in which the panel arches are slightly pointed in what Loudon would have called the 'Gothic' manner. There is no decoration and the top, without any form of moulding to the cornice, has an unfinished look, as though something has been removed to get the piece under a low ceiling.
1840-1850   *£3,500-£5,000*

4 A break-front bookcase of c.1840 with Gothic arching in the treatment of the glazing bars. The flattened arch of the lower doors is characteristic of the 1840s but is still to be seen in catalogues of the 1880s.
1840-1880   *£10,000+*

6 A burr walnut bookcase in four sections with arched doors on the outside sections. The adjustable shelves have scalloped leather dust aprons on the leading edges.
1850-1870   *£3,000-£4,000*

5 A walnut break-front secretaire bookcase of c.1850 with characteristically flattened-arch panels to the doors. The glazed door mouldings are embellished by carved applied floral decoration at the top.
1840-1860   *£5,000-£7,000*

7 In this example the arching of the doors has been retained in the upper, glazed section but the lower half is adopting the square panels and inlays of the 1860s. The use of figured walnut and satinwood 'shells' in the lower panels, the inlaid stringing and banding indicate a mid-Victorian type.
1855-1875   *£2,500-£3,500*

8 An interesting walnut break-front bookcase. The glazed upper doors and the lower doors are decorated with an arched fretted carving in a 'naturalistic' style. In form there is not much progress from designs of the 1840s and such pieces continued to be popular until the 1880s, often making dating difficult.
1860-1880   *£7,000-£9,000*

9 This walnut and marquetry bookcase or cabinet embellished by gilt-metal mounts could go into the display cabinet section since it has most of the characteristics of mid-Victorian display pieces. Decorative work of the type put into this piece is a result of the influence of the French *ébénistes* of the period.
1855-1875   *£3,000-£5,000*

10 A Reformed Gothic bookcase made by Marsh & Jones, showing many of the design characteristics typical of the type. Note the sloping architectural roof, with its 'tiled' effect achieved by clinker-built planking, and its gables which even include barge-boards. It is a roof style beloved by Burges but also used by other designers. Note also the incised decoration, the 'revealed' construction with pegged tenon joints and the 'structural' pillars which are, in fact, purely decorative. Inlaid ivory and ebony decoration complete the scene.
1860-1870   *£12,000+*
(Photo: Courtesy Jeremy Cooper Ltd.)

11 An oak revival bookcase of massive proportions of the type currently favoured in Germany. This kind of self-conscious medievalism illustrates how the desire for the 'Elizabethan' went through the whole period but this piece is likely to be late 19th or early 20th century.
1890-1910   *£5,000-£7,000*

12 A Georgian Revival bookcase in the Chippendale style, with blind fretting and a broken pediment with pierced fretwork. Now much sought after as an alternative to the real thing.
1875-1895   *£4,000-£6,000*

13 A Georgian Revival mahogany bookcase with satinwood cross-banding to the drawers and lower doors. The tapering short legs are inlaid with stringing lines which follow the front stiles. The panelled sides of the lower half are also inlaid with stringing and this is repeated on the base and top of the upper half, under the pediment, but not on the doors, which are glazed in Gothic arching and hence possibly a replacement.
1890-1910   *£1,500-£2,000*

14 A reproduction mahogany break-front bookcase in a style of the 1790-1810 period. It is a quite faithful reproduction in proportion and in treatment of the glazing bars. This popular item of furniture for wealthy bibliophiles is still being reproduced today, 'made up' from old wood or other items by less scrupulous 'restorers' anxious to pass the piece off as old, or simply reproduced to order and size by honest manufacturers. A hardy perennial of the furniture trade.
This example 1880-1920   *£5,000-£7,000*
                                        With marquetry £9,000-£12,000

15 A lesser version to follow the previous example, showing typical 'Edwardian Sheraton' characteristics in the satinwood banding around doors and drawers.
1900-1910   *£3,500-£4,500*

17 An Edwardian Sheraton mahogany secretaire bookcase painted with musical motifs, cherubs and floral decoration. It is also inlaid with satinwood stringing lines.
1890-1910   *£5,000-£8,000*

16 A 'Samuel Pepys' walnut bookcase, derived from the design made for Pepys and now in the Pepysian Library at Cambridge. The glazed doors have heavily carved mouldings above and below and the cupboards below these doors are of the low proportion associated with the design.
1900-1925   *£2,500-£3,500*

18 A Georgian Revival mahogany bookcase on a chest with ebony and satinwood inlaid stringing decoration and a blind fret under the dentillated top moulding.
1890-1910   *£2,000-£3,000*

19 A mahogany bookcase, with marquetry inlay, in the Sheraton manner, set on an 'outset' lower part which has two long drawers on four square tapering legs. The Edwardians were fond of these rather top-heavy pieces which look a little uncertain, on their slender tapering legs, of bearing the load expected of them. Sheraton and Hepplewhite used this form incorporating a cylinder bureau to the lower half. The illustrated version is nearly always 20th century.
1900-1910   *£1,500-£2,000*

20 A solid walnut secretaire bookcase of a type made by Norman & Stacey 1900-1910 and then available at a price of £11.11s.0d. It was also available in fumed oak or mahogany. The walnut used for this typical piece, with its bas-relief carved door panels and secretaire drawer, tended to be an American walnut of straight grain and reddish colour. The pediment of semi-broken type is also typical of the period and the handles are original. Note that the piece was also available without the secretaire drawer, but simply with cupboards below, for £7.18s.6d. The reader may note that the *Price Guide to Victorian Furniture*, published in 1973, illustrated the piece from Norman & Stacey's catalogue on page 218, and priced it at £80-£120. The above photograph is courtesy of Sotheby's Belgravia where the piece shown was sold in September 1979.
1900-1910   *£2,000-£2,500*

21 A solid mahogany bookcase not unlike the previous example, but with two drawers instead of a secretaire and of more severely Georgian characteristics in its dentillated top frieze, its fluted column-style decoration and its bracket feet in place of the typical Victorian apron.
1890-1910   *£1,600-£2,000*

22 An Edwardian mahogany bookcase, with typical bas-relief carving and pedimented top. Would also make a very useful kitchen dresser. No secretaire drawer, so not very highly priced.
1900-1910   **£3,000-£4,500**

23 A carved oak bookcase with broken pediment. The doors have leaded lights instead of glazing bars, a fashion quite popular with furniture from about 1890 onwards.
1900-1910   **£2,500-£3,500**

24 A bookcase of a form illustrated by the William Morris company c.1900 but in this case of more ornate appearance due to the fluted pillars between sections, the ornamented top moulding, and the fielded panels to the cupboard doors. It is doubtful, also, if William Morris & Co. would have used the bas-relief carving in triangular flashes in the corners of the arch curves. Made of solid American walnut and, although only suitable for large rooms, a handsome piece.
1890-1910
          £3,000-£4,000

25 A sub-classical 'Grecian' design of low bookcase in mahogany of a type used from the 1830s to the 1880s. The small scrolled brackets at the top of the reeded sides act as capitals in the manner so characteristic of this style. The adjustable shelves and panelled back add to value.
1835 -1865   *£2,000-£3,000*

26 A rosewood low bookcase of William IV characteristics emphasising the heavy approach of the 1830s. The turned side columns are carved with leaf forms.
1830-1840   *£1,500-£2,000*

27 A solid walnut side cabinet or bookcase in the Gothic Reformed style, in which the lowest of the three panels in each side door is not carved for some reason. A sort of Talbert-Eastlake piece, missing its top structure, which is characteristic of the 'revealed' construction and decoration of the genre.
c.1875   *£1,750-£2,500*

30 A single-door glazed side cabinet in walnut. See Colour Plate 17.

28 A rosewood bookcase with carved scroll and leaf decoration to the top rail of the same machine-produced form seen on chiffoniers and sideboards of the period. The side pillars and mouldings add the elegance that lifts this piece away from the commonplace.
1835-1845   *£1,500-£2,000*

29 A walnut music cabinet of a type conforming to the more severe outline of mid-Victorian popularity. There are both shelves and fitted vertical divisions and a brass gallery rail on the top.
1860-1880   *£600-£750*

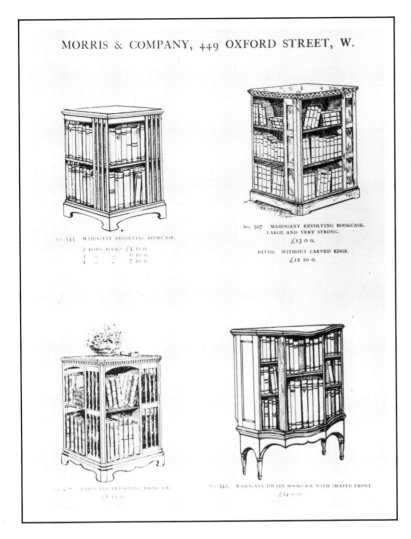

MORRIS & COMPANY, 449 OXFORD STREET, W.

No. 543. MAHOGANY REVOLVING BOOKCASE.
2 ROWS BOOKS £5 10 0.
3   "   "   6 10 0.
4   "   "   7 10 0.

No. 507. MAHOGANY REVOLVING BOOKCASE.
LARGE AND VERY STRONG.
£13 0 0.
DITTO, WITHOUT CARVED EDGE.
£12 10 0.

No. 518. MAHOGANY REVOLVING BOOKCASE.
£8 10 0.

No. 542. MAHOGANY DWARF BOOKCASE WITH SHAPED FRONT.
£14 0 0.

The earliest form of revolving bookcase appears to have been an 18th century tripod based type rather like a dumb waiter. Other inventions, including a cylindrical one at the 1851 Exhibition, followed, but the square type of table height shown here appeared during the second half of the 19th century.

31 A roofed Tabard Inn Library revolving bookcase in oak. See Colour Plate 18.

32 Three revolving bookcases and a dwarf bookcase from William Morris & Co.'s catalogue of c.1890. All three revolving versions are mahogany and vary from simple — plain mouldings, straight upright laths — to more sophisticated, with dentillated mouldings, shaped laths, arched spacings etc. These are all bracket foot types which do not illustrate the castored centre support beneath.
1890-1910   *£600-£1,200*

33 A simple mahogany revolving bookcase with inlaid stringing lines and straightforward uprights which include stringing. The centre rod on which the piece revolves is supported on a crosspiece on castors.
1890-1910   *£600-£900*

34 A slightly more sophisticated version which shows the features associated with Edwardian Sheraton, i.e. inlaid satinwood banding and centre 'shell' decoration to the top surface, and an inlaid top moulding.
1890-1910   *£700-£1,000*

35 An oak carved revolving bookcase of 'medieval' style. Instead of the vertical retaining laths there is a carved panel for each upright retainer of books and the flat top is elaborately carved in bas-relief with naturalistic forms.
1890-1910   *£800-£1,200*

36 A satinwood revolving bookcase with 'Japanese' fretting to the book divisions in the upper half and cabriole 'Queen Anne' legs to the open lower section with its shelf for magazines. Clearly made under the influence of the Aesthetic Movement.
1900-1910 *£800-£1,200*

37 A mahogany revolving bookcase on cabriole legs but this time with two tiers of bookshelves with spindle turned outer divisions.
1900-1920 *£850-£1,150*

BUREAU BOOKCASES

At the start of the Victorian period the bureau bookcase followed the bookcase in terms of 'Grecian' or 'Gothic' design, but the fall front appears to be less common than the cylinder or secretaire types even though fall fronts are illustrated in Loudon. As the century progressed the form was made in the styles then current, although here again the rococo appears to have been considered unsuitable. The Georgian Revival, however, was eminently suitable and large numbers were reproduced in that style.

At the end of the century a flatter, more elongated form makes its appearance. This form was often made in plain oak and the fall was either steeply angled or even vertical to allow for the shallower section of the piece. To it were added stylistically popular embellishments such as leaded glass and stained glass, art nouveau handles or capping, quaint fretwork, and so on.

At the same time, the Edwardian Sheraton version of the bureau bookcase, springing from the Georgian revival, was made in qualities ranging from the excellence of such firms as Edwards & Roberts down to mass-produced versions of a more hurriedly assembled nature.

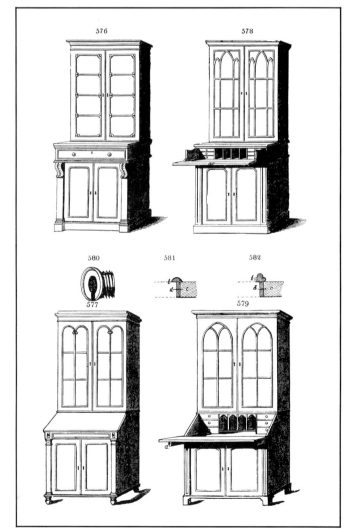

40 Bureau and Secretaire bookcases from Loudon's 1839 *Encyclopedia*, showing 'Grecian' (top left) and 'Gothic' (bottom right) types with mixtures between.

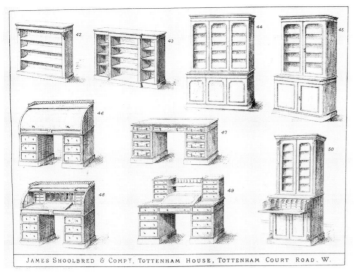

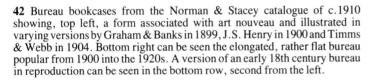

41 Library furniture from Shoolbred's catalogue of 1876 showing, bottom right, a secretaire bookcase similar to those illustrated by Loudon in 1833.

42 Bureau bookcases from the Norman & Stacey catalogue of c.1910 showing, top left, a form associated with art nouveau and illustrated in varying versions by Graham & Banks in 1899, J.S. Henry in 1900 and Timms & Webb in 1904. Bottom right can be seen the elongated, rather flat bureau popular from 1900 into the 1920s. A version of an early 18th century bureau in reproduction can be seen in the bottom row, second from the left.

43 A secretaire bookcase in mahogany which might have come straight from Loudon's 1839 publication and, equally, from Shoolbred's of 1876. The 'drawer' front folds down to give access to the pigeon-holed interior and is panelled inside with leather to provide a writing surface. The flattened arches of the panels and the small 'Grecian' scrolls under the secretaire drawer are characteristic.
1840-1880   *£1,900-£2,500*

44 A cylinder-front bureau bookcase in plain mahogany with flattened-arch panels, the whole piece rather unrelieved in severity and lack of ornamentation.
1840-1880   *£1,800-£2,500*

45 An ebonised Aesthetic Movement bureau bookcase with painted panel decoration depicting medieval scenes. Carefully designed and constructed, with typically turned column supports to the fall. (See Colour Plate 7.)
1870-1885   *£3,000-£4,000*

61

46 A mahogany secretaire bookcase with satinwood interior drawers showing plain rectangular or square panelling (missing one pane of glass to upper door).
1840-1860   *£2,000-£3,000*

47 The rather tantalising piece possibly by Godwin-Burges-Eastlake-Shaw discussed in the Furniture Styles section on the Anglo-Japanese period. Here it is shown with the fall open to reveal the carefully fitted interior.
c.1880   *Price at auction in 1978 £1,250*
               Estimate now £10,000+

48 A mahogany Georgian Revival bureau bookcase in a combination of the Chippendale (upper half) and Sheraton (lower half) manner, which combines the broken pediment and pierced frets of Chippendale's rococo pieces with the Adam inlaid decoration, square tapering legs and emphasised stringing lines of the Edwardian Sheraton.
1890-1910   *£2,750-£4,000*

49 (Far left) A more sober piece of mahogany Georgian Revival, closer to the 18th century original if of slightly elongated proportions. The astragal glazing bars are true to the period copied and the modest top cornice has a dentillated moulding.
1890-1910   *£2,500-£3,500*

50 An Edwardian Sheraton bureau book-case with a similar astragal glazing pattern but embellished with satinwood banding and Adam decoration to brighten the whole piece. For some reason the designer has chosen a very steep angle to the fall, which is not in keeping with the spirit of the original.
1890-1910   *£3,500-£4,500*

51 A mahogany bureau bookcase of George III 'design', with a broken pediment above the bookcase and satinwood banding throughout. A good 3ft. (91cm) wide reproduction which, apart from its missing or broken front bracket feet, follows the original line quite correctly. The Midland Furnishing Company sold an almost identical version for £6.6.0. in 1910. These bureaux are now standard 'trade' items and many of them still exist. The value of this example is helped by the curved broken pediment.
1890-1910   *£3,500-£5,000*

52 A mahogany bureau bookcase which aims at being a reproduction of a late 18th century piece. Once again, however, the Edwardian desire to go slightly one better than the original has given the game away. The falls of 18th century mahogany bureaux were not quarter veneered in the way this one has been, giving a diamond-shaped effect to the figure. Nor was the inlaid boxwood stringing arranged in an elaborately curved patterned panel. The glazing bar arrangement on the bookcase doors could also probably be shown to be a later form.
1900-1920   *£2,000-£3,000*

53 A Sheraton style bureau-cabinet on square tapering legs ending in block feet. The upper cabinet is fitted with bevelled plate glass doors. There is a hinged, folding top to the writing area, which folds over to give a greater surface area and is lined with leather. The roller shutter slides back to reveal pigeon holes and drawers inside.
1900-1910   *£2,000-£3,500*

54 A 3ft. (91cm) wide mahogany bureau bookcase on thin cabriole legs, of a type much produced from Edwardian times into the 1930s. The top, glazed cabinet has a reasonably robust approach to life but the legs are well and truly mean in proportion. It may be useful, it may be neatly made but the mass-produced look is deeply ingrained upon it.
1900-1930   *£1,200-£1,500*

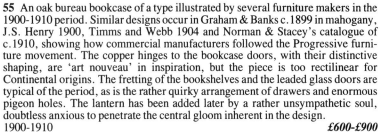

55 An oak bureau bookcase of a type illustrated by several furniture makers in the 1900-1910 period. Similar designs occur in Graham & Banks c.1899 in mahogany, J.S. Henry 1900, Timms and Webb 1904 and Norman & Stacey's catalogue of c.1910, showing how commercial manufacturers followed the Progressive furniture movement. The copper hinges to the bookcase doors, with their distinctive shaping, are 'art nouveau' in inspiration, but the piece is too rectilinear for Continental origins. The fretting of the bookshelves and the leaded glass doors are typical of the period, as is the rather quirky arrangement of drawers and enormous pigeon holes. The lantern has been added later by a rather unsympathetic soul, doubtless anxious to penetrate the central gloom inherent in the design.
1900-1910   *£600-£900*

56 An oak bureau bookcase with fall open to show the pigeon holes inside. There is a centre cupboard above the fall, with circular leaded-light door. Above this, the top shelf sports a weirdly-carved pediment and finials. The whole piece is a gesture towards the Progressive and art nouveau influences of the period. Small — 2ft.6ins. (76cm) wide and 5ft.3ins. (160cm) high — so really quite a desirable size for modern rooms.
1900-1915   *£250-£350*

57 An oak bureau bookcase which is only a brief development further from the previous bureau. Note the side bookshelves, also a feature of No. 55. The upper shelves are useful but the huge gap below the fall could surely have been used better. The fall is carved with scrollwork and the odd, quirky pierced decoration is, presumably, Progressive.
1900-1915   *£120-£180*

58 A more coherent oak bureau bookcase design with the flat capped top rail of the Edwardian period which stemmed from Voysey and the original Progressive designers. The centre cupboard above the open fall again has a leaded-light door but is rectangular in sympathy with the rest of the piece, including the panelled cupboard doors below the fall. The only place where over-exuberance may have set in is in the rather Islamic arching of the alcoves containing the vases.
1900-1915   *£300-£400*

59 An oak bureau bookcase with a conventional lower half but fitted with leaded-light doors to the upper glazed cupboard, incorporating stained glass, which adds to value.
1900-1915   *£250-£350*

60 An oak bureau bookcase with leaded-light upper doors incorporating two oval panels. The lower half has a drawer and two cupboard doors under the fall.
1900-1920   *£400-£500*

61 A more conventional version of the previous oak bureau bookcase without leading in the glass doors of the upper half. Back in 1910 or so the difference in price between this and the previous one was ten shillings — five bob for leading each glass door.
1900-1910   *£350-£450*

62 An oak bureau bookcase which owes something to the dresser in its design which is simple and pleasing. These pieces, of characteristically small proportions — 5ft.9ins. (175 cm) high and 2ft.9ins. (84cm) wide — will be enthusiastically collected for their use in small rooms one day.
1900-1920   *£175-£250*

BUREAUX

The fall-front bureau was essentially an 18th century piece of furniture which became somewhat superseded, for writing purposes, by the pedestal desk. As we have seen, however, the secretaire and cylinder bureau bookcases of the start of the Victorian period gave way, in the later part of the century, to Georgian Revival types. Much the same happened to the simple bureau which, although surviving in cylinder and other forms, was much replaced in mid-century by the davenport desk (q.v.). Nevertheless the fall-front 18th century type has proved an enduring form and by the end of the century had re-appeared as a Georgian Revival or Edwardian Sheraton piece. Another form was the 'medievalised' oak bureau, again of late 17th and early 18th century origin, profusely carved in bas-relief across its surfaces. In some cases this carved form incorporated lion-mask handles or motifs.

A variant on the fall-front bureau appeared at the end of the century in a small, vertical piece in which the fall was not always sloped but sometimes fitted flush with the vertical surface when closed. Large numbers of these small bureaux were made, with a variety of stylistic approaches to suit market requirements, including bureau bookcases (q.v.).

70 A painted Edwardian bonheur-du-jour. See Colour Plate 19.

71 A walnut bonheur-du-jour in the French manner. See Colour Plate 20.

72 An Edwardian Sheraton bonheur-du-jour cum cylinder bureau. See Colour Plate 21.

73 A walnut bonheur-du-jour of very French inspiration but in fact made by an English reproducer, with locks by a Birmingham firm. The boxwood inlays are of stylised flowers and semi-naturalistic forms. The two upper cupboards flanking the central mirror have glazed doors and pierced brass gallery rails above. The fitted interior has a well. An interesting example of how the Louis XV rococo style, popular in England in its own adapted form, could be more faithfully reproduced — with variations, of course — almost as the local English form was dying. C. and R. Light illustrate a very similar model in their 1881 catalogue.
1860-1885   *£3,250-£4,250*

BUREAUX - bonheurs-du-jour

The bonheur-du-jour is a piece of writing furniture which came to England in the late 18th century from the France of Louis XVI. After a strong vogue during the French Empire period it appears to have languished between the years 1830-1860 and then, perhaps as a result of the popularity of the rococo style and its French variants, came back into fashion. The French versions, including ebonised varieties, gradually gave way to Georgian Revival and Edwardian Sheraton types, which were of high quality and which, today, strongly resemble their early 19th century counterparts except for that exuberant inlaid embellishment which some Victorian and Edwardian makers were unable to resist.

Prices for these high quality, small, very decorative pieces of writing furniture are high and have continued to remain firm during a difficult period in the antique furniture market. The use of satinwood, painted and inlaid decoration has ensured the 'investment' attraction of such pieces, which would be difficult to reproduce economically.

74 This ebonised bonheur-du-jour is embellished with *pietra dura* (hard stone) which is a form of mosaic from the Italian Renaissance put together using various semi-precious and decorative stones and marble. These large ebonised bonheurs-du-jour with three upper sections, the centre providing a larger, break-front element, are not uncommon and were produced in the exhibition style by famous makers emulating the French *ébénistes*.
1860-1880   *£3,500-£4,500*

75 A late 19th century bonheur-du-jour or cheveret which emulates the form of one hundred years earlier with reasonable fidelity. The cross-banding in mahogany or kingwood is of high quality and the elegance of the legs is emphasised by the dark stringing lines down the corner edges.
1890-1910   *£2,000-£2,500*

76 A satinwood inlaid bonheur-du-jour with a central domed mirror flanked by cupboard doors inlaid with marquetry. The square tapering legs curve elegantly outwards towards the ends. Altogether a very delicate and finely-made piece of Edwardian lady's equipment.
1900-1910   *£3,250-£4,250*

77 An interesting late 19th century bonheur-du-jour which illustrates several features to be found on such pieces, namely

an arched central upper section with mirrored back

brass gallery rail round the top of the upper two sections

inlaid satinwood oval panels with painted floral decoration

painted floral and Adam decoration to the mahogany surfaces

satinwood banding to the drawer and folding top surface, which opens to provide the writing area

inlaid stringing lines to emphasise panels and edges of square-section tapering legs

legs united by an undertray with concave front (to avoid writer's pretty legs, well-concealed, of course, by pretty material) and inlaid stringing lines.
1890-1910   *£3,500-£4,500*

78 A mahogany bonheur-du-jour in the Sheraton manner on tapering square section legs ending in castors. The inlaid decoration is of flowers, paterae and husks. The front surface folds over outwards to provide an extra area of writing surface, supported by pulling out the drawer, which has a baize-lined top edge to prevent scratching.
1900-1910   *£2,500-£3,500*

79 A quite elegant writing table or bonheur-du-jour in the Edwardian Sheraton manner, with extensive inlays in boxwood and ivory. The drawers are banded in satinwood. The tapering square section legs end in brass castors and are connected by curving cross stretchers. The arcaded central section of the top is mirrored behind and the spindled top gallery sports characteristic finials.
1890-1910   *£2,500-£3,500*

80 An interesting rosewood variant on No. 72 (Colour Plate 21) but without the upper display case. Here the cylinder lid is shown open and the writing surface folded out. The piece is inlaid with floral and Adam decoration and has the undertray with scooped-out front, bordered by a pierced gallery. The letter slots and arrangements under the cylinder lid are very similar to those of davenports (q.v.), for which this is an elegant alternative without drawers except, presumably, one located under the writing flap.
1890-1910   *£2,000-£3,250*

81 A satinwood bonheur-du-jour of much later, greater proportions approximating to a sideboard but which is definitely intended as a piece of writing furniture. The flat centre surface is hinged and folds outwards to form a writing surface. The raised back has a central cupboard and flanking drawers. The central section is supported by flanking cupboards, each on four square tapering legs. The satinwood surface is crossbanded in rosewood and painted with vases of flowers, scrolls, birds, garlands and oval panels in the Angelica Kauffman manner.
1890-1910   *£5,000-£7,500*

BUREAUX - cylinder front

The cylinder front became a popular Edwardian form usually associated with higher quality bureaux. It was, of course, due to the popularity in revival of late 18th/early 19th century furniture of the Sheraton type that this vogue took place. Cylinder fronts still tend to be highly regarded despite the fact that they are somewhat subject to damage due to splitting and warpage in centrally heated conditions. Warpage can cause them to jam or lock in one position and repairs can be expensive.

82 A rather plain mahogany cylinder front bureau with three long drawers and mounted on bracket feet. The drawers and cylinder fall are crossbanded in satinwood in the characteristic Sheraton manner.
1900-1910   *£1,000-£1,500*

83 A cylinder front bureau in mahogany with satinwood cross-banding, inlaid stringing lines and a 'shell' motif inlaid into the fall.
1890-1910   *£1,200-£1,800*

84 A rosewood cylinder bureau, inlaid with marquetry dolphins, flowers and stringing lines. The arched cresting rail has an applied reeded or gadrooned vase and is a feature of much Edwardian furniture (without the vase). The square tapering legs end in castors. Inside the tambour top there is a pull-out writing surface and a fitted interior.
1890-1910   *£3,000-£4,000*

85 A simpler rosewood cylinder bureau with inlaid 'Adam' decoration but without the pull-out writing surface. The interior is fitted with pigeon holes and small drawers.
1890-1910   *£2,500-£3,500*

86 A rosewood cylinder bureau shown open. The inlays in this case are of boxwood, satinwood and ivory in the 'Adam' manner but the gallery round the top is pierced in Gothic arching. The two brass knobs at the front are to pull out the writing slide, which is surfaced in leather or baize.
1890-1910   *£2,500-£3,500*

BUREAUX - Georgian Revival and Edwardian Sheraton

The bureau seems to have languished (except in cylinder form or as a bonheur-du-jour) until nearly the end of the 19th century when it enjoyed a revival in various forms but particularly in reproduction Sheraton style. The illustrations in this section trace the main types of bracket foot bureaux. We have included those with solid plinths in this section also, since all the others are raised on legs of differing types.

87 A mahogany bureau of 18th century design, fairly faithfully reproduced. With three long drawers and a fitted interior. A fairly wide bureau — 3ft.6ins. (107cm) — on bracket feet, which is so simple in following the 18th century original without unnecessary decoration that one feels it might easily pass off as an 18th century piece.
1890-1930   *£1,200-£1,800*

88 A mahogany bureau of late 18th century 'design', inlaid with stringing lines in boxwood and with marquetry panels, in the centre of which is a chinoiserie scene. Such inlaid panels require considerable expertise to produce and it is a high quality piece, but, like so many Edwardian inlaid items, the decoration is just that little bit too flowery for comfort.
1890-1910   *£1,750-£2,500*

89 A mahogany bureau on 'Hepplewhite' splayed bracket feet and shaped apron, exhibiting the full treatment in the form of painted 'Adam' decoration. It is quite possible that this is an 18th century bureau to which the paint has been added later in order to 'improve' it.
1890-1910   *£3,000-£5,000*

90 A less florid version of mahogany bureau with Adam inlays of swags etc. and satinwood bandings. Again, this is possibly a late 18th century bureau to which inlaid decoration has been added after 1880.
1890-1910   *£2,000-£3,500*

91 A typical, almost classic, mass-produced Edwardian Sheraton bureau, 2ft.6ins. (76cm) wide, made in mahogany with satinwood crossbanding. There is a shell inlay in the centre of the fall, which is almost regulation, not to say *de rigueur*. Hundreds of these once-despised bureaux are now being sold by antique shippers to all parts of the globe.
1900-1910   *£600-£800*

92 A variation on the typical Edwardian Sheraton bureau of 2ft.6ins. (76cm) wide dimensions in mahogany. This one has the regulation satinwood crossbanding around the mahogany surfaces but has only one drawer beneath the fall and cupboard doors containing a shelf in place of the normal two lower drawers — hence less desirable, since it is less like the original 18th century piece from which it was copied, even if it may be more useful for some people's application.
1900-1910   *£400-£500*

93 A mahogany small bureau — 2ft. wide (61cm) — with splayed bracket feet in the Hepplewhite manner. Like several types of Edwardian bureau, it incorporates 'automatic action', which means that the lopers slide out automatically to support the fall when it is lowered. This obviates the need to pull them out manually and individually and is a security measure against lowering the fall without having the lopers extended, thus risking smashing the fall off at the hinges. Ah, progress!
1900-1910   *£200-£300*

94 A figured mahogany veneered bureau in late 18th century style. A very faithful reproduction in terms of proportion and restraint, with only the matched veneers on the drawers giving away perhaps the late origins of its manufacture.
1910-1930   *£1,200-£1,800*

95 A carved oak bureau which is characteristic in production and style. The lion-mask carved drawer handles are characteristic and the carving of the fall draws on 17th century models but adds 19th century arrangement to it. Note the solid frieze of the base — no concession to history there.
1895-1915   *£1,200-£1,600*

96 Another carved oak bureau with 'lion-mask' handles, this time on bracket feet but with the typical Edwardian addition of a shelf on top with a carved cresting rail.
c.1900   *£1,200-£1,600*

97 This is not a contemporary oak bureau. It is an 18th century bureau which has been carved up by a Victorian 'medievaliser' or creator of 'antiques'. Covered over with a penetrating black stain and carved with 17th century forms, the piece met the taste for medieval oak popular at the turn of the century.
1895-1915 for the carving *£1,400-£1,800*

BUREAUX - reproduction, on legs

This section covers several types of bureaux which emulate earlier styles with varying degrees of accuracy. They are mainly small pieces of furniture intended for occasional use.

98 A made-up oak desk on stand with an interesting contrast of styles which works quite well. The top desk section has been carved in 17th century style and has a false drawer with two rectangular moulded panels on the front. The base is pad-footed in the style of George II, say around 1730 to 1740, and has been carved to match the top. A decorator's piece.
1870-1890   *£500-£700*

100 A further bureau in the Sheraton-cum-William and Mary manner made, like the previous example, in mahogany. The overall effect is thin and cheap.
1900-1910   *£200-£300*

99 A mahogany bureau with rather striped cross-banding, on turned legs with inverted cups of William and Mary inspiration. A combination of styles from late 17th to late 18th century which is feeble, particularly in the inlaid central motif in the fall, which is neither one thing nor t'other. To be exported joyfully.
1900-1910   *£250-£325*

102 An oak bureau on stand with curved legs and shelf stretcher. The drawer under the fall, and the fall itself, are inlaid with the boxwood and ebony chequered banding ever popular in Arts and Crafts design. The top shelf is pierced to show a motif of indeterminate sort.
1900-1915   *£120-£180*

101 An oak bureau of Queen Anne inspiration in style, on tapering legs ending in pad feet. It has a lot of pigeon holes inside, two long drawers under the fall and, like many of these Edwardian pieces, is rather small — 2ft.6ins. (76cm) wide.
1900-1910   *£200-£300*

103 An oak bureau on stand with bobbinised front legs to give an 'old oak' effect, relevant to the moulding on the fall, slightly 'Jacobean' in character. The ring handles are a Sheraton design.
1900-1920   *£70-£120*

BUREAUX - elongated Edwardian

Following the popularity of the Progressive designers and the influence of Voysey and others, there was a move by the trade, around 1900, to produce designs in the required manner. This resulted in a unique species of elongated bureaux, slightly, but ever so slightly, art nouveau in manner, using a much thinner depth of section, few drawers, if any, and often with elongated hinges to the fall in an 'artistic' design. The following section shows a selection of the bureaux; the bureau bookcases have a separate section to themselves.

105 An oak fall-front elongated bureau of the 3ft. (91cm) wide, but much less deep, version preferred by the early 20th century. These slenderer — or should it be narrower — versions of the old 18th century invention, seem to have met a need for bureaux for smaller rooms. This is a very straightforward version with a simple interior and three drawers under.
1900-1920   *£80-£120*

104 A typical example of the elongated species with stamped bronze handle and elongated hinges to the fall. Note that there are no drawers — only bookshelves below and a typical bookshelf round the top, formed by a solid wooden cresting rail.
c.1900-1910   *£120-£180*

106 A roll-top version of these oak bureaux with shelf above, pigeon holes inside but no drawer under — just shelves. Roll top adds to price.
1900-1920   *£140-£180*

107 A fall-front oak bureau with a pierced fretted gallery round the top (also of oak) and with a drawer and two shelves under the fall. This generic type has been utterly despised until lately, when the use of the piece, the way it occupies little space, and the fact that it has been cheap, have suddenly made it a regular feature of many 'antique' shops.
1900-1920   *£80-£120*

109 An oak bureau which has a variation from the previous examples in the classic Edwardian shaping of the top rail. That central semi-circular arch is a very popular feature of the period (see Sideboards for similar examples). It may be thought that since these bureaux have only recently become a feature of the stock of 'antique' shops, there will have been little incentive to fake them or gerrymander about with them as yet. Not so: the author was offered one which turned out to have been re-fitted inside, repaired, improved and generally cobbled together from bits. So be warned.
1900-1915   *£100-£150*

108 A small oak roll-top bureau with a wooden top gallery rail intended as a bookshelf. The inside is neatly fitted with pigeon holes and there is a drawer and shelves under.
1900-1920   *£140-£180*

110 An oak fall-front bureau with a pierced top shelf which exhibits a heart shape and two art nouveau-ish leaves. Otherwise nothing remarkable.
1900-1915   *£70-£90*

111 A small oak bureau, 2ft.2ins. (66cm) wide, of the same genre but with a dash of art nouveau shaping to the top shelf. Pigeon holes inside and shelves under, as before.
1900-1915   *£60-£90*

CABINETS

The 19th century might well be designated, for furniture collectors, the Age of the Cabinet. The 18th century never saw such a mania for display and ostentatious storage except in the case of the rich. Increasing affluence in the upper and middle classes created a demand for a wide variety of side cabinets which had nothing to do with books or dining room requirements. They were intended for the drawing room, for places of public display, and the enormous furniture industry of the country turned them out in every possible taste.

The sub-classical style did not lend itself to the rather exuberant business of display and Loudon, in 1833, confined himself to dining room sideboards (q.v.) or chiffoniers (q.v.), the latter possibly for use between windows in place of a pier table, if you couldn't afford the proper thing, or as a sort of morning sideboard for light refreshment which might be used in a lady's parlour or library, but not as a cabinet in the sense covered by this section. It was the rococo, with French overtones, which set off the popularity of side cabinets and what have come, inaccurately, to be called credenzas. Subsequent variations, high and low, are to be found in nearly all the styles covered by the Style section, culminating in Georgian Revival or 'Edwardian Sheraton' versions.

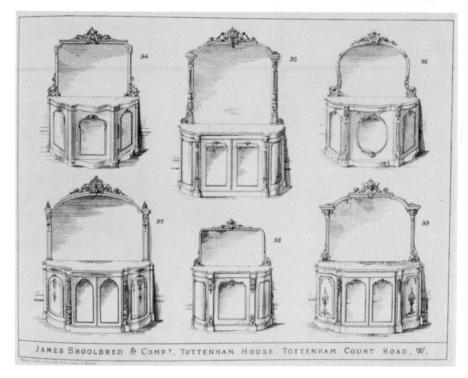

120 Drawing room cabinets from the Shoolbred catalogue of 1876, showing versions with pier glasses above. In many cases these mirrors would now be removed. The style is an adaption of the rococo and such pieces would date from the mid-century onwards.

121 Further drawing room cabinets from Shoolbred's 1876 catalogue showing pieces without pier glasses and a more rectilinear, later approach to style, with designs probably dating from the 1860s onwards.

Colour Plate 17. A single-door glazed side cabinet in walnut with applied carved decoration incorporating scrolls, and with a marble top. Very similar to one illustrated by Shoolbred and possibly one of a pair. Used in this instance as a bookcase but clearly adaptable to any display.
1860-1880   *£1,200-£1,800*

Colour Plate 18. A roofed Tabard Inn Library revolving bookcase in oak, inscribed with the quotation 'The True university of These Days is a Collection of Books — Carlyle' in Gothic script. Designed in a rather free 'Queen Anne' style in the manner of a follower of Richard Norman Shaw, who designed the Tabard Inn at Bedford Park c.1870. These bookcases were also produced in mahogany and were part of a lending library system that was quite extensive.
1870-1880   *£1,000-£1,600*

Colour Plate 19. (Top left) A painted Edwardian bonheur-du-jour with its cylinder fall depicting a *fête-champêtre* and flowers decorating the two short drawers below. The fluted turned legs have gilt metal mounts and gilt metal is used for the pierced top gallery and moulded borders to the panels.
1900-1910   *£3,500-£4,500*

Colour Plate 20. (Above) A walnut bonheur-du-jour in the French manner, on wavy cabriole legs with gilt metal mounts. The upper structure has mirrored doors and a pierced brass gallery above. High quality manufacturers showed variants of this popular piece during the mid-Victorian period.
1860-1880   *£3,500-£4,500*

Colour Plate 21. An Edwardian Sheraton bonheur-du-jour cum cylinder bureau in mahogany with satinwood inlaid decoration in the Adam manner centring on an oval 'shell' decoration which is considered classic to this form. The gently-inclined slope and the cylinder section open to provide a generous writing surface. The square, tapering legs are united by a concave-fronted undertier. Above the cylinder section there is a display cabinet of three sections and a brass gallery rail is provided round the sides and back of the top surface. The piece is almost identical to No. 80 and illustrates the crossover in terms of definition of writing pieces of this small, decorative type. It is a restrained, elegant, cheerful piece which has an enthusiastic following.
1890-1910   *£4,000-£6,000*

Colour Plate 22. The ebonised side cabinet in the French manner was highly regarded by Victorians of certain tastes, and was made usually to a high standard. *Pietra dura* (literally, hard stone) was used for decoration, consisting of hard stones, agate, jasper, lapis lazuli and fragments of coloured marble inlaid into a surface as a mosaic and highly polished. In this case the *pietra dura* decoration is floral and the gilt-bronze mounts, mouldings and stringing lines are typical of the type.
1850-1860   **£2,500-£3,500**

Colour Plate 23. An ebony and amboyna side cabinet (or credenza, a word derived from a serving-table for vessels, originally sacred vessels) with pilasters flanking a central ebonised door inlaid with an oval within a border inlaid with anthemia. (An anthemion is a Greek decoration of curves characterised by formalised honeysuckle flowers and leaves, with a band or scrolls to link them.)
1850-1870   **£2,000-£2,750**

Colour Plate 24. A red Boulle side cabinet of serpentine outline with ebonised mouldings and sides. André Charles Boulle (1642-1732) was a French artist-craftsman who practised a form of inlay using tortoiseshell and metals such as brass, or even silver, in a very complex decorative form. The style had a resurgence in the 19th century although often the tortoiseshell was replaced by horn painted on the reverse to simulate red tortoiseshell.
1850-1860   *If tortoiseshell £3,000-£4,000*
                                 If simulated £1,500-£2,500

Colour Plate 25. White marble was the normal material used for the top of many side cabinets of this type and this example with its scroll and naturalistic decoration of applied mouldings, carving and inlaid floral marquetry, shows clearly the rather stark contrast which has led to many pieces having the original tops replaced with wood or fabric covers. The flattened arch of the sub-classical period is retained in conjunction with a later over-exuberance.
1850-1860   *£3,500-£4,500*

Colour Plate 26. Two variants on the burr walnut side cabinet with marquetry inlays and gilt-bronze mounts. Both have curved glazed display shelves to the sides of the solid central door but whereas one has simple curved doors the other has the serpentine form. There is not much to choose in terms of values; the simpler curved-door version has a more decorative marquetry panel and concave-moulded top whereas the serpentine example has bolder gilt-bronze mounts.
1860-1880   *£3,000-£4,000*

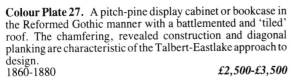

Colour Plate 27. A pitch-pine display cabinet or bookcase in the Reformed Gothic manner with a battlemented and 'tiled' roof. The chamfering, revealed construction and diagonal planking are characteristic of the Talbert-Eastlake approach to design.
1860-1880   *£2,500-£3,500*

Colour Plate 28. This walnut side cabinet, with its ebonised bandings and panels inlaid with 'Adam' decoration, is an early example of the revival of 18th century motifs in Victorian furniture. A rectilinear approach capped by a broken pediment is a rejection of the rococo in no uncertain terms, but by the 1880s commercial catalogues were full of such pieces.
1870-1880   *£2,500-£3,500*

Colour Plate 29. A satinwood display cabinet on rather uncompromising square legs. The doors are decorated with chinoiserie panels and floral trails are painted on the legs and frame stiles. There is a Chippendale-style blind fret on the frieze below the glazed doors.
1900-1910   *£2,500-£3,500*

Colour Plate 31 An ebonised and Boulle side cabinet inlaid with tortoiseshell and cut brass, with metal mounts and mouldings. The two glazed doors reveal shelves inside and are flanked by foliate mask gilt metal mounts.
1850-1870   *£1,500-£2,500*

Colour Plate 30. A mahogany corner cupboard with satinwood banding and marquetry inlay of the style known as Edwardian Sheraton. All the resurrected Georgian features — broken pediment, Gothic glazing bars, 'Adam' inlays, bracket feet — are present but the makers have brightened the severity of the original concept by the abundance of decoration.
1890-1910   *£4,500-£5,500*

Colour Plate 32. A mahogany display cabinet inlaid with marquetry and decorated with oval plaques in the style of Jasperware (i.e. Wedgwood). A fussy version of Edwardian Sheraton which had no intention of providing modest background to enhance the items on display. 1890-1910

£2,500-£3,500

Colour Plate 33. A side cabinet or chiffonier accompanied by a davenport desk which is part of the same satin and ebony suite. The upper shelf of the cabinet has a pierced brass gallery and is supported on turned columns linked to the mirrored back by a low, spindled rail. The mouldings are ebonised, as are the door bandings, contrasting sharply with the main satinwood surfaces.
1865-1885   *£1,500-£2,500*

Colour Plate 34. A satinwood Canterbury with turned legs and divisions which has some kinship with the earlier bobbin-turned example but is of a later date. This rather specialised, whimsical but high quality form is often difficult to pinpoint in the chronology of Victoria's reign but is a desirable piece as far as retail values go.
Probably c. 1870-1880   *£1,500-£2,000*

122 The chiffonier as seen by Loudon in 1833. Arched door panels, a shelf supported by brackets and 'usually' a white marble top.

CABINETS - chiffoniers

The chiffonier was introduced in the 18th century as a set of shelves for books with a cupboard or drawers below. In 1833 Loudon illustrated a 'chiffonier pier table' for placing between windows and said that such tables were usually finished with white marble tops, with plate glass behind, and a shelf supported by brackets for holding ornaments. The panels of the doors could be silvered plate glass or fluted silk. He said they were a cheap alternative to pier or console tables and could be used as a sort of morning sideboard for any light species of refreshment. For some reason, both the sideboard and the chiffonier attracted the opprobrium of the progressive designers, who regarded the mass-produced mahogany piece of dining-room furniture with loathing. It is true that in many cases there was little quality about such pieces and that ornamentation was shoddy. Many Victorian chiffoniers, however, have been turned into Regency pieces by the alteration of the doors to square panelling instead of arched; the addition of brass latticing with watered silk behind; and the simplification of the upper shelf and back.

123 A better quality small Victorian chiffonier in mahogany which has eluded alteration because the scrolled mouldings and pillars to the lower door panels are decorative enough to avoid the treatment handed out to the flattened-arch type. The upper structure could pass for William IV, but the lower part is unmistakably Victorian.
1835-1845   *£900-£1,200*

124 The characteristic early Victorian chiffonier-sideboard made from the 1840s onwards. Panelled doors with the flattened arch and 'feather' mahogany figures; ogee moulded drawer fronts; acanthus leaf carving; solid plinth and carved curvy back. Cheaply made and mass produced; hated by all 'progressive' designers. This one is too wide for alteration to a 'Georgian' type.
1840-1880   *£700-£900*

126 A mahogany chiffonier of similar date with heavy, scrolled bas-relief carved upper section (which a 'converter' would remove, leaving only the severe shelf), moulded drawer front, scrolled shelf supports and applied panels with bobbined edge decoration. The fluted feet are associated with the 1830s.
1835-1845 *£600-£900*

125 A small mahogany chiffonier which has the moulded drawer front of the 1830s but lacks the arched door panel characteristic of Loudon's sub-classical types, even though the scrolled brackets are in place. The square-panelled door with lattice in brass and silk backing has possibly been altered to provide a more 'Regency' or 'William IV' look. The upper part, with turned supports and pierced brass gallery, is severe enough in style to get away with this 'de-Victorianisation'.
1835-1845 *£2,250-£3,250*

127 A papier-mâché side cabinet or chiffonier with inlaid pearl-shell and painted floral decoration. The papier-mâché process was much applied to chairs (q.v.) but tables, cabinets and beds were produced in this characteristic Victorian style, which is associated with Jennens and Bettridge of Birmingham. The upper shelf is supported by scrolls and the top is exuberantly outlined in scroll forms as well.
1855-1875 *£2,000-£3,000*

128 An ebonised Aesthetic Movement side cabinet or chiffonier with shelves below and two cupboard doors decorated with Oriental — presumably Japanese — decoration depicting fish and birds (storks). The upper structure is also decorated with Japanese motifs and a short spindled rail to the sides of the top shelf.
1870-1880 *£2,400-£3,000*

129 The 'vulgar' chiffonier, much hated by 'progressive' designers, did not really change very much over a period of fifty years as these three examples from a 1910 catalogue show. Add a bit of spindled gallery, the occasional broken pediment or turned pillar, a bit of machined carving in bas-relief but leave the basic format the same, seems to have been the rule of thumb. Some versions — the better ones — are in solid mahogany; some — the nastier ones — are cheap thin veneer on a cheap deal frame, or even stained deal.
1910   *£400-£600*

130 An ebonised side cabinet in the French manner. See Colour Plate 22.

131 A ebony and amboyna side cabinet. See Colour Plate 23.

132 A red Boulle side cabinet of serpentine outline. See Colour Plate 24.

133 Marquetry side cabinet with white marble top. See Colour Plate 25.

134 Two burr walnut side cabinets. See Colour Plate 26.

135 A walnut side cabinet with pier glass and mirrored doors of high rococo style. The white marble top is surmounted by a pier glass in three sections, the large central mirror being decorated with naturalistic carving and a carved bust depicting someone like Robin Hood in the manner of a 'Romayne' panel. There is much scroll and leaf carving throughout.
1850-1880   *£1,500-£2,000*

136 A more restrained glazed walnut side cabinet with marquetry inlay and brass mounts, retaining its upper pier glass which so often has been removed. Obviously intended for display purposes. Whilst entirely original, the mirror does not add to the elegance of the piece and it is quite likely that the cabinet will eventually end up without it.
1860-1880   *£1,200-£1,800*

137 A later walnut side cabinet with smaller upper mirror showing the advent of the bespindled gallery to British furniture as the 1870s progressed and various design influences affected commercial manufacture. The central door is panelled and decorated with a Wedgwood plaque. The mouldings are ebonised and the fluted columns are capped with brass Corinthian terminals. Here again, it is likely that the upper spindles and mirrors will be removed since they do not add to the desirability of the piece.
1865-1885   *£2,500-£3,500*

138 A walnut side cabinet of considerable quality, serpentine in form, with Corinthian capitals, ebonised mouldings and sophisticated inlays, bandings and patterns. The deeper burr veneer in the door is probably amboyna, giving emphasis to the inner satinwood and kingwood banding panelling the central walnut area with its marquetry inlay of box and ivory. The slanting key pattern inlaid under the top moulding is also a fine quality feature.
1860-1880   *£3,000-£4,500*

139 A walnut single-door side cabinet with ebonised mouldings and painted porcelain panels in the door and top frieze. Gilt-bronze mounts emphasise the panels and embellish the front in the place of pillars. The base is shaped using ogee curves and the stringing lines used throughout emphasise this shaping.
1860-1880   *£2,500-£3,500*

140 A walnut serpentine double-door side cabinet of considerable embellishment, using floral marquetry panels and gilt-bronze mounts throughout. Again the base is shaped in ogee curves, which lightens the rather heavy impression that the solid apron bases of other examples can give.
1860-1880   *£3,500-£4,500*

141 A later Victorian side cabinet in thuya, with ebonised mouldings and banding. The more rectilinear shape and the break-front section with its pillared spacing beneath the doors reflect the influence of the new cabinet designs from Collcutt, Collinson & Lock (q.v.) etc. in the 1860s.
1870-1890   *£2,500-£3,250*

142 A burr walnut side cabinet of the 'D' shaped type with burr maple banding. There is a porcelain panel in the centre door, depicting cherubs, and there are gilt-metal mounts round the edges of the frieze and on the main frame panels. The curved glazed side doors enclose curved shelves. A very popular piece of the 1870s and 1880s but originating in early sideboard-chiffonier designs of the 1850s.
1860-1890   *£3,000-£4,000*

143 Another walnut D-type side cabinet with gilt-metal mounts and porcelain panels. Very similar to the previous example but with extra gilt-metal mounting around the top edge of the base and the whole piece jacked up on turned feet. The top does not have a moulded edge, nor does the base, and there is less panelled decoration in the veneering. There also appears to be less variation in the figure and burr of the walnut.
1860-1890   *£2,500-£3,500*

144 A fully ebonised side cabinet with serpentine glazed doors either side enclosing shelves with shot-silk lining. The piece is inlaid with boxwood stringing and has gilt-metal mounts throughout. The centre door has a porcelain panel. It would be tempting to associate this jet black furniture with the death of Prince Albert in 1861, after which Victoria herself wore the colour, but the revived use of ebonising probably followed the great Exhibitions, particularly that of Paris in 1855 — great French cabinet makers were not known as *ébénistes* for nothing. The commercial catalogues of the 1870s and 1880s show, however, that such pieces must have continued in popularity for a long time. Definitely now a specialised taste — the market does not like black.
1875-1890   *£1,500-£2,500*

145 A kingwood side cabinet decorated in the grand manner with an inlaid trellis diamond flowerhead pattern in the frieze, repeated as a decorative motif throughout. The diagonal treatment of the kingwood veneer banding around the doors and on the base is in the French manner and can be seen behind the trellis marquetry of the centre door with its glazed oval panel. There are porcelain panels painted with figures and gilt metal mounts with masks and leaf casts as additional decoration. Although it is an English piece, it has leant heavily on French inspiration and Exhibition stimulus. The curved side doors are glazed to reveal further display shelves.
1860-1880   *£6,000-£8,000*

146 A walnut side cabinet with two central cupboard doors each having oval porcelain plaques painted with couples in 18th century dress. The curved side doors are glazed and reveal shelves intended for display. The frieze is also inset with porcelain oval plaques and there is a stamped gilt metal gadrooning around this frieze, the top edge of the base and the centre door edge. The central door panels also have gilt metal decoration and are symmetrically quartered with carefully-chosen veneers.
1860-1880   *£4,000-£5,000*

147 A kingwood side cabinet showing 'French' diagonal treatment of the veneer figure, but with glazed doors at the centre instead of veneered panelled ones. The tops of these central doors and the curved glazed side doors, with serpentine, dipping shape is not usual on English pieces. The bun feet are ebonised and there are gilt-metal mounts throughout.
1860-1880   *£2,500-£3,500*

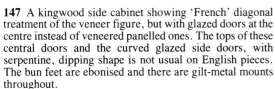

149 In the 1860s and 1870s the exhibition style of furniture led to the incorporation of porcelain and painted plaques on many pieces. A more rectilinear approach hinted at a return to 18th century proportions. This satinwood display cabinet has Sèvres-style porcelain insets and gilt-metal mounts and contrasts quite strongly with the rococo-influenced designs of the 1850s.
1860-1880   *£2,500-£3,500*

148 A walnut music cabinet inlaid with satinwood stringing. The upper tier, with pierced brass gallery, is supported by turned pillars with scrolled corbels and there is a mirrored back. The lower part has elegant glazed doors and the piece is on short turned legs with castors.
1855-1870   *£1,000-£1,500*

150 A burr walnut and marquetry dwarf cabinet of French influence, with gilt-metal mounts and floral decoration.
1855-1875   *£1,500-£2,000*

151 A pair of mid-Victorian cabinets in walnut with marquetry decoration and gilt-metal mounts. These ostentatious cabinets, like the so-called credenzas, were intended for drawing-room displays to impress visitors.
1860-1880   *£4,000-£6,000*

152 A more restrained pair of satinwood cabinets which show the direction which taste was taking — away from the exuberance of the rococo and towards the restraint of the Georgian Revival. Gilt-metal mounts and brass gallery rails embellish what are quite severely rectilinear proportions of considerable elegance.
1860-1890   *£4,000-£6,000*

153 A display cabinet designed by Clement Heaton with a glazed three-panel upper part and a painted lower part with scenes from Aesop's Fables. An unusual version of late Reformed Gothic work. c.1880   **£10,000+**

154 An ebonised Aesthetic Movement cabinet with bespindled top gallery, mirror, fielded solid panels and painted panels of floral decoration. In the base there is a sort of 'pot board' shelf with further turned and fluted pillars at the sides. Note the small circular inlaid 'pies' at the carcase joints.
1870-1880   **£800-£1,200**

155 A very interesting ebonised and inlaid Reformed Gothic display cabinet by Gillows & Co. The pillars, with their architectural, 'roofed' bases, turned collars and ornamental capitals are of the sort of structural stonework design that one associates with the style. So is the moulded edge around the top and the brass gallery rail at the back with quatrefoil pierced design. The door hinges are of the strap, 'revealed' type but the inlays are perhaps a little bit more floral than the Reformed Gothic pieces of the early 1860s.
c.1870   **£6,000-£8,000**

156 An ebonised inlaid side cabinet of Aesthetic Movement characteristics — spindled gallery, decorative panels, bevelled mirrors, 'pot board' shelf beneath with ring-turned columns — but, unusually, drawers inlaid with amboyna or some other burr wood. One is led to believe that this is a commercial manufacturer's version of Art Furniture, with concessions to popular taste and the fact that Edwards and Roberts, the renowned reproducers, both made and stamped it, reinforces this view.
c.1880   **£1,750-£2,500**

157 An ebonised mahogany display cabinet of commercial design, with a rather Japanese glazing arrangement in the central doors and upswept ends to the top surfaces.
c.1890   *£750-£950*

158 An ebonised side cabinet of mixed Aesthetic and commercial origin, with painted panels depicting an owl and a cockerel. The fluted columns and inlaid decoration are acceptable commercial practice; the spindled lower gallery and painted panels are purely Aesthetic. The lower panels are satinwood inlaid with flowers.
1880-1890   *£1,750-£2,500*

159 An amboyna and ebonised side cabinet showing the more severe style and increasing use of ebonising, which had both become more fashionable than the rococo plasticity of curve during the 1860s. There are three drawers in the frieze below the top which have porcelain plaques and gilt-metal bandings to decorate them. The central area has two cupboards set with porcelain plaques in the doors and an open area below, euphemistically termed a gallery. This centre section is flanked by glazed doors enclosing velvet-lined shelves. The workmanship and finish require the highest order of craftsmanship.
1865-1880   *£2,500-£3,500*

160 A burr walnut and ebonised bonheur-du-jour is included in this section because it is tempting to compare it with 159, and to speculate whether the same maker was involved in both pieces. There is the use of the two cupboards with porcelain-plaqued doors; there are the three frieze drawers with porcelain plaques and gilt-metal bandings, this time the central drawer fitted for writing. Even the burr wood panels are similarly handled, save for an extra crossband set around them. From there on the piece departs from 159, however, for the pillars are fluted and gilded — the use of turning has made them thus flashier. The top has a brass gallery rail around it and, again, the columns are turned and the fluting emphasised by gilt. 159 is more restrained. Perhaps it was simply that gilt-metal mounts, bandings and porcelain plaques all came from one manufacturing source — a sort of Beardmore's of the 1870s — so there was little choice for the cabinet maker.
1865-1870   *£3,500-£4,250*

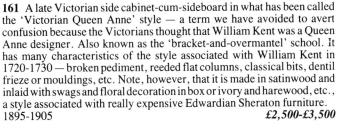

161 A late Victorian side cabinet-cum-sideboard in what has been called the 'Victorian Queen Anne' style — a term we have avoided to avert confusion because the Victorians thought that William Kent was a Queen Anne designer. Also known as the 'bracket-and-overmantel' school. It has many characteristics of the style associated with William Kent in 1720-1730 — broken pediment, reeded flat columns, classical bits, dentil frieze or mouldings, etc. Note, however, that it is made in satinwood and inlaid with swags and floral decoration in box or ivory and harewood, etc., a style associated with really expensive Edwardian Sheraton furniture.
1895-1905   **£2,500-£3,500**

162 A rosewood inlaid side cabinet with a broken pediment above. An example of how 18th century designs returned to fashion at the end of the 19th century. Although of the 'bracket-and-overmantel' school of the late Victorian period, it would now be sold as Edwardian Sheraton due to the boxwood and ivory inlays of Adam/Sheraton inspiration.
1890-1900   **£1,500-£2,000**

163 A satinwood break-front display cabinet in very 18th century style, but showing more restraint than one often associates with Edwardian reproductions. The glazing bars on the doors are in keeping and the broken pediment, with its dentil moulding, is a good proportion. The drawers are crossbanded and the side drawers additionally inlaid with oval panels. The tapering square section legs are connected by a platform stretcher and end in block feet.
1900-1910   **£6,000-£8,000**

164 An art nouveau mahogany display cabinet of rather flimsy construction, with stained glass decoration to the leaded glazed door and inlaid with beechwood flowers. Rather Liberty's in design but a bit more sophisticated and individual.
c.1900   *£1,000-£1,500*

165 An art nouveau bow-fronted display cabinet with glazed side door decorated with leaded mauve leaves. The bowed doors are inlaid with apple tree motifs and the tapering baluster columns in the central shelf section are purely decorative.
c.1900   *£1,500-£2,500*

166 An interesting side cabinet of art nouveau design of English origins, the only sinuousness perceptible being in the inlays. The use of much-leaded glazing appears to have been a feature of later English art nouveau which emulated some Arts and Crafts Movement designers. Certainly leading was used in the 1920s to give a sort of 'craft' look. The thin tapering legs are straight, not splayed in 1950s Danish fashion — the one on the left has been dislodged.
c.1900   *£1,000-£1,750*

167 An art nouveau cabinet of a design possibly emanating from Liberty's, who were much associated with art nouveau furniture. The cabinet is of mahogany with inlaid decoration. Note the flat square feet like the 'caps' on art nouveau uprights and the exaggeration of the flat top.
c.1900   *£1,000-£1,750*

168 An 'art nouveau' hall cabinet, attributed to Waring & Gillow, showing the whip-lash form in the inlaid floral decoration. Although it is this decoration which would, nowadays, bring the 'art nouveau' description to the piece, it must be observed that the construction owes nothing to art nouveau, being panelled, stiled and corniced in rectilinear traditional cabinet work of quite severe proportion.
1900-1910   *£2,500-£3,500*

169 A side cabinet by Gardner & Son of Glasgow, in the art nouveau manner. Note the flat capped uprights, echoed by the feet. The stained glass in the glazed doors is balanced by the inlays in the solid doors, although the 'whiplash' above is not very consistent with the geometric curves below.
c.1900   *£1,000-£1,500*

170 An art nouveau display cabinet in mahogany with decorative inlays of floral motifs. Note, again, the flat capped uprights so favoured by Voysey and the pernickety grouping of the 'balusters' in the top gallery in threes and fives.
c.1900   *£1,500-£2,000*

171 A mahogany side cabinet, the design of which is the result of a union between art nouveau principles and the characteristic Edwardian upper shelf with centrally arched back, this time pierced into the ever-popular broken pediment. The result is that the top has a curiously inglenooked effect while the rest of the cabinet is conventional enough, with some art nouveau inlays.
c.1900   *£1,000-£1,400*

172 An interesting oak cabinet with folksy-artistic leaded glazed doors above and below, the upper ones being curtained. The central door panel has a stained glass still-life scene, depicting a steaming bowl and ladle, a drinking mug or glass, a lemon and a decanter. The author naturally supposes the piece is intended for the storage of the makings of hot punches for winter nights but then some people will think of a drink when confronted with almost anything . . .
c. 1900 *£350-£500*

173 (Top right) A satinwood display cabinet in the Grand Edwardian Sheraton manner, with a moulded central glazed door and convex-glazed side doors. The decoration is all painted, relying on the 18th century for its origins, with swags, flowers, young ladies and cupids.
1900-1910 *£5,000-£7,000*

174 A satinwood and marquetry display cabinet which is less faithful to 18th century English origins than 163, and more to Franco-Dutch ones. The serpentine shaping, dwarf cabriole legs and rather fancy broken pediment are not severe enough for the English taste and the piece is most likely to end up on the Continent. None the less, a high quality reproduction in an expensive wood.
1900-1910 *£6,000-£7,000*

175 A grand form of mahogany display cabinet or bookcase incorporating many 'Chippendale' features such as a carved broken pediment on top, fretted with leaf carving of real distinction, and a carved concave top moulding. The glazing bars, in the Gothic style, are beautifully moulded and also incorporate scroll and leaf carving. The lower half has a top edge which is gadrooned and a blind fret under this top edge. The ogee or serpentine feet are carved with scrolls and bas-relief motifs of an almost Chinese inspiration. Very high quality craftsmanship required for this.
1900-1910 *£5,000-£7,000*

176 (Right) A display cabinet of art nouveau style, probably intended as a music cabinet. It is made of mahogany with box-wood and ivory inlays. The top has sinuous curves in the Continental art nouveau fashion with hearts and tulip shapes incorporated in the fretwork and carving.
c.1890   *£450-£550*

177 (Left) Another small mahogany cabinet with art nouveau tendencies, also probably intended for music. A much simpler shape, with flat capped shaping to the top and 'whiplash' forms in the inlays.
1890-1900   *£350-£450*

178 A mahogany display cabinet with glazed door to the central cabinet and mirrored upper shelves. There are both turned and square-section tapering columns as well as turned and reeded legs. These legs and the inlays are more Adam in design than Sheraton, as are the cherubic panels.
1900-1910   *£1,100-£1,600*

179 A characteristic 'Edwardian Sheraton' display cabinet with a broken pediment above. Made in mahogany with inlays and satin-wood bandings and with glass shelves inside.
1900-1914   *£1,200-£1,600*

180 A mahogany display cabinet, in a later version of the Edwardian Sheraton manner, on somewhat flimsy cabriole legs connected by a platform stretcher. The inlay is of stylised flowers and foliage and the top cresting shows the flattened moulded top rail so favoured at the time and derived from the art nouveau-progressive designers. A somewhat eclectic piece, now popular for china display or for collectors.
1900-1910   *£1,100-£1,500*

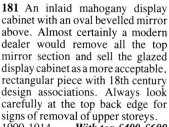

181 An inlaid mahogany display cabinet with an oval bevelled mirror above. Almost certainly a modern dealer would remove all the top mirror section and sell the glazed display cabinet as a more acceptable, rectangular piece with 18th century design associations. Always look carefully at the top back edge for signs of removal of upper storeys.
1900-1914   *With top £400-£600*
           Without top £600-£850

182 Another example of a small display cabinet which nowadays would almost certainly have the top mirror section removed and be sold as a nice, squarish, Sheraton type of cabinet.
1900-1914   *£400-£800*

184 This display cabinet is an example of how first class inlaying can be used to no avail. The piece is in rosewood and might have been quite attractive had not the upper half gone completely awry and out of proportion. The two flanking curved mirrors jar hideously in the total design. A shipping goods dealer would be tempted to take the whole top off and sell the bottom half as quite an elegant sideboard.
1890-1910   *£1,600-£2,200*

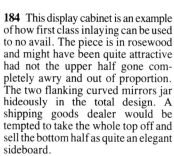

183 A mahogany glazed display cabinet in the rococo Chippendale manner, on small thin cabriole legs ending in ball-and-claw feet. Complex to carve all that fretted work.
c.1900   *£1,200-£1,600*

185 An ebonised china cabinet made in cheap deal, with bevelled swerving mirrors and machined fretwork plastered all over it. Inside it has plate glass shelves. The makers describe it as a 'Louis' style, perhaps originating the famous derogatory phrase 'in the style of All the Louis!' Looking at this and the subsequent pieces, one can understand and sympathise with the obsession of Percy Wells and other designers to get back to clean, functional lines without dust.
1900-1914   *£300-£400*

186 Another ebonised china cabinet in the 'Louis' style, plastered with French rococo fretwork, with a top that has swollen up to grotesque proportions. Since the top unscrews quite easily, it would now almost certainly be removed by a dealer and the lower half sold as a more manageable piece.
1900-1914   *£400-£500*

187 An ebonised piece described as a 'Dainty Music or China Cabinet', this time with a fashionably progressive leaded-light door.
1900-1914   *£300-£400*

188 Mahogany with central glazed door and chamfered glazed sides. The maker has run the front cabriole-type legs down the entire vertical height from the top shelf to the ground and secured these legs below the lower chamfered side shelf by means of an elaborate bracket. The tops of the front legs have quaint fretted brackets to secure them to the upper shelf and this eccentricity of shaping is repeated in the shelf form itself, the lower shelves — which have an odd, bitten-out centre to avoid the descending front legs — and in the absurd top which has spur-like accoutrements on the scrolled ends. When Percy Wells spoke of 'flashy and flimsy furniture with embellishments and meretricious ornament', he might have had this in mind. Highly destructible.
1890-1910   *£350-£450*

189 A single-door display cabinet of 'Edwardian Sheraton' style in mahogany crossbanded with satinwood and inlaid with 'Adam' motifs.
1890-1910   *£1,000-£1,400*

191 A mahogany corner cupboard of Hepplewhite inspiration in the elegant splayed legs and bowed form. Decorated with inlaid ebony stringing lines and dentillation under the top moulding.
1890-1910   *£750-£1,150*

190 A decorative mahogany corner cupboard of more 'Hepplewhite' than 'Sheraton' origin (illustrated as Colour Plate 11 in the Georgian Revival section). The use of banding round the elegant 'feather' veneer door panels and the stringing lines, with their diamond and key pattern designs, indicate a carefully considered piece of considerable quality.
1890-1910   *£2,000-£3,000*

193 A much more elegant Edwardian Sheraton display corner cabinet with a broken pediment above, profuse marquetry inlays in the Adam manner and central glazed upper door arched with inlaid spandrels in the top corners.
1890-1910   *£3,000-£4,000*

192 A single-door 'Edwardian Sheraton' display cabinet of corner cupboard variety. The essentially 18th century form, including bracket feet, has been lightened by the use of inlaid 'Adam' marquetry.
1890-1910   *£1,200-£1,600*

194 A pitch-pine display cabinet or bookcase in the Reformed Gothic manner. See Colour Plate 27.

195 A walnut side cabinet with ebonised bandings and panels inlaid with 'Adam' decoration. See Colour Plate 28.

196 A satinwood display cabinet. See Colour Plate 29.

197 A mahogany corner cupboard with satinwood banding and marquetry inlay. See Colour Plate 30.

198 An ebonised and Boulle side cabinet. See Colour Plate 31.

199 A mahogany display cabinet inlaid with marquetry and decorated with oval plaques. See Colour Plate 32.

200 A side cabinet or chiffonier accompanied by a davenport desk from the same suite. See Colour Plate 33.

CANTERBURIES

The name Canterbury is said to come from one of the Archbishops who liked mobile furniture, possibly a supper trolley, but also an atlas stand and the now accepted music stand which is defined by the term. The music Canterbury was always supposed to be mobile, i.e. mounted on castors, and the early form, which appeared c.1800, was a restrained piece of mahogany furniture with flat divisions. It did not take long for decorative treatment in prevailing styles to occur although certain fashions appear to have by-passed it; Reformed Gothic and Aesthetic Movement Canterburies have not come to the author's attention.

210 Two music Canterburies from Loudon's 1833 *Encyclopedia*, reprinted in 1839. The one above would supposedly be considered to be in a 'Grecian' sub-classical style whilst that below in a Regency, or perhaps more accurately French Empire version. Loudon described it as 'of elegant but rather expensive construction'.

JAMES SHOOLBRED & COMPY, TOTTENHAM HOUSE, TOTTENHAM COURT ROAD, W.

211 A page of Canterburies (and two corner whatnots) from Shoolbred's catalogue of 1876. The form has developed an upper shelf in three cases and the use of fretwork has become universal.

212 A Canterbury taken almost straight from the pages of Loudon's *Encyclopedia* described above. The use of the rather military laurel wreath and the 'flying' dividers between sections emphasises the Regency character of the piece.
1830-1840   *£900-£1,100*

213 This rosewood Canterbury was made just a little before Victorian times but shows how, already, the form had lent itself to exuberant treatment. Students of bobbin-and-reel turning of the 17th century will recognise the inspiration for the piece.
1825-1835
£1,000-£1,400

214 From the 'Loudon' example with its laurel wreath and flying divisions joined by turned spindles to this walnut rococo example with acanthus leaf carving is but a short step. The concave moulded base has a flush-fitting drawer set in it.
1850-1870 *£900-£1,300*

215 A walnut Canterbury not far removed from the previous example but with fretted, rather than carved divisions. The circular panel is painted with birds and flowers.
c.1860 *£1,000-£1,400*

217 A walnut Canterbury with fretted divisions and sides in scroll forms. The top is hinged and lifts up to form a writing slope.
c.1860 *£1,000-£1,300*

216 Another variant on the fretwork type of division in the Canterbury, this one showing completely flat fretted divisions with scroll and leaf forms but otherwise a similar, simpler type.
1850-1875 *£800-£1,100*

218 A papier-mâché music Canterbury decorated with shell and mother-of-pearl inlays. A high quality version valued for its uniquely Victorian character.
c.1860 *£1,100-£1,300*

219 A walnut Canterbury with fretted divisions and sides. It has a flush-fitting drawer in the concave bottom moulding and fixed top shelf with fretted gallery.
1850-1870   *£900-£1,100*

220 A satinwood Canterbury with turned legs and divisions. See Colour Plate 34.

221 A burr walnut Canterbury of a kidney shape with scrolled fretwork divisions below and a pierced brass gallery rail around the top.
c. 1860   *£1,600-£2,000*

222 A design advertised in the 1850 catalogue of W. Smee & Co. He shows it as a single decker but, given Victorian taste, it was no doubt ordered as a double to provide a useful top.
1850-1870   *£1,400-£2,000*

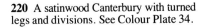

223 Bamboo has always been an adaptable material for furniture making and the Canterbury is a piece which obviously lends itself to the medium, being light, strong and suitable for open work of this kind.
1880-1900   *£120-£180*

224 A bamboo Canterbury of a type made from about 1880 onwards. Painted decoration in panels is frequently to be found on these pieces.
1880-1910   *£150-£250*

225 A rosewood music cabinet-cum-Canterbury with a glazed display door to the tiered cupboard below and a galleried shelf supported on four turned columns.
1890-1910   *£500-£700*

CHAIRS

CHAIRS - bentwood

The steaming and bending of chair bows and stretchers was a standard craft of Windsor (*see* **Chairs — country and kitchen**) chair makers, but the Austrian, Michael Thonet (1796-1871), perfected the technique and presaged the tubular steel chair. The introduction of Thonet's bentwood chairs, seats and tables to England in the mid-19th century led to their enormous popularity and prolific sale for almost every kind of establishment. The seats were usually caned. London furniture catalogues from 1851 onwards illustrate a wide variety of forms.

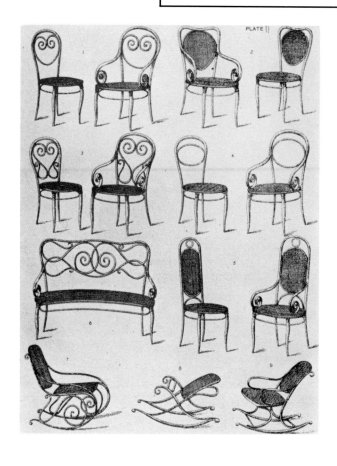

230 A selection of bentwood chairs from *The Cabinet Maker's Pattern Book* published by Wyman in 1877. They show the versatility and elegance of which this furniture is capable.

231 A further selection of bentwood furniture from Wyman's catalogue of 1877. Again the extraordinary versatility of this type of furniture is clearly illustrated.

232 An illustration from Thonet's catalogue which shows — No. 14 and No. 13 — two of the examples illustrated here.

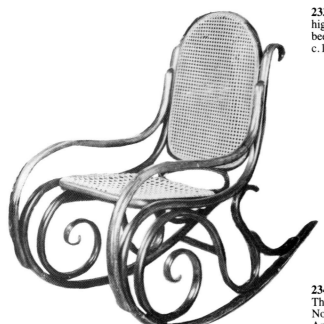

233 Bentwood rocking chair of a highly popular form which has been much reproduced.
c.1860 *£300-£400*

234 A bentwood armchair of Thonet production itemised as No. 20 in the Thonet catalogue. An elegant chair of pleasant proportions.
c.1860 *£120-£180*

235 A plain bentwood chair, catalogued as No. 14 by Thonet, and his best selling item at nearly fifty million since 1859. As used in cafés throughout Europe. During the 1870s Thonet was said to be turning out 1,200 of this model daily — see Gillian Walkling, *Antique Collecting*, December 1979.
c.1860 *£20-£30*

236 An unusual, high, bentwood office chair, adjustable in height and with a revolving seat. The circular seat is impressed with the pattern one associates with bentwood furniture.
1900-1920 *£120-£150*

237 Chair No. 13 from the Thonet catalogue. Of more complex form but very strong structurally.
1850-1870 *£150-£200*

238 A form which is to be seen in Wyman's 1877 catalogue and which was presumably imported from Thonet.
1850-1880 *£70-£120*

239 A more rectilinear bentwood form with turned front legs and moulded arms and uprights.
1860-1880 *£140-£200*

CHAIRS - country and kitchen

To the 'early' Windsor and country chair enthusiast, mention of the Victorian and Edwardian period brings forth the compressed lips, the furrowed brow. The whole of the 19th century, especially post-1830, is viewed with considerable suspicion, for it is the time when the 'hand' crafting of country chairs was supplanted by industrial methods.

While it is true that chair manufacture, especially in relation to solid wood or rush-seated chairs of traditional type, moved from an individual craftsman's work to that of a team of specialists backed by power saws, the change was very gradual. Many of the methods used, even when individual parts were the work of different specialists, were pure cottage-industry ones. The pole lathe, in existence for at least 150 years, was still used extensively. Large manufacturing establishments, such as Edwin Skull's and the High Wycombe mass-producers, by no means dominated the rural trades. Amateur films of the 1930s show chair makers, turners and bodgers, still turning out work in time-honoured fashion.

There were, on the whole, two schools of traditional country chair makers. These were:
1. Solid-wood chair producers of the Windsor, smoker's bow and industrial variants of the Windsor such as scroll-back, lath-back and similar types.
2. Rush-seated chair producers based originally on the North West tradition of chair-making but which gave rise, ironically, to the William Morris 'Sussex' type.

At the start of the Victorian era the solid-wood chair had evolved from its 18th century comb-back and later, stronger, bow-back into types based on the bow in various forms, the 'scroll' back and the 'tablet' type of Mendlesham or Oxford chair with its squarer, Sheraton influences. From these eventually came the smoker's bow, the Lancashire/Yorkshire variant of the high bow-back Windsor, and the scroll backs which evolved into the Roman spindle and lath or lath-and-baluster variants. The bow-back Windsor, whether of high or low-back form, was still in production throughout; it never ceased to be popular and 'reproductions' — if a simple continuance of a popular form can be called a reproduction — have continued to the present day.

The rush-seated chair from the North West — Cheshire, Lancashire, Westmorland and Cumberland — whether of slatted or spindled back, appears to have been the inspiration for several architect-designers, who eagerly seized on the form. Not all were like William Morris' 'Sussex' chair, said to have been based on a traditional, Hurstmonceux maker.

Because of the continuance of production over a long period, many traditional forms of country chairs have become difficult to date. Machine turning is usually distinguishable from pole lathe work and the later bulbous turning from earlier, slenderer forms. Within a certain time scale, however — perhaps forty years — many country chairs, like town designs, are very difficult to pinpoint.

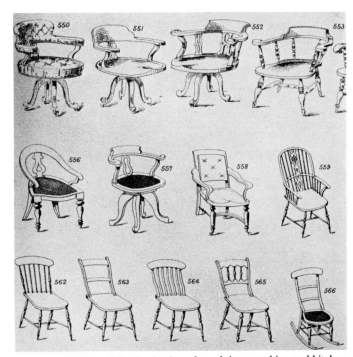

240 Single bow-back Windsor and scroll-back chairs shown by Loudon (1833) as kitchen chairs. Seats of elm, hollowed out, the Windsor one with back stays, are bored with holes to allow the legs and the back uprights to be inserted. Loudon gives a recipe for staining the Windsor red, like mahogany.

241 A selection of revolving, smoking and kitchen chairs from Shoolbred's catalogue of 1867. There is a high bow-back Windsor (centre row, extreme right) and a selection of scroll-back chairs on the bottom row, from left to right: spindle, simple scroll, lath-back, Gothic scroll and a rocking chair.

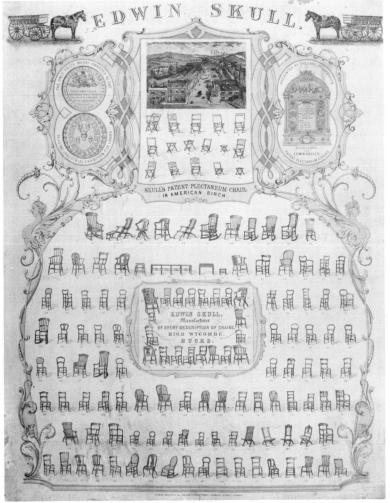

242 The display card used by Edwin Skull of High Wycombe, 1865-70. The variety of chairs is outstanding, with many variants of Windsor such as high and low bow-backs, wheelbacks, splatbacks and, in addition, smoker's bow, scroll, lath, spindle, Gothic scroll, lath-and-splat, rocking and steamer chair varieties.

243 A page of traditional Lancashire rush-seated chairs from the catalogue of H.J. Berry of Chipping, Lancashire, actually published in the 1930s. The long continuance of manufacture of this type of chair, from the 19th century to the present day, can make a dating of individual examples extremely difficult.

244 (Left) This chair may be seen on the right-hand side of the William Morris catalogue advertising the 'Sussex' range of rush-seated chairs. Originally they were birch, ebonised or stained dark green, using Ford Madox Brown's discovery of a green stain. The design of the chair is said to be traditional, and it is stronger than it looks. The posture required of the sitter is a bit severe. Note the way that the inclined arm supports go right through the seat rail and down into an extra cross stretcher, where their finely-tapered ends locate through the stretcher, like dowels, to add to strength. These chairs set a fashion for many other rush-seated types.
1865-1895   *Singly £90-£120*
                                              In sets, each £100-£140

245 A variation on the previous design, using the same arm-support extension down through to an extra cross-stretcher. The back design is a variant on the 'wavy-line' ladderback.
c.1870   *Singly £90-£110*
                                              In sets, each £100-£130

246 A bamboo rush-seated chair in which the influence of William Morris, the Arts and Crafts Movement and the Japanese or 'quaint' style are gaily intermingled. By the 1870s, leading firms were producing bamboo furniture cheaply to cater for the popular Japanese vogue. In this chair the traditions of Sussex and Tokyo have been determinedly blended.
1870-1910   *£30-£40*

247 Not all country chairs were made by simple country craftsmen. This oak armchair with rush seat was probably designed by R. Norman Shaw about 1876 and retailed by William Morris. It rests at the Victoria and Albert Museum, who note that it was at the Tabard Inn, Bedford Park. The high back, with turned uprights and simple straight splat, owes a good deal to early 18th century chairs, but the turning on the front legs is much later in concept.
c.1876   *£400-£600*

248 A fruitwood chair designed by Ernest Gimson. The rush seat is conventional. Note the careful proportion and the spacing of the ladder back — a very satisfying chair to look at.
1880-1910   *£600-£800*

249 A cleaned-off rush-seated armchair with an unusual back incorporating wavy, slightly 'quaint' slats with pierced circles in them. Made of birch and originally stained black.
c.1885   £100-£130

250 A rush-seated 'art nouveau' chair with round-capped uprights to the back which are echoed by the front legs. Although it looks simple, it is a deceptive chair, in which the plain oak surface in the back has a simple fielded panel carved in it and the spacing of the flat cross slats beneath has been very carefully designed and proportioned. It is a chair of traditional country ancestry but redesigned in a modern, arts and crafts form which indicates an architect behind it somewhere.
1890-1910   £90-£110
(If by 'known' architect designer, then £250-£350)

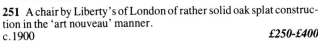

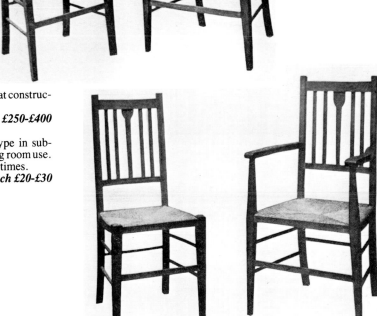

251 A chair by Liberty's of London of rather solid oak splat construction in the 'art nouveau' manner.
c.1900   *£250-£400*

252 Four small rush-seated chairs of mass-produced type in sub-Sheraton designs which were intended for kitchen or dining room use. A large variety of this type were turned out in Edwardian times.
1900-1920   *In sets, each £20-£30*

253 The spindle and ladderback country chair was made throughout the 19th century and much reproduced in the 1920s and 1930s when both types suited the vogue for oak 'Jacobean' dining rooms. There were many producers of such chairs. On the left is a spindle-back rush-seated chair of a Lancashire or Yorkshire type made from the 18th century onwards. On the right a 'wavy-line' ladderback of similar dating. Both are popular country chairs and have continued to be sought after. It is likely that many 20th century versions, with a bit of wear knocked into them, would be sold as being of much earlier date.
1830-present day
In sets, each £500-£600

254 A bobbin-turned yew chair with rush seat designed by Ernest Gimson. The bobbin-turning dates back to the 17th century and the style is derivative of that earlier period. Evidence again of the late 19th and early 20th century desire to get back to simpler and more natural styles.
c.1905
£1,000-£1,500

255 A remarkable example of a low-backed ladderback chair with rush seat illustrated by Maurice Adams in 1926. The distinctive top rail is derived from the 'Macclesfield' design of country chair originating in 1790-1830. It is almost a faithful reproduction but the back design is not quite true. Would probably be sold nowadays as an 'early 19th century' chair.
1920-1930
In sets, each £100-£150

CHAIRS - country and kitchen: *wooden seated, 1860-1930*

This section also includes chairs for institutional and office use, made in large quantities by mass-production methods. On the whole they are more durable than rush-seated chairs and tend to be perennially favourite types such as the Windsor which is still going strong. In the mid- and late 19th century large quantities of simple chairs were produced for the expanding markets available. Some of them were of attractive design and are now coming to be appreciated as cheap, pleasant and functional chairs.

256 Starting with the Windsor, which goes back to the beginning of the 18th century (see *British Antique Furniture, Price Guide and Reasons for Values*), some forms of chair have been produced over very long periods. The illustration shows a typical 19th century Windsor with robust baluster turning (look at the arm supports) and a curved, or 'crinoline' stretcher. This stretcher adds more value than an ordinary, turned one. Manufacturers' catalogues show such chairs up to the 1914-18 war. Later versions tend to be less robust, however.
1830-1920
If with yew wood, seat in elm £1,400-£1,800
If in other wood £400-£500

257 A version of the wheelback, without the two diagonally-sloping extra spindles of 258. The turning of the legs is elegant and lacks the extra turned collars which embellish the later types and make them look more mass-produced.
1830-1870   ***Arm £300-£400***
                                        Single £120-£160

259 A high bow-back armchair from Nottinghamshire. This chair is made of beech, with an elm seat, and is of a type made in thousands for use in homes, clubs, institutions and pubs. It could be produced very inexpensively to meet the demands of an expanding market. Everything is designed for simplicity: the splat is simply shaped and pierced; the front arm supports are simply turned, and even the triple-ring turned legs were designed for speed and economy of manufacture.
c.1850-60   ***£600-£800***

258 (Below left) The 'Windsor' chair remained in use and manufacture throughout the period, as indeed it still does. Below are some straightforward mass-produced Windsors as retailed by almost every department store and furnisher.
1830-present day

Wheelback arm £100-£180

Wheelback single £60-£80

260 A high bow-back Windsor from Worksop, made of yew, with an elm seat. This type of chair was made in both the North East and the Thames Valley.
1835-40
£1,600-£2,000

Spoke-back arm £60-£90

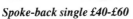

Spoke-back single £40-£60

261 A low bow-back Windsor from Nottinghamshire, made of yew, with an elm seat. The finely-cut and shaped centre splat is made in two halves.
c.1845
£1,400-£2,000

262 A low bow-back Nottingham Windsor. See Colour Plate 35.

113

263 A scroll-back armchair and side chair with horizontal splat incorporating turned boss decoration. The seats are elm but these attractive chairs are otherwise made of fruitwood. The form of the seat and understructure are similar to low bow-back Windsors but the scroll top was easier to manufacture and was soon into mass-production.
c.1840   *£250-£350*

265 Lancashire or Yorkshire bow-back Windsor. See Colour Plate 36.

266 A slightly later variant on the smoker's bow chair. See Colour Plate 37.

264 Tablet-back armchair by Stephen Hazell of Oxford with diagonal back stays of a form which is celebrated to this maker. At the intersection of the diagonal stays a ring decoration derived perhaps from the bosses or wheels of earlier chairs ties the design together.
c.1850   *£1,100-£1,600*

267 The 'bergère' variant on the smoker's bow armchair. The horizontal arm-bow of the previous examples has been replaced by a higher curved back supported by longer turned spindles and the arms flow over the front supports in a continuation of the top curve. The lower half of the chair is similar to No. 275.
c.1860 onwards   *£400-£600*

268 A late 19th century chair which is a cross between a Windsor and a kitchen or office chair. It is very ornate, as the turning and the fretting of the centre splat show. There are still plenty of them about, although there has tended to be a drain of all these types of chair, particularly the smoker's bow, to the export trade.
1850-1940   *£400-£500*

269 A typical kitchen armchair of the 19th century, on turned legs, much beloved of schools and other institutions up to the present day. Usually made in birch or beech and stained or varnished a dark colour. Sometimes the seat is made of elm. When stripped of stain or varnish to their natural colour, these chairs are often a pleasant golden brown.
1850-1940   *£100-£140*

270 A Gothic scroll-back chair with pleasant arched and spindled decoration in the back, made of beech with an elm seat. This more sophisticated version of the scroll-back was used for a long time and may be seen in Edwin Skull's trade card as well as that of Shoolbred in 1876.
c.1850 onwards   *£160-£220*

271 A very pretty late 19th century chair with a seat which has been re-covered. Usually these chairs had an impressed plywood seat, with a pattern embossed by pressure in it, usually finished in a lighter colour than the background.
1870-1900   *In sets, each £140-180*

272 A 'Roman spindle' single or side chair often known as a Worksop chair. It has a double bow top cresting rail with 'Roman spindle' upright supports below and the elm seat is raised on heavily turned legs with tulip feet. On Allsop's trade card of 1871-87 this chair is described as a 'Roman' chair.
c.1860 onwards   *£400-£600*

273 Lath-back Windsor armchair with double 'H' stretcher and turned arm supports, attributed to the High Wycombe area. Of a type illustrated by Edwin Skull and made in large quantities and sizes. The back uprights were shaped and sawn but in this case have no turning. The turned members are heavily decorated with baluster and vase forms.
c.1850 onwards   *£350-£450*

274 Lath and splat Windsor single or side chair with double 'H' stretcher. In this case the back uprights have been sawn, shaped and turned with ball decoration at the top. The centre splat is pierced and shaped. Typical of kitchen chairs of the mid- and late 19th century.
c.1850 onwards   *£50-£70*

275 Lath and baluster or lath and splat armchair with double 'H' stretcher and dished and saddled elm seat. A variant in which an attractive centre splat, of a design clearly drawn from earlier Windsor antecedents, is placed in the back. Handsome turned arm supports, the arms scrolled over at the ends.
c.1850 onwards   *£300-£400*

276 A 'Roman spindle' armchair with full 'Roman spindle' back spokes and nicely-shaped top cresting rail arched between spokes. The elm seat is raised on baluster turned legs with tulip feet united by a double 'H' stretcher. Probably North Midlands.
c.1860 onwards.   *£300-£400*

115

CHAIRS - dining

The chair provided a fertile field for the Victorian application of styles. When Loudon produced his *Encyclopedia* in 1833 he illustrated Gothic, Grecian and Elizabethan chairs although he clearly favoured the Grecian (expression, suitableness as a seat, simplicity, great effect from few lines) over the Elizabethan (merely a curious piece of antiquity) and his subsequent reprintings into the 1860s did not modify this view. The sabre leg, however, gradually faded from fashion, and the straight front leg, continuing through the period, vied for a time with the cabriole legs of occasional chairs. For solid seating over a period of the day — like, say, lunch or dinner — there is no doubt that the straight front leg, in reeded, fluted, turned, faceted, chamfered, square or a combination of all these forms, prevailed. The light, cabriole-legged balloon-back, for example, was not intended as a dining chair. It is in Loudon that the early, straight-legged, 'dipped' balloon-back makes its appearance together with an upholstered single chair, both described as drawing room chairs and rather deprecated by the author, along with many other chairs, for the contrast between front and back legs.

By the 1840s, in catalogues and design books of such retailers and manufacturers as Toms (1840), Whitaker (1847), Wood (1848) and Smee (1850) the 'rococo' single chair of cabriole-legged balloon-backed form was well established. This type of chair, initially sometimes with stretchers to unite the legs but increasingly without, ran in harness with the straight-legged chair for the next thirty to forty years, appearing in Blackie (1859), Yapp (1879) and C. and R. Light (1881) with little alteration. The straight-legged chair, with a wide variety of back designs but of unmistakably Victorian appearance, has not been as highly valued by collectors as the balloon-back cabriole, but may increasingly be appreciated, in better quality versions, for its durable and comfortable properties.

The Reformed Gothic, the Aesthetic, Arts & Crafts/Art Nouveau and Anglo-Japanese styles all had their expression in chairs following these fashions but Georgian Revival and Queen Anne, from the 1870s onwards, began to dominate dining chair design. Edwardian catalogues such as those of Norman & Stacey (1910) show full-blooded Chippendale, Hepplewhite and Sheraton reproductions which are simply a continuance of the examples to be seen in Heal's (1884) and similar retailers.

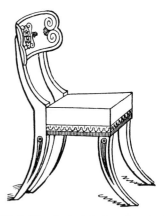

277 A 'Grecian' chair from Loudon's *Encyclopedia* of 1833-1867, actually taken from Thomas Hope. The sabre leg gradually died out during the 1830s and was no longer fashionable after the 1840s.

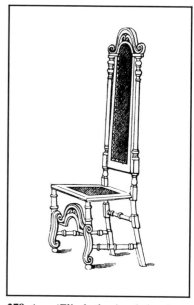

278 An 'Elizabethan' chair from Loudon (1833). Most so-called 'Elizabethan' furniture owed its design to the Stuart period but it is instructive to reflect on this furniture being reproduced from the 1830s onwards. See chair No. 327 for an almost identical specimen.

279 Two 'Drawingroom' chairs from Loudon (1833) the left-hand one showing the 'depressed' balloon-back form. Loudon commented unfavourably on the contrast between front and back legs.

280 Two straight-legged chairs of the 'depressed' balloon-back style. See Colour Plate 38.

281 A combination of the 'Grecian' (sabre leg) and the 'Gothic', probably c.1840 and influenced by Pugin.

£250-£350

282 The classic balloon-back, cabriole-legged Victorian chair, made in walnut, rosewood and mahogany, usually in sets of six. Owing a great deal to French Hepplewhite, this type of chair, particularly with scroll or carved leaf decoration to the back, has come to symbolise the collector's Victorian dining chair but was originally intended for occasional, drawing room use.
1840-1880 *£350-£500*

284 A Georgian Revival dining chair of the Hepplewhite 'shield back' variety, made in mahogany. The shield back form returned to favour in the late 1870s and is to be seen in Heal's catalogue of 1884. This is a high quality, crisply-carved version which, in sets of six or eight, is now quite a costly collector's target. Such chairs were also made in solid satinwood versions which are now very expensive.
1870-1900 *£600-£800*

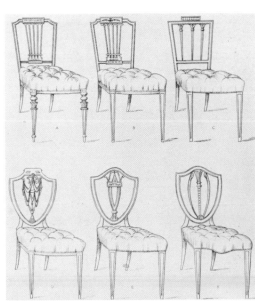

283 'Edwardian' chairs of a type made in mahogany, American walnut and other hardwoods from the later 1870s onwards. The use of a scrolled broken pediment is perhaps more characteristic of the 1880s onwards when the Georgian Revival was making its influence felt but examples in the catalogues of Shoolbred (1876), Wyman (1877) and C. and R. Light (1881) show very similar chairs with a shell motif (Queen Anne) or similar embellishment to the bas-relief machine carving of these examples.
1830-1890 *£250-£350*

285 A page from *The Cabinet Maker's Pattern Book* published by Wyman & Sons in 1877 showing chairs in the 'Chippendale' style. This illustrates the Victorians' love of misnaming earlier styles since the chairs above are in styles much more attributable to Sheraton, Adam and Hepplewhite. However, it is likely that these 18th century designs were extremely well copied and would now be hard to distinguish from the originals without disassembly.
1870-1890 *£220-£300*

286 Late 19th century 'Queen Anne' chair. A reasonably faithful reproduction, in walnut, of an early 18th century design of the stretchered variety. It is possible that the first 'Queen Anne' reproduction chairs were those designed by Richard Norman Shaw (q.v.) for Willesley in 1865, but the form was more numerously reproduced somewhat later. At the end of the century and on to 1910, they are exhibited prominently in catalogues.
1880-1910　　　　　　　　　　　*£300-£400*

287 Late 19th century/early 20th century 'Chippendale' chair of heavy mahogany with a rococo approach to the splat design and carving. The lower edge of the front seat rail is gadrooned. The chair exhibits the characteristic Victorian lack of feel for 18th century proportion in the weak relation of seat and front legs to the bold back — the cabrioles are a classic example of Victorian weakness at the ankle. Still a very collectable chair.
1880-1910　　　　　　　　　　　*£500-£750*

CHAIRS - balloon back, Victorian

The balloon-back chair was quite a perennially popular form and has been appreciated by collectors since the 1960s. It is worth reiterating that most balloon-back chairs were not intended as dining chairs, which are structurally heavier. The light cabriole-leg balloon-back was for occasional use in the drawing or sitting room.

288 A standard Victorian mahogany chair of a type made from the 1840s to the 1880s. Not actually a balloon-back but showing how it could easily come about as a sequence of this design. The legs are a bit pumpkin-like and the top rail is heavy.
1840-1880　　*In sets, each £200-£250*

289 A mahogany balloon-back chair with some carving appended under the top rail. It would probably have been wiser to restrain this sort of decoration to the lower rail, since the appended upper carving detracts.
1840-1880　　*In sets, each £250-£350*

290 A classic example of an oval walnut balloon-back chair with a wool-work covered seat. The amount of carving on the back and on the 'knee' of the cabriole legs, which end in scrolled feet, is restrained and pleasant.
1850-1880
In sets of six or more, each £350-£500

291 A late, turned-leg version of the balloon-back in mahogany, with a central carved splat instead of a horizontal rail. The back is quite attractive but the legs, with their rather clumsy collars, the large upper ones carved with vaguely leaf forms, are not harmonious with the curves of the back.
1850-1880   *In sets, each £200-£300*

292 A variant of the balloon-back on cabriole legs but with Gothic influence in the shaping of the back. The dot-dash grooving in the flat surface and the sudden cranks in the shaping are tell-tale characteristics of the later varieties of Victorian rococo.
1850-1880   *In sets, each £250-£350*

293 A mahogany variation on the principle, this time with a French Louis XV shape to the back, which is upholstered. Still rococo enough for Victorian tastes and of a shape which is a perennial favourite. Sometimes known as 'French Hepplewhite'.
1860-1880   *In sets, each £250-£300*

294 An oval upholstered chair with a buttoned back, painted and decorated with carving. Again a French design which returned to popularity in the 1870s, conveying an impression of lightness and elegance whilst still being stronger structurally than the cabrioled balloon-back. The oval back is perhaps a little heavy.
1870-1890   *In sets, each £300-£400*

295 A variation on the seat covering showing deep buttoning on this rosewood cabriole-leg chair which has acanthus-leaf carving on the back and central rail.
1840-1880   *In sets, each £250-£350*

296 Another variant in the back, which has been scrolled into two cusps on the top rail and has acanthus-leaf carving on the central rail.
1840-1880   *In sets, each £250-£350*

CHAIRS - straight front legs, Victorian

Chairs with straight front legs in this section are generally dining chairs but, obviously, occasional chairs of this type exist as well. The variation in style is greater and most of the major schools of influence had their effect on the dining chair. Indeed, the almost sacred aura connected with the business of eating made this imperative — dining rooms were sometimes larger and more carefully furnished than sitting rooms. This is consistent with an ecclesiastical work ethic, which advised that one should be either working — out of the house or in a study — or eating, or sleeping but not idling about in a sitting room frittering away one's time.

297 A mahogany chair of a design made from the 1830s to the end of the 1850s, from which this example dates. Its form clearly gave rise to many variations in back and legs but was essentially the basic upright Victorian chair's original.
1850-1860 *In sets, each £350-£450*

299 An oak chair, described as being 'in the Eastlake manner' due to the spindled arched gallery in the back, but with slab-like front legs connected to the back ones with rather nicely-turned, baluster-formed stretchers. Acorn finials and 'money' pattern carving decorate the uprights.
1870-1890 *In sets, each £100-£120*

298 Another mid-19th century design in oak which persisted in various alternatives until later in the century. C. and R. Light illustrate an upholstered chair with a similar back in their 1887 catalogue. The desire for a vaguely medieval form is evidently satisfied by the caned panels and carved decoration.
1840-1880 *In sets, each £140-£180*

300 Another oak chair with an arched spindled gallery in the back and a panel, strangely turned with concentric rings. The front legs are turned with a multiplicity of collars. Again, the influence of Eastlake, Talbert — any 'reformers' will do.
1870-1890 *In sets, each £60-£80*

301 Another oak chair with turned spindled galleries, of a type popular in the 1870s and 1880s. This is the armchair out of a dining set using single chairs of similar design. The triangular top rail is carved in bas-relief with floral scrolls and the leather covered upholstery has a Prince of Wales' feathers motif on the back.
1870-1890 *In sets each £160-£220*

302 An interesting 'near pair' of chairs of very high quality. There is an aura of the Aesthetic Movement about the spindled galleries but the quality of turning and the latticing of the back of the right-hand version lead one to feel that one of the celebrated designers may have had a hand in them, Godwin perhaps, for there is an Anglo-Japanese feel to them, or even Norman Shaw, who designed similar chairs for Lord Armstrong's house, Cragside. In fact, they are by Waterhouse, an architect who designed furniture for a manufacturer called Capeland, and was a close friend of Norman Shaw.
1870-1880

Set of six £4,000-£5,000

303 An occasional chair in mahogany, of a design found in manufacturers' catalogues of the 1870s and 1880s with incised, or 'scratch', decoration. Usually part of a suite of chaise-longue, armchairs and six singles, akin to balloon-backs.
1870-1880   *In sets of six or more, each £140-£180*

304 Another similar chair of lighter construction, incised with dot-dash grooving and inlaid with boxwood motifs.
1870-1880   *In sets, each £120-£160*

305 A 'Gothic' design of oak chair made by Shoolbred. Not a happy termination to the top rail which leaves the outsides chopped off in mid air.
1880-1890   *In sets, each £100-£120*

306 An oak dining chair, the 'carver' from a set of singles, of rather elaborately carved design using leaves and flowers, gadrooning and scrolls, intended to impress with the owner's importance.
1870-1890   *In sets, each £220-£280*

307 This oak chair would nowadays be auction catalogued as 'Gothic' but the Victorians might equally have described it as 'Elizabethan'. It is very close, almost identical, in design to a chair shown in W. Blackie's *Cabinet Maker's Assistant* of 1853 to 1859, in which most of the styles are described as 'Elizabethan'. Blackie's version has buttoned upholstery rather than the striped and patterned plush of this one.
1850-1860   *For set of six £900-£1,200*

308 This rather heavy stuffed and padded dining chair in mahogany with considerable carving in leaf and scroll form is characteristic of the more solid approach to dining room chairs. Quite often available in sets of more than six, they are becoming appreciated for their comfort.
1840-1880   *In sets, each £250-£350*

309 A mahogany 'Chippendale' chair with a back of quite faithful reproduction. The seat is, however, smaller than the original would have been and the seat rail has been made the same width as the legs. The original would have been more likely to have a deeper seat rail even if the legs were of the same proportions.
1880-1900   *In sets, each £350-£400*

310 A mahogany 'Chippendale' ladder-back chair with carved pierced rails to the back, which is well executed. The seat and the square legs are, again, small and thin compared with the 18th century original; the seat rail is not deep enough.
1880-1900   *£400-£600*

311 Typical mass-produced 'Chippendale' style chairs with rexine (imitation leather) covered drop-in seats. No problems of confusion with the originals here; both 'carvers' and single chairs are of proportion and dimensions well away from the 18th century. The Gothic style back splat is quite a good copy of an original design.
1890-1930   *In sets, each £120-£160*

312 A mahogany 'Hepplewhite' chair of very good proportion, on moulded square tapering front legs. The back is a variation of the shield back, curved in shape with carving on the rails. The seat is full and bold, serpentine-shaped at the front and worthy of the original.
1880-1900　　*In sets, each £500-£600*

313 A classic shield-back 'Hepplewhite' chair with carved Prince of Wales' feathers in the back design. The tapering square legs and slightly bowed seat are copied faithfully from the original and the proportion is good. A well-made chair like this was very much more expensive than a mass-produced, thin 'Chippendale' design — about nine guineas for this as against one and a half for the mass-produced item.
1890-1920　　*In sets, each £600-£700*

314 A mahogany wheel-back 'Hepplewhite' chair of good proportion and workmanship. The carving of the back is a considerable achievement and, with wear, and without sight of the unpolished areas, such chairs can be difficult to tell from an original period chair.
1890-1920, but could be made even now — at a price　　*In sets, each £500-£600*

315 Another 'grand' chair in mahogany of semi-medieval design with leatherette or rexine covering to the upholstered parts. A popular style from the 'Abbotsford' influences onwards.
1880-1890

As a single armchair £200-£240
A set of two plus four singles
£1,800-£2,500

316 A late, straight, 19th century chair with a needlework covering and ring-incised, turned front legs.
1880-1890　　*In sets, each £90-£120*

317 Another simple, straight chair with a spindled gallery and ringed front legs.
1880-1890　　*In sets, each £80-£100*

The return to 18th century styles in the 1880s affected chairs almost more than other furniture. Chippendale, Sheraton and Hepplewhite chairs were produced in varying grades of quality and exactitude. Queen Anne cabriole legs with 'fiddle' backs soon followed and, of course, the medieval oak craze had to be met by chair makers . . .

320 A mahogany armchair in Sheraton style with inlaid boxwood stringing lines as decoration. There is also an inlaid oval satinwood and marquetry panel in the broad top rail. These panels were available ready-made by machine from the trade.
1890-1910   *In sets, each £220-£280*

318 A mahogany 'Chippendale' chair of some considerable quality. The carved splat is of Gothic style in its origins and the scrolled cabriole legs end in ball-and-claw feet. It is still unmistakably Victorian, however, from its slightly narrow proportions.
1880-1900   *In sets, each £500-£600*

319 A highly-carved 'Chippendale' chair with a wool-work tapestry seat. The narrow proportions, particularly of the back, proclaim it to be Victorian. The cabriole legs, which are elegantly carved, show that incipient bandyness and weakness at the ankle which are also characteristic.
1880-1900   *In sets, each £600-£750*

321 Not quite Sheraton and not quite Edwardian 'own brand', these small chairs still owe more to the late 18th and early 19th century than to the 1900-1910 period in which they were made. The back is a Sheraton design-book copy and the tapering square legs end in block feet.
1890-1910   *In sets, each £70-£90*

322 An example of the mahogany 'Queen Anne' style of dining chair which had a great vogue from around 1900 to 1940. They do not seek to emulate original Queen Anne period chairs too closely — these examples are usually mahogany or stained to look like it, and mahogany was not used in quantity until after 1730 — and they are mass-produced in unmistakably economic ways, so there is little problem in differentiating them from the originals.
1900-1940   *In sets, each £120-£150*

323 Elegant mahogany chairs based on a Queen Anne design and of a shape quite popular in the early 20th century. The front legs are an English variation on the cabriole, usually associated with country makers. The back curves are restrained without being stiff. The central panel of the back is caned and the pincushion seat is covered with a striped tapestry. Intended as an occasional chair but would now be sold for dining.
1900-1920   *In sets, each £140-£200*

324 Typical 'Jacobean' chairs, in oak, of a type also very popular from 1890-1940, made to go with the bulbous-legged refectory-style table of the 'Jacobethan' dining room. Twist turning is the key to these chairs which owe their form to the second half of the 17th century.
1890-1940   *In sets, each £60-£160*

325 (Above right) Four more variations on the popular 'Jacobean' chair theme, with pincushion seats covered in rexine (an imitation leather). More expensive than the previous examples because the stretchers between the legs are turned as well, not just left square for cheapness. The top pair on the right have abandoned the twist turning normally used and have turned pillar supports capped by finials instead. (The rather elaborately carved top rail was not popular on post-1920 versions.)
1890-1920   *In sets, each £150-£200*

326 The end of the line for the 'Jacobethan' style. An oak chair with twist turning in prominent places and cheap square sections elsewhere. The drop-in seat is covered in rexine.
1920-1930 *In sets, each £40-£65*

327 An oak arm and a single chair in 'Carolean' style with caned back and seat panels. They are fairly faithful reproductions of chairs of the Restoration period of 1680-1690, showing the elaborately-carved scrolled front stretcher between the front legs echoed in the top rail of the high back. They would be detected by the lack of age and wear apparent in them, and by their colour. Such chairs were originally made of birch, beech, oak or walnut and stained black. They are very decorative but not popular as dining chairs due to the weakness of the seat jointing to the back and legs; the very thinness of the seat frame makes the joints very susceptible to breakage by weight or leverage. Nevertheless, this design, of all reproductions, is probably the one most faithfully copied.
1830-1910 *Each £350-£450*

329 An oak chair of square design in emulation of the 1650-1670 period and often known as 'Cromwellian'. The turning on the front legs is not of a period type.
1890-1920 *In sets, each £130-£160*

328 A pair of oak bobbin-turned chairs in the style of 1660-1680 with leather covered backs and seats, peppered with large brass-headed studs like a pair of Restoration Hell's Angels! These must surely have met the taste for medievalism with a vengeance. The bobbin-turned stretchers and the legs, with their square-section joints, look like faithful copies of the originals.
1880-1930 *In sets, each £140-£180*

330 Another pair of oak chairs, known as Cromwellian in style, which emulate those of 1650-1670. They are similar to the previous examples but the more severe column turning of the legs, with plain square stretchers joining them at ground level, is perhaps more apposite to the Protector's time. Covered in velvet and just right for that big reproduction refectory table in the dining room.
1890-1930 *In sets, each £100-£120*

CHAIRS - small Edwardian oak

The period from 1900 to 1914 saw the mass production of a large number of small chairs of rather square proportion, made in oak. Some had drop-in seats, some were rushed, some simply webbed and upholstered with a shiny rexine covering. Their design was quite simple and functional; the legs were either square section tapering or turned and the back, fairly severe in outline, leant sometimes to the 18th century and sometimes to more modern, art nouveau designs for its style. Individual comment on each version would be either unrewarding or unwise. Suffice it to say that they are still a source of cheap matched seating.

331 Two of the many variations of small Edwardian oak chairs that were made from 1900 to 1914. *In sets, each £40-£60*

CHAIRS
Arts and Crafts, Art Nouveau and after: 1860-1930

The reader is not going to be bored by another harangue on the differences between the Arts and Crafts Movement and Art Nouveau. That is done frequently throughout other sections of the book. Some of the chairs here will be known loosely as 'art nouveau' by the trade and many collectors. So be it.

332 A William Morris rush-seated 'Sussex' type of armchair as shown in the firm's catalogues of the 1870s. This chair is also featured in the Country and Kitchen section (No. 244) but it is legitimately shown here because the middle-class trendies who bought Morris & Co. furniture used these chairs for dining and occasional use, thus reflecting the genuine role that Morris & Co. played in the Arts and Crafts Movement. Many rush-seated chairs were produced in emulation of this precedent. 1865-1895 *Singly £90-£120*

333 A rush-seated chair by William Burges (q.v.) painted dark green, with painted decoration. It has been remarked (by Michael Whiteway) that the chair looks like something out of a modern Italian café. Possibly slightly pre-dates the William Morris chairs but at this point Burges and Morris were fairly close. c.1865 *£250-£350 (because by Burges)*

334 The celebrated design by A.H. Mackmurdo of the Century Guild. A chair with a high back and original upholstery with characteristic 'heart' shapes. A similar chair is in the Victoria and Albert Museum.
c.1885   *£1,000-£1,500*

335 Another chair by the William Morris firm, in which the tulip motif has been used in the inlaid panels in the back uprights. Again, based on a traditional form but this time the width of the back and the length of the arms is a bit attenuated.
1900-1912   *£200-£275*

336 (Left) The use of rush seating seems to have been an almost morally-inspired move by the members of the Arts and Crafts Movement, as though rush seats and plain oak, with their 'country' connotations, were somehow less decadent than stuffed Victorian upholstery. But then architects have always been puritans at heart. Add to that characteristic the socialist principles of William Morris and where do you land? On something fairly hard, usually. It was Voysey and others, designing in what is known as the 'vernacular' tradition, i.e. in the native idiom, who produced chairs in clean lines made of plain oak and with seats of rush. This chair exhibits all these characteristics and the motifs, now associated with 'art nouveau', such as the heart shape, used by Voysey.
1890-1910   *If attributable to a known designer, £250-£350*
                                                    If not, £70-£90

337 (Top right) Plain oak, rush seat, but not particularly likely to have been made by a 'known' designer — too stiff, a bit pinched.
1880-1910   *In sets each, £40-£50*

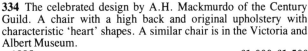

338 An oak rush-seated chair in a style going on from progressive art nouveau towards something more modern, as evidenced by the arched cross-stretcher between the legs. The tapering back with the pierced 'handle' looks most uncomfortable.
1905-1915   *In sets, each £40-£50*

339 More rush seating, more vertical discomfort. Very much a 'clean' architect's design, the back following a model by William Birch.
c.1900   *In sets, each £200-£300*

340 Chair designed by Charles Rennie Mackintosh of Glasgow, now famous for the elongated shape, the low proportion of the seat and the strange motifs, weepy eyes, seagulls-viewed-end-on and other Mackintosh hallmarks.
Before you mock or turn away, reflect that Mackintosh designed his furniture to make specific impacts in rooms of high proportion or in the now-famous cafés and tea rooms where other designs would have been unnoticed. His work now sells as 'art' rather than furniture, hence the price.
1890-1910   *£12,000+*

341 An art nouveau armchair with decorated back panel in characteristic floral design. The wavy arm supports are a 'quaint' feature. Possibly Liberty's. May have had a rush seat subsequently covered over.
c. 1900   *£200-£250*

342 A more commercial art nouveau chair with characteristic heart shapes cut through. The seat looks like a repair job.
c. 1900   *£90-£120*

343 Commercial oak chair with a rexine or leatherette seat cover fixed by brass studs. Owing something to 'art nouveau' styles due to the tapering back and legs ending in 'block' feet but fairly mass-produced in appearance.
1890-1910   *In sets, each £80-£95*

345 Arm and single chair of commercial production with drop-in rush seats.
c. 1900
Singles in sets, each £35-£50
Arm, each £60-£85

344 Another oak art nouveau chair, quite good quality and stiffened for strength by the curved apron under the seat. An enduring design.
c. 1900   *In sets, each £40-£60*

346 A somewhat Scandinavian-looking chair with leather panels in the bobbined back and a leather seat. The panels are moulded with flowers and birds. Very 'arts and crafts'.
c. 1900   *£250-£350*

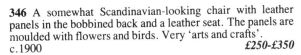

347 A typical turned spindled rocking chair of a type made in large numbers. This example has been re-covered.
c.1880   **£250-£350**

348 A typical Edwardian child's chair in birch or beech, originally either white-painted or stained. The lower mechanism allows the chair to be set in a lower position or, additionally, to rest as a 'rocker' on the ground. Quite a common and popular child's chair in the pre-1914 period.
1900-1914   **£250-£325**

350 A mid- to late Victorian child's steamer chair of unusual embellishment, with pierced leaf carving, ivory dot inlays and the usual caned seat and back panel.
1860-1900   **£400-£550**

349 A folding 'safari' chair, shown both open and closed, suitable for collapsing and portage by a bearer. The turned legs unscrew from the frame for further dismantling and carriage. It is made of mahogany with cane seat and back and is quite strong. When the lady concerned was tired, the chair was easily set up and she could be carried by native bearers. Made by Ward & Co. until the 1920s.
1880-1920   **£300-£400**

There seems to have been a revival of the corner chair, which had languished after the end of the 18th century, in the 1870s. Why is a mystery, for it is an essentially masculine, leg-separating and inconvenient form. Richard Norman Shaw (q.v.) designed rush-seated corner chairs for J.C. Horsley's house Willesley, with a cabriole front leg and rather early 18th century form, stained green, in the late 1860s and, before that, a type based on late 17th century models for his own office. The corner chair fascinated Shaw, so perhaps he is responsible for its revival; his interiors show several types. It is clear from furnishers' catalogues that, by the end of the century, there was a steady demand for them.

351 Here is an early 20th century reproduction of a 'Chippendale' type, with a drop-in rush seat. The square legs and turned back supports are correct copies of the original, as are the fretted splats which are a Chippendale design. This version is made in oak to accord with the 'country' connotations of the rush seat. If made in mahogany, the drop-in seat would be upholstered. Would almost certainly be sold as 18th century.
1900-1910   *£350-£400*

352 A mahogany corner chair of much more Edwardian form but still based on 18th century design, this time late Sheraton. The drop-in seat is covered with tapestry and the back has an inlaid satinwood 'shell' in it.
1900-1914   *£140-£180*

353 Another more Edwardian variant in the mahogany corner chair — the splats are of 18th century design origin but the top rail at the corner has been embellished with the pedimented shape so dear to Edwardian hearts. The seat upholstery is fixed and finished with brass studs round the edge.
1900-1914   *£140-£170*

354 A rather feebler version with a half-circular back rail and a single central splat inlaid with a Sheraton 'shell'. The thin seat and spindly legs make it look easily destructible. An intermediate step to a rounded chair — the next stage is to make the seat round instead of square.
1900-1914   *£70-£100*

355 And here it is — the fully rounded 'corner' chair in which the seat as well as the back rail are of circular shape. There is now no particular reason to think of it as a corner chair except for the centrally-placed front leg, which ensures a limb-separating posture for anyone seated straight on the chair.
1900-1914   *£70-£100*

CHAIRS - papier-mâché

Papier-mâché, a material made by pulping paper, originated in the Middle and Far East, but was introduced to Europe during the 17th century. (The term, in French, literally means mashed or pulped paper.) It was used to imitate carving and, when japanned, or black lacquered, was painted with flowers or festoons. Boxes, trays and small tables were treated in this manner. Henry Clay of Birmingham patented a production method, in 1772, for pasting sheets of paper over a mould, then baking the result. He called this 'paper ware' but his successors, Jennens & Bettridge, marketed their wares as 'papier-mâché' and the process was used for all sorts of furniture, often inlaid with pearl shell (mother-of-pearl) as well as being painted. In the 1850s and 1860s it had a considerable vogue, giving rise to a particular species of Victorian furniture.

359 A more solid form tending towards a scoop-back profusely inlaid with pearl-shell in naturalistic forms with birds. The decoration of the cabriole legs is much worn at the knee and the upholstery needs renewal.
1850-1870   **£800-£1,500**

357 An unusual papier-mâché and brown lacquer chair, showing the versatility of the manufacturing process and the forms which could be produced. The elegance of this cabriole-legged variant of the spoon-back does not require floral or pearl-inlay decoration; key-pattern banding and heart-shape embellishment are sufficient. The caned seat is covered by a squab cushion.
c.1850   **£350-£450**

358 Papier-mâché chairs and table. See Colour Plate 39.

356 A spoon-back papier-mâché chair with inlaid pearl-shell decoration in floral designs of the highest quality. The cabriole front legs and caned seat are typical of this type of chair which, if in good condition, can be highly valued. Damage to this sort of chair is, however, very difficult to remedy and the collector who is not expert in this field is advised to avoid damaged papier-mâché chairs. The brilliance of the decoration makes this an expensive chair.
1850-1870   **£1,500-£2,000**

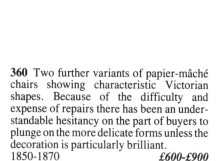

360 Two further variants of papier-mâché chairs showing characteristic Victorian shapes. Because of the difficulty and expense of repairs there has been an understandable hesitancy on the part of buyers to plunge on the more delicate forms unless the decoration is particularly brilliant.
1850-1870   **£600-£900**

CHAIRS - prie-dieu

The prie-dieu chair is intended for praying or kneeling on. Generally the back has a slight rake and widens out at the top, the front legs are turned and the back legs splayed outwards. It was popular from about 1840 to 1880 not only for prayers but for ladies with broad crinoline skirts to sit on (although the prie-dieu chair preceded the crinoline skirt). High Church religious observance became fashionable in the 1850s and gave, perhaps, an impetus to the form and nomenclature — they were also known as devotional chairs.

361 Three prie-dieu chairs with Berlin woolwork coverings from *Cheval & Pole Screens, Ottomans etc.*, by Henry Wood, published c.1850. All three show the influence of the 'Elizabethan' style, but particularly the two outer chairs with their spiral-turned uprights and finials.
1840-1850   *£350-£500*

364 A prie-dieu chair with highly coloured Berlin woolwork. See Colour Plate 40.

362 A typical prie-dieu chair. The horizontal top is used to rest the arms on during prayers. The legs are fairly typical bulbous turned ones, but the covering is rather more decorative than many of the period which were somewhat sober in design or religious in inspiration.
1840-1880   *£300-£500*

363 A low chair with strong prie-dieu influence in the shape of the back. The carving shows a marked naturalistic turn with its leaf motifs, but the extremely ripe-looking turned and carved bulbous front legs, with thin aggressive white castors, cancel out any leanings to French slenderness. Nevertheless, an extremely well-made chair in mahogany with crisp carving.
1840-1870   *£300-£400*

CHAIRS - upholstered

The upholstered armchair to be seen at the start of the Victorian period followed, not surprisingly, a solid post-Regency sub-classical form. Even as far into the new reign as 1850, versions of 'classical' armchairs were quite current. The rococo style, with both turned leg as well as cabriole, soon became equally current and, in its button-back form, has become synonymous with the 'Victorian' armchair in modern collecting parlance. Taken from the 'set of nine' i.e. a chaise longue, an arm (gentleman's) and armless (lady's) and six occasional (now dining) chairs, the button-back arm and single chair are now highly valued.

It is tempting to assert that, as the century wore on, comfort supplanted style in the design and manufacture of armchairs. Many catalogues exhibit more attention to upholstery — buttoned, padded and overstuffed — than to other features. By the 1860s the wooden arms tend to vanish under stuffing and fabric and, except for specific designers' chairs, a rather lumpy heaviness seems to have arrived. The examples in Norman & Stacey catalogues of 1910 are openly lounge and fireside-seeking, with reproduction 18th century saddleback and sub-Sheraton alternatives. The 'open' armchair did, however, continue to be available as well as the fully-upholstered variety. Towards the end of the century the scrolled arms of the rococo were supplanted by a straighter 'Louis XVI' approach in which the horizontal, padded arms were supported by spindled turning. These spindles eventually spread to the backs of the chairs, either below or above the padded area, in response to an 'Aesthetic' approach to design. Small tub chairs, now very popular, made their appearance, initially as library or smoking-room seating but eventually for wider use. The open-arm chair was also given the Georgian Revival and Edwardian Sheraton treatment, with inlaid 'Adam' motifs.

  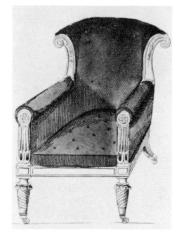 

365 Chairs from Taylor's catalogue of 1850, showing armchair designs virtually unchanged from the 1830s. The use of sub-classical, Egyptian, Grecian and 'Empire' motifs appears to have remained fashionable until this date.

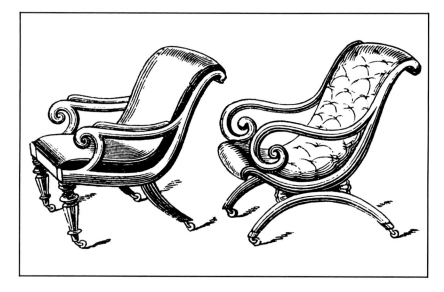

366 Upholstered chairs from Loudon (1833) which he refers to as 'easy reclining chairs for a library, parlour or other sitting room. They are covered in morocco leather, with button tufts; and they are very easy to sit upon.'

134

367 The form of chair in No. 366 is not very far different from these examples, which have retained the turned and heavily-reeded front legs, but allowed the rococo to take over the arms and the small scrolls of the back. The right-hand, armless chair is a type much produced, with turned or cabriole legs, for occasional use throughout the century.
1835-1855   *£600-£850*

369 Button-back Victorian armchair with solid arms, showing a scrolled back shape and carved floral decoration of a form found from 1845-1880. Presumably re-covered in floral fabric at a later date.
1840-1880   *£1,600-£2,200*

368 The classic form of Victorian button-back arm and single upholstered chairs, probably taken from a set of nine, in which a chaise longue and six single occasional chairs would have made up the set. The curvilinear scrolling, cabriole legs and rather exaggerated arm sweep are typical examples of this form, to be found from the late 1840s to the late 1880s.
1840-1880   *Arm £1,200-£1,800*
                                                      Single £1,000-£1,300

370 A chair from C. and R. Light's 1881 catalogue showing the spindled approach to arm support which has spread to the back, both above and below the padded area. Produced perhaps in response to the Aesthetic Movement's influence of the 1870s and possibly intended to be ebonised, this form of chair received much subsequent stricture for its ability to harbour dust.
1870-1890   *£500-£700*

371 Three varieties of 'tub' chair, with open arms and back, from C. and R. Light 1881. This form of chair, re-upholstered in buttoned leather, has enjoyed an expensive vogue in recent years as a form of 'club' armchair.
1870-1890   *£650-£850*

372 A button-back closed armchair. See Colour Plate 41.

CHAIRS - upholstered: *Victorian spoon backs*

The spoon back chair, usually with buttoned upholstery to the back, has become an accepted 'standard' in the antique trade following its revival in the 1960s. Many such chairs are elegant, cheerful and, as with much rococo-derived furniture, slightly frivolous in appearance. The cabriole-legged variety is the most highly valued, followed by turned-leg chairs with backs that are still in flowing curves. The later, straighter types on turned legs are not prized as highly as the early, curly ones.

373 A good example of an open-armed Victorian button-back chair, in the rococo style, with some naturalistic carving on the front cabriole legs and the top rail of the back. An elegant, cheerful chair, fit to bring a scowl to the brow of an architect for, as Handley-Read has pointed out, the style is essentially frivolous and, therefore, not liked by architects. It was, and still is, tremendously popular. Although probably in its heyday in the 1850s and early 1860s, this style was still being made in the 1880s, as manufacturers' catalogues testify.
1850-1885   *£1,200-£1,800*

374 The 'ladies' chair' companion to the previous example. The same excellence applies: crisp carving, smart proportion, deep buttoning, flourishing cabriole legs. A classic spoon back that was popular and made throughout the period. Unfortunately, many versions were made much more cheaply and in woods much inferior to the mahogany of this example. Walnut and rosewood (rare) are in a similar quality bracket to mahogany, but beware the stained birch or beech of later examples.
1850-1885   *£1,000-£1,200*

375 Another open-armed armchair with an oval back, not buttoned in this case, although it could be. Missing its castors. Again, carved with naturalistic flora and scrolls. It can be seen that these curvaceous chairs were not for the heavier members of society: they do have a tendency to break at the joints.
1850-1885   *£1,100-£1,500*

376 Another mid-Victorian chair, usually a partner to an armchair of the previous examples, with floral carving. In this case the 'waist' of the spoon is not quite as positively narrowed as one would wish — that of 374 is a better example.
1850-1885   *£650-£850*

377 A much rounder version of the spoon back with later characteristics in its rococo style — the start of cranks appearing in the flowing curves of the back. Like the other chairs, it is low and would allow the easy spread of complicated garments around it without creasing them.
1850-1880   *£500-£750*

378 A more elaborately-carved version of the open-armed spoon back with buttoned upholstery to the back. There is a lot of detailed naturalistic carving, strongly in the spirit of the rococo of its time.
1850-1870   *£1,500-£2,000*

379 A scoop-back variant with button upholstery, also with naturalistic carving and scrolling of the rococo.
1850-1870   *£1,100-£1,800*

380 A rather stiffer version in which the angular back does not have the accentuated 'waist' of the spoon back and the junction of the cabriole legs with the arm uprights does not flow in the manner of other examples. Possibly Continental.
1850-1870   *£900-£1,400*

381 A squarer low chair which is a successor to the spoon back. It has turned legs instead of cabrioles but the back is inlaid with burr walnut or amboyna and has boxwood inlays in the top in marquetry floral forms.
1860-1880   *£500-£700*

382 Square, turned-leg chairs marking the return to straighter styles prevalent from 1870 onwards. Similar to the previous example but in plain mahogany and with the characteristic dot-dash grooving (incised decoration) so typical of later semi-rococo chairs.
1870-1890
     Arm chair £600-£900
     Single chair £500-£700

As the wavy curves of the rococo died out, so a new, severer, heavier and altogether more stolid form appeared. Built rather too enduringly and associated with the graver, more portentous side of Victorian life, these chairs have not yet found great popularity and many more would have been broken up if they had not been quite so strongly built.

383 This chair almost takes up where the last chairs of the previous section leave off. The back design is very similar but the arms and legs are altogether different. Note the heavy turning and the spindled gallery under the arms — very popular in the 1870s.
1870-1890   *£500-£800*

384 A successor to the spoon back but with classical additions, including pillars and a pedimented top. Note that the chair is missing its castors.
1880-1890   *£500-£750*

385 The classical and 18th century revival has arrived — note the use of the slightly Hepplewhite back, Adam-ish pillars and earlier 19th century legs but with a bit of incised grooving on the seat rail. A similar design occurs in C. and R. Light's 1881 catalogue.
1880-1895   *£400-£550*

386 A heavy single chair, possibly intended for the dining room, with upholstered seat and back. The seat has an overstuffed appearance and it is clearly built for heavy use.
1880-1890   *£100-£140*

387 Another heavily-built chair with rexine upholstery using sub-classical design and carving. The broad, curved top rail with its bas-relief carving of acanthus leaves, is approaching the Edwardian type.
1890-1900   *£200-£400*

388 The style of 'the Louis' has intervened. A sub-French design of the turn of the century which is to be found in suites of furniture for about twenty years. In a sense, the rococo is back, but in a much less attractive form.
1895-1915   *£300-£400*

389 An oak armchair of Gothic reformed design, with all the hallmarks of the movement in its motifs, its 'revealed' construction and decoration. The use of the leather upholstery with impressed sun or sunflower motifs is also very interesting and characteristic of the interest in Japanese design at the time. The chair is a version of a popular Victorian open-arm tub chair, much found in more conventional Victorian versions.
1860-1870   *£1,700-£2,500*

The architects who were involved in the various design movements from 1860 onwards tended to produce chairs that were rather puritan in concept, perhaps as a reaction from the stuffed upholstery of Victorian comfort. A small selection is shown here — chairs by famous designers tend to be individually hunted and expensive.

390 A leather-covered armchair which provides an interesting comparison with the previous 'Gothic' chair with its impressed Godwinesque 'suns'. This is the traditional Victorian version, with baluster and bulbous turning to the legs and arm supports, made in an uncompromising mahogany and with a distinctly 'club' or institutional look about it.
1850-1880   *£700-£1,000*

391 A chair designed by E.W. Godwin (q.v.) for the William Watt catalogue of Art Furniture of 1877. A chair subsequently much copied, particularly the back, which was admired by the Arts and Crafts Movement (q.v.).
c.1880   *£600-£900*

392 This mahogany chair with tulip-pattern upholstery is of a design derived from Godwin, particularly the back, which is similar to an Anglo-Japanese type in which the uprights continue vertically well clear of the back panel. Would now be loosely called 'art nouveau' particularly due to the tulip upholstery, but it is in fact much more of an Arts and Crafts Movement chair of carefully considered design. Note the incised ring turning on the front legs and back uprights and the way in which the arm supports sweep right down through the seat rail to the stretchers between the front and back legs.
1885-1895   *£300-£400*

393 A stained beechwood chair, also of the Arts and Crafts Movement, with twist-turned arm supports. The use of vertical straight turned spindles is rather overdone but it is, again, a very carefully thought-out design.
c.1890   *£250-£350*

394 A more flagrantly art nouveau chair, using the flat capped uprights associated with Voysey in conjunction with inlaid 'whip-lash' floral marquetry in the rather sinuous back rail. There is a strange use of short curtain-like screens to the sides and back.
c.1900   **£1,000-£1,500**

395 A simpler and more satisfying art nouveau chair, again with flat-capped uprights and inlaid marquetry, but this time in a more solid, almost 'hall-porter's' or 'saddleback' derivation for totally enclosed comfort.
c.1900   **£1,200-£1,600**

CHAIRS - upholstered: *occasional*

396 The turn of the century saw an onslaught of a type of chair, neither for dining nor for long-term comfortable seating, which is aptly named 'occasional'. They were made in a variety of styles and we show a selection which covers most of the normal types. Rather than dwell individually on the stylistic origins of each chair, we are sure that our well-informed readers will derive pleasure from identifying the chairs for themselves. The principal characteristic of most of them is their spindly nature, a surety that, were they to be used more than occasionally, they would suffer from damage.
1900-1920   **£50-£75**

Upholstered chairs clearly were produced to meet the demands of fashion like any other furniture. By the end of the 19th century most types of 18th century and earlier design were being produced. Some of these chairs were very well made and are now quite difficult to distinguish from the originals; others are not so successful.

399 Not upholstered at all, but a good example of a 'wainscot' chair in oak emulating a mid-17th century design. The carving on the back, shaping of the arms and frieze under the seat proclaim its modernity — apart from colour and method of construction, of course.
1900-1920   **£250-£350**

397 A 'French Hepplewhite' chair of high quality made in a dark mahogany. Every edge appears to be carved with gadrooning and the legs and arm supports are carved with leaves. It is very close to an 18th century chair, probably an exact copy taken from a genuine original. One can see how this design, given a little more rococo eccentricity, can become the open-armed spoon back of mid-Victorian taste.
1880-1900   **£900-£1,200**

398 A painted armchair with caned seat and back, again in a 'Hepplewhite' design but with other 18th century connotations. Designed for drawing room use.
1910-1920   **£250-£350**

400 A perennially popular armchair (look at any modern reproduction catalogue) in the square-legged 'Chippendale' style with curved arm supports and fully upholstered back. From a catalogue of 1910.
1900-present day
        Depending on material and condition
                     £450-£650

401 A shield-back French Hepplewhite revival chair in mahogany with good carving and acanthus leaves on the moulded arms. The legs are reeded.
1890-1900   **£1,100-£1,700**

402 The bergère, or caned, armchair was a popular type from about 1900 well into the 1930s and has never really died. These oak and mahogany versions are derived from similar chairs of the late 18th and early 19th century except that the oak version has been 'Jacobeanised' by the use of bobbin turning.
1900-1930   *Left, chair oak version £100-£150*
settee oak version £150-£200
Right, chair mahogany version £300-£400
settee mahogany version £300-£450

CHAIRS - upholstered: *arm and easy, 1890-1930*

A mixed bag of chairs for leisure. It is not quite clear when the fully upholstered 'lounge' chair came about: probably from the 1870s onwards, when manufacturers' catalogues start to show them.

403 An armchair with inlaid decoration of the type usually associated with 'Edwardian Sheraton' furniture. The circular design of the chair is fairly typical of the Victorian period, and the front legs with their collars and fluted treatment also follow the turns that later 19th century manufacturers appear to have found irresistible.
1880-1890   *£900-£1,200*

404 An armchair showing again the return to 18th century designs. In this case the legs show a Sheraton influence, particularly in the stringing and crossbanding of the seat rail.
1890-1900   *£250-£350*

405 Six wing easy chairs from a catalogue of c.1910.
Depending on material and condition £150-£400

406 Six more armchairs from the same catalogue of c.1900, showing two surprisingly '1920s' looking chairs with wooden arms and supports (bottom row left and centre) and a rocking chair (bottom right).
Top row, depending on condition £300-£400
Bottom row, left and centre £80-£120
Rocking chair £80-£110

407 Easy chair and settee from Maurice Adams, 1926. Out of date for some years but now coming back. *Easy chair, depending on material and condition £120-£180*
Settee, depending on material and condition £250-£450

408 Two more easy chairs from Maurice Adams, 1926. The right-hand one is of little interest but the left-hand caned 'bergère' chair is of a type very popular in the 1930s.
Right, depending on material and condition £100-£150
Left, depending on material and condition £350-£450

409 A Turkey carpet cover distinguishes this Edwardian armchair from other examples and provides an instance which demonstrates that a quite pedestrian shape can be much enhanced in value by a fashionable, ethnic and colourful fabric. c.1900 *£350-£500*

144

CHESTS

CHESTS - chests of drawers

The chest of drawers, which in the 18th century had played a decorative as well as utilitarian role, suffered a decline in Victorian times. It was relegated to the bedroom and its place in more public rooms was taken by the display cabinet and chiffonier. Loudon, in 1833, even disparaged the chest of drawers' role upstairs, referring to it as a 'common substitute for wardrobes, but far inferior to them for keeping clothes.' He grumbled about the 'useless labour in pulling out and pushing in drawers' as against opening one wardrobe door.

Other designers, retailers and manufacturers show an equal reduction in the decorative treatment of chests of drawers. The article becomes functional, plain, unexciting. There is a degree of quality in construction and the use of decorative veneers on the drawer fronts helps to break the massive solidity of Victorian chests somewhat but, apart from bow-fronted quality pieces, they are more prized for use than ornament. Perhaps the modern fitted bedroom unit, wardrobe and drawers combined, provides an endorsement of the Victorians' view of this piece of furniture.

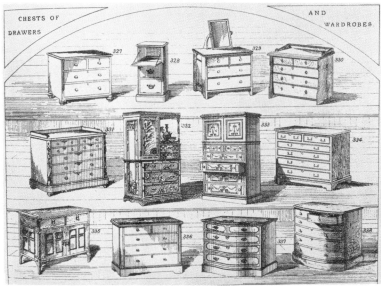

420 A page from Shoolbred's design book of 1876 which collects chests of drawers and wardrobes together, emphasising the purely utilitarian, bedroom role of the Victorian chest of drawers, which did tend to be incorporated in many wardrobe designs. The majority in this display are fairly straight-forward, functional affairs with little stylistic change from their 18th century forebears except in a heaviness of treatment and the substitution in several cases of turned feet or solid aprons to replace bracket feet.

421 A forerunner of the Victorian chest of drawers — a 'Regency' or 'William IV' chest with gadrooned edges and the applied, turned decoration to the vertical sides characteristic of the 1820-1840 period. The rather disc-like turning of the feet presages the Victorian turning of later decades. The quality of both turning and figured mahogany veneers is high and the bow front helps to relieve the overall solidity. One is tempted to believe that, due to its wide proportion and three long deep drawers, this is the lower half of something but this is just the prejudiced eye of 18th century proportion reimposing itself.
1820-1840   *£900-£1,400*

422 A mahogany chest of drawers with twist-turned columns down the sides and a heavy, serpentine-moulded top drawer. The mahogany veneers used are of high quality, with well-matched figure repeated from drawer to drawer, but the overall effect is heavy. It is a type popular from the 1840s onwards, although by 1880 it must have been out of fashion.
1840-1870   *£450-£650*

423 Another chest in mahogany of sub-classical design of a type originating in the 1840s and based on French classical types. Well made, with well matched veneers but nowadays considered ponderous.
1840-1860   *£500-£750*

424 A mahogany chest with three deep drawers at the top. Sometimes the middle deep top drawer is fitted as a secretaire, which adds to value. The quality of veneers is good but the effect is ponderous, particularly the bottom apron which appears to have a drawer in it. These chests, like the previous two, were built usually of deal, with mahogany veneer, for cheapness and many now suffer from missing pieces of veneer due to wear. It is not difficult to repair small missing pieces but the effect before repair tends to put purchasers off.
1850-1870   *£300-£450*

425 Another ponderous chest, but this time bow-fronted. Not really of the correct proportions for modification to an '18th century' bow front on splayed feet by a 'converter', so has to be sold more or less for what it is.
1850-1880   *£400-£550*

426 Possibly the epitome of the good quality Victorian mahogany chest of drawers — tall, bow-fronted, with splendid use of 'feather' mahogany veneers. Capacious, well-built and with drawers fitted to run smoothly. The wooden knobs have been turned with some decorative ridging which refines the bluntness of the ordinary bulbous knob. The bun-shaped and tapered turned feet are also typical. The gradation of the drawer depths is also well handled on this example. Altogether a very professional piece of furniture but, unlike 18th century chests, not very suitable for rooms other than the bedroom and therefore restricted in price accordingly.
1850-1870   *£500-£750*

427 A chest made by Shoolbred & Co. in emulation of a French Empire style, with a marble top. It is made in solid mahogany with mahogany veneered drawer fronts and solid mahogany mouldings, so must have been expensive. Now considered somewhat dark and sombre, so not particularly valued.
1870-1885   *£200-£300*

428 Back to the 18th century — a mahogany bow-fronted chest on splay feet in the 'Hepplewhite' style but with original wooden knobs, whereas Hepplewhite would have had pressed brass plates and handles. Made in quite large quantities and now often 'converted' to an 18th century piece by modification back to brass handles. If a bit tall for 18th century proportion, then it might be further modified by having a drawer removed and the carcase re-jigged.
1880-1900   *£500-£750*

429 Satinwood, satin birch and satin ash were used for better quality chests of drawers, along with ebony stringing lines or pokerwork inlays. The form here is traditional, with an apron base and interesting ring handles of a perhaps consciously 'art' form.
1860-1880   *£500-£800*

431 A mahogany serpentine-fronted chest on chest incorporating two short drawers, six long drawers and a brushing slide. The canted corners are embellished with blind fretwork of Chippendale pattern and the top moulding is dentilled. Although the quality of workmanship appears to be good, the proportion is too cramped for 18th century work. Doubtless a useful piece for the smaller rooms of the early 20th century.
1910-1930   *£500-£700*

430 A 'Chippendale' mahogany serpentine fronted chest of drawers, with a brushing slide and canted corners with blind fretted decoration, on bracket feet. A good reproduction of a mid-18th century chest.
1900-1910   *£600-£900*

434 Another typical Edwardian form of chest, known at the time as a 'Scotch' chest. The drawer edges are bevelled or fielded. The arrangement of the top drawers, with one deep central unit and pairs of small drawers flanking it, dates back to press chests of the 18th century. Available in walnut or mahogany.
1900-1910   *£150-£200*

432 An Edwardian mahogany chest of drawers, on a solid plinth base, with satin-wood crossbanding and oval pressed brass handles to give a 'Sheraton' look.
1900-1910   *£160-£220*

433 A typical Edwardian chest of drawers, with solid plinth base. Available at the time in either 'satin walnut' — which is a kind of solid yellow-brown wood, imported from America — or oak. It has pressed bronze handles and plates. The incised horizontal moulding machined across the drawer fronts and down the sides is a feature of the period.
1900-1910   *£100-£150*

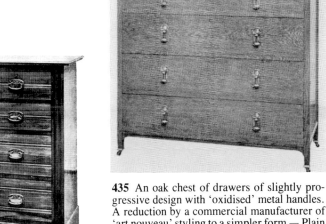

435 An oak chest of drawers of slightly progressive design with 'oxidised' metal handles. A reduction by a commercial manufacturer of 'art nouveau' styling to a simpler form — Plain Furniture is on the way.
1900-1910   *£50-£80*

CHESTS - dressing

The dressing chest appears to be a Victorian invention and, although out of favour for some years, it was quite a good idea. The addition of a mirror to a normal chest of drawers was a quite common form but sometimes the chest top was modified into a minor dressing table top with small drawers and cubby holes. A lot of such chests have had the mirrors removed to convert them into ordinary chests of drawers, but the pine dressing chest appears to be less subject to such modification.

436 A bamboo and rattan dressing chest with a small drawer under the mirror and three long drawers below. Decorative and now quite fashionable.
1890-1900   *£300-£375*

437 Two pine dressing chests with characteristic, shaped cresting rails to the mirrors, also shown under Pine Furniture, as 613.
1890-1920   *£300-£400*

438 An Edwardian pedimented dressing chest, available in a stained oak or mahogany colour, with the characteristic broken pediment to the top rail of the mirror. The top of the chest has been fitted with two small drawers under a shelf.
1900-1920   *£200-£250*

439 An oak dressing chest known as a 'combination' chest due to the tiled splashback to the washstand section, the swing mirror and the cupboard, with a towel rail to the side. A combination of washstand and dressing chest or table with incised grooving across the drawers.
1900-1920   *£100-£200*

440 Another 'combination' chest, this time white enamelled, with tiled splashback and towel rail. Note the shaped cresting rails above mirror and splashback.
1900-1920   *£100-£200*

441 A white enamelled chest with mirror between turned uprights. Many such chests have had the mirror removed and been treated to the pine stripper's caustic tank.
1900-1920   *£100-£200*

CHESTS - military

442 A mahogany military chest fitted with a secretaire drawer. This secretaire arrangement can be extended for the whole drawer length or confined to a smaller central section as shown here.
1845-1865   *£1,750-£2,000*

443 A military chest on turned feet. These chests were used by army officers up to the 1870s. The flush-fitting drawer handles and brass-reinforced corners are their characteristic features, as are the carrying handles to each half. Usually made in mahogany, but padouk, cedar and camphorwood examples are found. Now much reproduced in a variety of woods, including 'distressed' yew veneers and available in large quantities in reproduced form. There is not a lot of difference in price between reproductions and 19th century examples.
1800-1870   *£1,500-£2,000*

444 A camphorwood military secretaire chest of Anglo-Indian origin. This example is slightly more ornate than usual, since it includes a wooden gallery rail around the top which incorporates scrolled carving for decoration. The style of the carving derives from rococo ornamentation of earlier Victorian popularity. The central secretaire section contains a fitted interior. The brass reinforcing plates at the joints and the flush handles are characteristic and the turned feet are removable. A high quality version in a desirable wood.
c.1860   *£2,750-£3,750*

CHESTS - Wellington and specimen

Wellington chests should more correctly be called specimen chests, since that is what they are for. Why the Great Duke's name has been used for them is not clear; he was an inventive man, although he disliked inventors, but there does not seem to be any record of his hand in their design. The lockable flaps, which hold the drawers in place, might make the piece a useful campaign item but when Loudon illustrated a similar chest in 1833 the Duke had not campaigned for nearly twenty years. The type was long-lived, being illustrated by Smee (1850), Shoolbred (1876) and Light (1881).

445 A rather plain Wellington chest of sub-classical Loudon-like design made in mahogany. The third and fourth 'drawers' down are in fact false; the fronts are *trompe-l'oeil* on a single flap which lowers for a writing surface, revealing secretaire fittings inside.
1830-1860
£1,000-£1,500

447 A figured walnut secretaire Wellington chest with the usual turned wooden drawer knobs. Again there is a sub-classical scroll at the top of the locking side flaps like that used on 445. Similarly, the third and fourth drawers conceal a secretaire section and are on a false front which lowers to act as a writing surface. The wood surfaces are more decorative and lighter in tone — hence the higher price.
1850-1880   ***£1,200-£1,800***

446 (Above right) A Wellington chest in feathered satinwood with ebony stringing lines. There is a brass gallery rail around the top. Furniture in woods with 'satin' finishes is often associated with Holland & Sons who produced items in this style in the 1850s and 1860s.
1850-1870   ***£2,500-£3,500***

448 A carved oak 'Wellington' chest with lion-mask carved handles to the drawers. A version of the popular form of Wellington or specimen chest which meets the vogue for carved oak furniture of medieval appearance which started in the 1880s.
1880-1910   ***£1,000-£1,400***

449 Not really anything to do with Wellington chests, but a 20th century specimen chest-on-chest made of oak with wooden drawer knobs having carefully-faceted front surfaces. Very much designed in the manner of Gimson or one of the Arts and Crafts—Cotswold school of the first quarter of the 20th century.
1900-1925   ***£1,000-£1,500***
If attributable to, say, Gimson £3,500-£4,500

450 A collector's specimen cabinet in maple, with spiral pillars at the sides, and a glass panelled door enclosing the twelve drawers. The carved decoration has a mask and leaf form over the door. Quite a remarkable specialist piece.
c.1860   *£5,000-£7,000*

451 An ebonised exhibition-style specimen chest with sophisticated inlaid decoration and a brass gallery round the top. It has ormolu mounts and reflects the rather grand exhibition styles of the mid-19th century influenced by French designers. Known as a semanier, because of the seven drawers — one for each day of the week.
c.1850   *£3,000-£4,000*

452 An Edwardian Wellington chest, made by the celebrated firm of Edwards and Roberts, who have, as usual, used all the decorative motifs associated with Sheraton — satinwood inlaid shells, ribbons, husks, etc., etc.
c.1900   *£2,000-£3,000*

453 A walnut veneered Wellington chest with pleasantly curled figure of almost burr type.
c.1855   *Walnut £1,000-£1,400*
             Bird's eye maple £1,000-£1,250

454 A plain oak Wellington chest similar to the previous example.
c.1855   *£500-£700*

CHESTS - coffers

The coffer endured a revival in the 1860s. After all, it is a medieval piece of furniture. The revival led to an outright spate of reproductions, rebuilds and fakes. It was not difficult to embellish the many plain three-band coffers which existed by adding carving to them. Some coffers must have been 'made up' by using the three-panel heads of small beds.

455 A painted chest by an enthusiast of the late 1860s or 1870s, with heavy strap hinges in wrought iron and matching wrought iron reinforcing frame on the top. The painted flowers have the appearance of sunflowers (Gothic-Anglo-Japanese-Aesthetic) and the piece follows the vogue for painted Gothic furniture associated with Burges (q.v.) who liked painted flamboyant pieces but was not too fussy about Gothic purity of motifs — he used Gothic, classical and Renaissance illustrations indiscriminately to get the flamboyant effect he liked. Attributed to Morris & Co.
1865-1875   *£2,000-£3,000*

456 A 'hall coffer' by Gillows based on an adapted design of Talbert (q.v.). Reformed Gothic features include the pillars, dentillated and incised carving. The domed top is normally considered a drawback in the British Isles because the piece cannot then be used for a table or seat.
1870-1880   *£800-£1,200*

457 From original interpretations to an out-and-out reproduction of high quality. It is possible that this was a plain, three-panel oak coffer of correct period, to which carved and inlaid decoration has been added. There is an honest look about the feet, formed by carrying down the joined frame, but the carved decoration and inlays give rise to doubts. Certainly, the arcaded panels (used often enough in 'correct' coffers) have a new, crisp look about them and the decoration inlaid into the three panels does not ring true to period.
1890-1920   *£600-£800*

458 This rather handsome mule chest, which would originally have resembled the example from *British Antique Furniture* illustrated on the right, has been extensively carved over in bas-relief with guilloche and sunflower motifs (the sunflower was the fertility symbol of the Gothic Revival, Aesthetic and Arts and Crafts Movements) which, at one time, would have ruined the piece in the eyes of any antique dealer. The interior-decoration role of the antiques trade of today, however, ensures a ready market for such pieces, but not with the purist collector.
Originally mid-18th century
Carving late 19th century   *£1,200-£1,800*

Oak mule chest of c.1770, showing the original plain surfaces and panels.

DESKS

Written communication and clerical effort accelerated in the Victorian period. It is not surprising that writing furniture, including tables (q.v.) and bureaux (q.v.) became a major part of the cabinet maker's range. Whether small and incidental, like davenports and bonheurs-du-jour, or large, imposing and directorial, like pedestal or partners' desks, or even elegantly decorative, like the reproduced Carlton House writing table, there were many versions and presentations of the writing surface.

Most of the forms used — like the pedestal desk, the bureau and the davenport — came from earlier periods, from before 1800. Naturally, the Victorians added their own presentation to these forms; the Georgian Revival brought back an 18th century accuracy to the pedestal desk, a piece of furniture which had never really ceased production throughout the period, but there were Victorian variants on the form. The davenport, a square, severe, almost nautically bare piece of functionalism in Gillows' design book of the 1790s, acquired classical columns or Gothic tracery in the 1830s, scrolled cabrioles in the 1850s, diagonal planking in the 1860s, ebonising in the 1870s, incised grooves in the 1880s, while all versions overlapped merrily with each other.

To define the term 'desk' in rather haphazard fashion for this section, which essentially consists of davenports and pedestal desks, may seem a little narrow. After all, a bureau is a desk and so is a bonheur-du-jour. Some writing tables veer towards the pedestal desk. However, it helps to retain an alphabetical arrangement which has become trade and auctioneers' practice.

470 The 'Devonport' as Loudon saw it in 1833 — sub-classical pillars (left) or scrolls (right). Both feature the top, sloping section being able to slide forward over the knees of the writer (shown right) and both have side slides (shown right) 'to hold papers, a candle etc'. Both have real drawers down one side and imitation drawers on the other. They are on castors so that 'industrious young ladies' will find them not only useful but mobile.

DESKS - davenports

The davenport desk was a late 18th century piece, said to come from an order entered in Gillows' cost books of the 1790s, 'Captain Davenport, a desk'. In 1833 Loudon referred to it as a 'Devonport (so called from the inventor's name)' and categorically removed the piece from the military or nautical masculine to 'drawing room writing-cabinets used by ladies'. Perhaps the gallant Captain intended his for his lady. The davenport was produced in all the stylistic varieties of the period but, apart from the Regency versions which now go from £4,000 to £8,000, the burr walnut piano-top version of the 1850s and 1860s leads the collecting field.

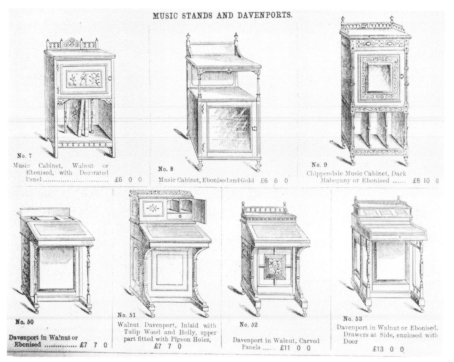

No. 7
Music Cabinet, Walnut or Ebonised, with Decorated Panel £6 0 0

No. 8
Music Cabinet, Ebonised and Gold £6 6 0

No. 9
Chippendale Music Cabinet, Dark Mahogany or Ebonised £8 10 0

No. 50
Davenport in Walnut or Ebonised £7 7 0

No. 51
Walnut Davenport, Inlaid with Tulip Wood and Holly, upper part fitted with Pigeon Holes, £7 7 0

No. 52
Davenport in Walnut, Carved Panels £11 0 0

No. 53
Davenport in Walnut or Ebonised, Drawers at Side, enclosed with Door £13 0 0

471 A page from Heal's catalogue of 1884 illustrating davenports and music stands. The four davenports shown, on the bottom row, exhibit the characteristics of the later mass-produced items particularly in the use of machine-turned columns. All the examples shown were available in walnut, but three were also available in ebonised finish as an alternative. That on the right has a 'piano' top.

472 A satinwood davenport of the very early 19th century showing the restrained early design, a brushing slide at the top of the drawers.
c.1820   *£6,000-£8,000*

473 Made in rosewood, with a 'Gothic' arched door, flat Corinthian pillars. A restrained and elegant piece, not unlike a design shown for 1835.
1830-1840   *£3,000-£4,000*

474 An 'Elizabethan' or medieval davenport which conforms to the popular baronial style of the 1830s and 1840s. The heavy carving and rather parqueted surface to the fall pander to the medievalism which persisted throughout the early Victorian period and was revived in the late, post-1880 era.
1840-1860   *£2,000-£3,500*

475 The severe, early Regency form of davenport. See Colour Plate 42.

476 A burr walnut 'piano-top' davenport. See Colour Plate 43.

477 A slightly more severe 'piano-top' davenport. See Colour Plate 44.

154

479 A high quality burr walnut 'harlequin' davenport with a 'piano' shaped top with a lid that lifts to reveal a pull-out writing slide. The superstructure has a hinged letter rack operating on a spring mechanism released by a button inside a short drawer. The piece has inlaid boxwood stringing and stylised flowers. The drawers down the side in view are genuine sliding drawers, whilst on the other side there are four dummy drawer fronts. This is the normal, and preferred arrangement except for examples where the drawers are contained inside a cupboard door. An example which has all the high quality features and gadgetry associated with the highly-prized versions. A very similar model is illustrated in Shoolbred, 1876.
1860-1880   *£3,500-£5,000*

478 A rococo davenport with scrolled corbels and twist-turned supports which has fretted panels in naturalistic motifs for decoration. Similar panels are shown on a davenport illustrated in Smee's catalogue of 1850.
1850-1860   *£1,750-£2,500*

480 An interesting form of burr walnut davenport of a design shown in catalogues of the 1870s and 1880s but which owes something to the 1860s in its use of veneers and naturalistic fretted carving. The two top upper doors open to reveal letter compartments and, in some versions, small drawers. There is a frieze drawer which contains a hinged writing slope. A side door in the lower section, panelled with a carved fretted adornment, opens to reveal four drawers. The piece is inlaid with boxwood stringing and stylised flowers. Not as expensive a form as the piano top but still a highly-prized piece.
1860-1880   *£2,500-£3,500*

481 A rosewood davenport of the cabriole leg type of front support, using the scrolling rococo form popular in the 1850s. A design which was still made for another twenty years, though it must have been thoroughly out of fashion by the 1880s. The fretted top gallery shows an alternative form to the lidded stationery compartment of protruding type shown in the other examples.
1850-1880   *£1,750-£2,500*

482 A davenport veneered in amboyna with bandings in a dark, ebonised style influenced by the exhibition cabinets of the 1850s and 1860s. A rather rigid severity has supplanted the scrolled curvaciousness of the rococo.
1855-1875   *£1,750-£2,500*

483 A walnut davenport in which the 'pop-up' section has been replaced by a fixed superstructure with small drawers flanking a letter-rack under a curved lid in the style of contemporary bonheurs-du-jour. Inlays of amboyna banding and stringing provide panelled effects.
1860-1880   **£1,500-£2,500**

484 A rosewood davenport of an unusual and amusing form with candle-holder attached. There are Adam inlays and stringing lines, coupled with a multi-panelled lower front surface. The superstructure has a 'piano' type of lid and writing slide below an upper shelf capped by a shaped rail with a small broken pediment. The piece is raised on four curved legs.
1890-1900   **£1,200-£1,800**

485 An interesting and unusual oak davenport in Gothic style with clustered column supports. Gothic style davenports were illustrated by Pugin himself in 1835 — but a much more Regency, elaborate 'Gothick' form — and in the Reformed Gothic manner by Richard Charles in 1866 and C. and R. Light in 1881. The style of this davenport is more of the earlier Victorian unreformed variety but could have been repeated by later makers.
1850-1860   **£1,750-£2,500**

486 A figured (but not burr) walnut daven-port of simple design but a perennial one. The top lid opens to give access to a letter rack; the sloping writing surface lifts to give access to a fitted interior. Four real drawers on one side, four dummy ones on the other.
1870-1890   **£1,000-£1,400**

487 An Aesthetic Movement ebonised davenport with characteristic design features — painted panels, this time of birds, panelled construction and rather fussy turning. At the top of the pillars there is a curious Anglo-Japanese bracket just to show that the makers had kept up with Godwin and the latest taste.
c.1880   **£1,000-£1,500**

488 A really late Victorian form in mahogany with little pretension to elegance and very stiff in execution. The turned columns have lost their way and are not sure what form to take. The base is plain and rigid. A panel has been suggested by applied mouldings. The top retains the features of the earlier davenports, however, and the inherent usefulness of the type.
1885-1900   *£500-£750*

489 A bamboo davenport with japanned and painted surfaces decorated with Oriental designs. The bamboo structure is left un-adorned and is emphasised by these panels. The fixed top structure provides a rack for paper, letters etc.
1880-1900   *£900-£1,200*

490 The end of the line for davenports from a catalogue of c.1910. No pillars, an inlaid 'Sheraton' satinwood banding and no decoration to speak of on the cheap stained mahogany, doubtless finished with French polish.
c.1910   *£400-£500*

DESKS - pedestal

One of the most enduring of 18th century pieces of furniture, the pedestal desk must have been in continuous production from the time of its inception. It was not an incidental writing place like the davenport or the bonheur-du-jour. It was — and is — a serious piece of furniture, something to work upon. One example illustrated by Loudon, with a writing slope which can be elevated by a rack, is little different from an 18th century desk. Although the Victorians, with their offices, dens, libraries and dealing rooms, used a wide variety of forms — cylinder, roll-top, upper-structured or unusual — many of them must have been straightforward, working desks of plain appearance in undecorated oak or mahogany. Since modern office furniture is tax-deductible, the period pedestal desk has attracted much 'investment' money and has tended to be expensive.

One of the interesting consequences with the pre-occupation about health and disease due, mainly, to poor drainage, which became prevalent at the end of the 19th century was that new furniture design lifted pieces off the floor on legs which allowed air to circulate at lower levels. The effect upon pedestal desks was to lift them from their pedimented bases on to four initially short legs and then higher ones as the later decades passed, virtually converting them into writing tables (q.v.). A man who wants a pedestal desk does not want a writing table or something halfway between. For this reason the value of a pedestal desk is diminished rather than enhanced in proportion to the height of the space beneath the bottom drawers of the pedestals.

491 A mahogany pedestal desk of the type Loudon might refer to as 'cabinet maker's Gothic' due to the pointed arch panelling of the doors which cover the drawers inside the pedestals. Similar desks with the characteristic flattened arch of the 1840s used to be very cheap but are now highly regarded.
1830-1845   *£3,500-£5,000*

492 A walnut pedestal desk with elaborate columns and panelled doors which lock over the drawers within the pedestals. The flattened arch of the 1830s and 1840s has been modified, with scrolled applied carving to emphasise a 'rococo' look.
1850-1860   *£5,000-£7,500*

493 A solid walnut and rosewood pedestal desk whose inlaid decoration suggests a tinge of Arts and Crafts influence and, via that influence, a measure of Reformed Gothic, especially in the bevelled edging of the structural stiles framing the drawers.
1870-1880   *£5,000-£7,000*

494 This type of desk, with a fixed upper structure incorporating a writing slope panelled in leather, is illustrated in catalogues such as Blackie (1859), Shoolbred (1876) and C. and R. Light (1881). The drawers in the upper structure are locked in place by hinged side flaps. The space under the slope, which is hinged, can be used in the same way as a normal school desk. This example is in mahogany but the spindled gallery behind the upper shelf is turned, with vase-shaped spindles identical to those on the walnut example which follows.
1855-1885   *£2,000-£3,000*

495 A handsome burr walnut pedestal desk with superstructure including a sloping writing surface, drawers and a turned baluster gallery. A type of desk once rather despised for its superstructure, which was often removed to convert the piece into a flat-topped pedestal desk of more Georgian appearance. Now, however, the form is coming into its own as a genuine Victorian one with its own usefulness.
1855-1885   *£2,500-£3,250*

496 A mahogany cylinder bureau with a kneehole. The pedestals each have three drawers and under the sliding tambour there is a writing surface with six small drawers and letter compartments. It is a type illustrated in several catalogues of the 1870s and 1880s, although the design goes back to earlier George III forms. This is a very plain version.
1870-1890   *£1,800-£2,500*

497 A highly decorated Reformed Gothic desk in a style which brings Burges, Seddon, Talbert and Eastlake to mind. Burges and Seddon would go for such lavish decoration; all of them would use the diagonal planking and pillared columns with central collars. It is interesting to compare this version of Gothic with that of 'Chippendale' shown in No. 512 in this section.
1860-1870   *£50,000+*

498 An interesting variant on the 'writing slope' type of desk which exhibits the features of the end of the 19th century: pedimented back with bas-relief machine carving; spindled gallery and mirrors; space beneath pedestals achieved by lifting the piece on turned legs.
1890-1910   *£1,000-£1,500*

499 A walnut kidney-shaped writing desk by Gillows of Lancaster. See Colour Plate 45.

500 An Edwardian satinwood kidney-shaped writing desk by Maples of London. See Colour Plate 46.

501 A mahogany kidney-shaped desk with satinwood inlay and marquetry. See Colour Plate 47.

502 A satin-birch pedestal desk with painted decoration. See Colour Plate 48.

503 A burr walnut pedestal 'partners' desk. See Colour Plate 49.

504 A kneehole desk (dressing table) in mahogany and harewood with marquetry inlay. See Colour Plate 50.

505 The designer of this pedestal desk has imbibed more than a little of the spirit of Reformed Gothic — note the panelled sides and slightly 'revealed' construction, with shaped feet.
c.1880   *£7,000-£9,000*

506 A mahogany pedestal desk of a type made fairly continuously throughout Victoria's reign and onwards to the present day. There is a tooled leather top, three drawers in the frieze and three drawers in each pedestal. The moulded edge is a fairly bold type and so is the thumbnail moulding around the base.
1860-1890   *£3,500-£4,500*

507 A plain mahogany pedestal partners' desk of large dimensions — 3ft. x 6ft. (91.5cm x 183cm) — with drawers in each opposing side, the concept being that the two partners involved could work at the same desk, facing each other.
1870-1890 but a type made on into the present day   *£6,000-£7,500*

508 A carved oak pedestal desk with characteristic lion-mask carved handles to the drawers. The late Victorians and Edwardians were fond of carved oak — a taste for the medieval transmitted to them by the work of the Gothic reformers, who would have hated this piece.
1895-1915   *£1,750-£2,500*

509 A further version of a carved oak pedestal desk with lion-mask carved handles. The 'Elizabethan' effect has been taken a stage further by the inclusion of reeded bulbs on the legs. More carving has been packed on in foliage form and the top edge is also carved with leaf forms.
c.1900   *£2,500-£3,500*

510 A mahogany cylinder bureau or pedestal desk on serpentine feet with a pierced brass gallery rail around the top. The piece is inlaid with marquetry of 18th century inspiration (Adam, Hepplewhite and Sheraton all spring to mind) including the splendid central vase in an oval panel on the cylinder front and swags, husks, leaf and floral decoration elsewhere. It has been said of other 'Edwardian Sheraton' pieces that the craftsmen of this period had a tendency to over-egg the pudding and this piece is inclined towards an example of this trait. There is just a bit too much decoration, a tendency to flashiness which distinguishes the piece from its 18th century original. A handsome piece, nevertheless, requiring some first class craftmanship to execute.
1890-1910   *£6,000-£8,000*

511 A mahogany partners' pedestal desk on carved serpentine bracket feet in 'Chippendale' style. The canted corners are carved with leaf and foliage decoration and the top edge is gadrooned. The top is inset with tooled leather. A straightforward high quality piece which states that it is reproduction from the carved decoration.
1910-1930   *£5,000-£6,500*

512 A mahogany pedestal desk in the early Georgian manner, with clustered columns on the pedestal corners and Gothic blind fret tracery around the frieze. There are three drawers in the frieze on the viewed side, with three drawers in each pedestal below. The out-of-view side has three drawers in the frieze and cupboards below — an arrangement normally fitted to a partners' desk but in fact allowing the desk to be viewed favourably from both sides. The quality of workmanship and carving is high — note the carved moulded edge to the top and the plinth around the base.
1920-1940   *£6,000-£8,000*

513 A walnut 'Queen Anne' kneehole desk, made as an accurate reproduction of a period piece. The top is quarter veneered and the drawers have a diagonal banding and lip moulding round the edges. The pierced handles are a little late in design for the period of the desk, but otherwise the proportions and restraint of the veneers are a good copy.
1920-1930   *£1,300-£1,700*

514 A mahogany partners' desk inlaid with stringing and satinwood banding to the drawers of a type, on bracket feet joined by an ogee curve, which is close to those of one hundred years earlier.
1890-1910   *£3,000-£5,000*

515 A somewhat 1930s interpretation in the use of matched figured walnut veneers on the drawer fronts but without excessive over-figure or burring ('Queen Anne' versions of pedestal desks, with feather banding, etc., etc., were not uncommon in the 1930s). The choice of ring handles, however, if original, is odd.
1920-1930   *£5,000-£7,000*

516 An inlaid mahogany kidney-shaped pedestal desk or writing table in the Sheraton manner, with boxwood inlaid stringing lines and set on square tapering legs ending in brass castors. The top is inset with tooled leather. The kidney-shaped desk is a perennial favourite and can often be highly decorative, with burr veneers and marquetry adding enormously to value.
1890-1930   *£4,500-£6,500*

518 A high quality mahogany pedestal desk, on square tapering legs, with inlaid boxwood stringing lines. There is a brass gallery rail about 4ins. (10cm) high at the back, which has a diamond-pattern fret. By using the stringing lines to describe panels on the drawer fronts and facings of the frame, the makers have managed to convey the impression of a restrained, quality piece.
c.1900   *£2,250-£3,000*

517 A rather spindly cabriole-legged writing table-cum-pedestal desk, half way between either definition, which shows how, in Edwardian times, there was a movement towards versions of the 'Queen Anne' style which heralded the outburst of burrs and cabrioles of the 1920s. In this case the decoration of the drawers is late 18th/early 19th century Sheraton in origin, whereas the legs are somewhat apologetic cabrioles, i.e. a version of an early 18th century style. The piece is in mahogany, which is not a Queen Anne wood.
1900-1910   *£450-£600*

520 A mahogany half-pedestal desk of Sheraton style with drawers banded in satinwood. The top is inset with tooled leather. 1900-1910 *£200-£300*

519 A mahogany writing desk on turned legs, with bow-fronted pedestal drawers but straight central drawer. It is a general rule in pedestal desks that the longer the leg, the lower the value and this early 20th century piece exhibits a high profile. 1900-1910 *£900-£1,200*

DESKS - roll-top

521 A rather fine oak roll-top desk in which something of Eastlake's preaching on Gothic reformed furniture has taken effect. Note the panelled sides, the incised line decoration on the drawers and the carved trefoil motif on the slope frame. Undoubtedly intended for use by some professional of 'reformed' leanings. c.1875 *£5,000-£7,000*

522 An oak roll-top pedestal desk with panelled sides shown open to reveal a generously complex fit-up of pigeon holes, small drawers and letter racks inside. There are four drawers in each pedestal and a pull-out shelf at either side. 1900-1920 *£1,200-£1,800*

523 An oak roll-top desk similar to the previous example but with a simpler inside fit-up, no foot rail and not panelled at the back.
1900-1920   *£800-£950*

524 An oak roll-top desk with a wooden top gallery intended as a bookshelf and fitted with metal drawer handles. The inside has a relatively simple fit-up of two drawers, pigeon holes and ink wells. There is a foot rail and the back is panelled. The piece is on castors.
1900-1920   *£800-£950*

525 A half-pedestal oak roll-top desk with metal drawer handles based on the previous model in design.
1900-1920   *£150-£250*

526 An oak roll-top desk with ring handles to the drawers. It has a solid frieze around the bottom but is mounted on castors. Quite a complex fit-up to the interior but not as desirable as the example shown in No. 522.
1900-1920   *£700-£850*

DESKS - Wootton Patent Office (Wells Fargo)

This form has become a category almost to itself, with a ready market in the USA, from which it originates. Usually made in American walnut with figured panels in more desirable versions, but also found in mahogany. The genre originates from around 1870 and appears in a variety of designs of single- or double-opening types with more or less complicated interiors. Really complex large decorative versions are highly sought after and price is affected accordingly. Often referred to, loosely, as a 'Wells Fargo' desk by those fond of watching TV.

527 A good quality walnut Wootton Patent Office desk of the double-doored type, shown closed. Note the fielded panels with ebonised moulding, the figured woods and the highly-carved top shelf. There are letter boxes fitted in the doors so that correspondence can be delivered to the owner while he is away and the piece is locked up.
c.1870   *£6,000-£8,000*

528 Another Wootton desk, this time shown with the doors open to illustrate the quantity and variety of pigeon holes and drawers in the piece. The writing surface, which conceals more fitments, is shown in the 'up' position, i.e. closed. The top is not carved like the previous example and the wood is mahogany.
c.1880   *£6,000-£8,000*

529 Another Wootton desk, this time of the single-opening door type, but with panels and drawers veneered with decorative burr walnut. Although the single-door is not always as convenient as the double-door and tends to off-balance the piece, this version has a complex and attractive interior.
c.1880   *£3,500-£4,500*

530 A large double-door version with elaborate interior and carved top similar to 527, shown closed. A handsome piece.
c.1880   *£7,500-£10,000*

DRESSERS (see also the Pine section)

The dresser, being a piece of kitchen furniture originating in the country, met with Loudon's approval in 1833. He was, after all, writing a book on cottage as much as villa furniture. The dressers he illustrates were almost certainly of widespread types and in common use, indeed 'essential to every kitchen but more especially to that of the cottager, to whom they serve as both dressers and sideboards'.

The word 'dresser' comes from the side table used for dressing food in medieval times. The dresser of 17th and 18th century type comprehensively illustrated in *British Antique Furniture* had, by the start of the Victorian era, changed only a little, perhaps growing in solidity, size and permanence at the expense of the design. The extensive growth of housing stock in Victorian towns was of a type in which kitchen cupboards and shelves of a utilitarian nature, fixed to the wall, presaged the built-in kitchen of modern times.

Many of the Victorian dressers must have been made of deal or pine (q.v.). Indeed, the Victorian era is that of the pine dresser. In most cases they would have been painted, either white or to conform to the same colours as the rest of the kitchen. The dresser was not used as a sideboard (q.v.), of which there were plentiful types, until somewhere round the turn of the century, when the return to fashion of oak medievalism brought 'Jacobethan' and similar styles back to the dining room. In fact, many so-called 'sideboards' of turn-of-the-century catalogues are no more than variants on the traditional dresser, which was clearly enjoying a popularity which has proved an enduring one.

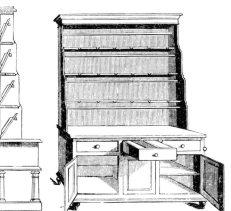

540 Two dressers from Loudon (1833). The one on the left is based on a traditional pot-board dresser whereas the one on the right, with cupboards under, is a more standard type often known as a 'Welsh' dresser, although the term is misleading; both cupboard and pot-board dressers were made not only in Wales but all over England with wide regional variations. These examples would have been made from pine (q.v.).

541 A mid-19th century version of the South Wales pot-board dresser of five drawers, all cock-beaded, in an arrangement which is characteristic. The three turned balusters support the whole at the front, terminating on the pot-board. The upper structure is simple and has wide pine back boards.
1840-1860   **£3,000-£4,250**

542 In many areas the traditional regional variety of dresser continued to be made for local requirements. This is an Anglesey break-front dresser with applied turnings and 'star' inlays which are associated with the Anglesey type. The turned knobs with ivory or mother-of-pearl inserts are also characteristic.
1840-1860   **£3,500-£4,500**

543 A Shropshire oak dresser with characteristic side cupboards to the upper half, these cupboards terminating before the uppermost shelf. The drawers in the lower half and the cupboard doors are crossbanded in mahogany. The piece is raised on cabriole legs at the front and straight square-section legs at the back. Even though cabriole legs are associated with the early 18th century such dressers were made over a long period and these rather less than robust legs are 19th century.
1830-1860   *£1,500-£2,500*

544 A simple pine 'dog kennel' dresser of the type originally made in Pembrokeshire. (The term dog kennel is due to the space in the centre where the dog was supposed to sleep.) Popular because it was designed to fit into smaller houses in what was a poorer part of Wales and very plain in construction with uniform boarded sides, no panelling and a plain cornice. Made in large numbers.
1830-1870   *£1,500-£2,000*

545 A better quality but later variant of the dog kennel dresser. This has panelled sides and the upper structure is more sophisticated, having in some cases glazed doors to the side cupboards. Bracket feet add a further touch of quality.
1840-1870   *£2,500-£3,000*

546 The elemental pine dresser of three-door lower half, two drawers and simple upper construction. The inner edges of the door panels have been chamfered and there is a bold moulding round the top cornice, otherwise the piece is very plain and would have been painted originally.
1840-1890   *£1,100-£1,500*

547 Two oak 'sideboards' from a William Morris catalogue of c.1900. These dressers represent the desire to return to earlier and simpler forms of Tudor and other inspiration. The wood was left unstained and in its natural state, which is extremely dull.

The upper example is an adaption in design from original 17th century dressers. Features which include the scalloped central arch in the top and the leaded glass doors are 19th century additions to the original concept.

The lower example is possibly closer to the original 17th and early 18th century dressers it emulates, but the Art Nouveau influence has provided the shaping of the back uprights and the sharp squareness of the overall outline.
c.1900   *£400-£1,000*

548 An oak sideboard of commercial manufacture which comes quite close to the spirit of the original period from which it derives. It seems that the designers of such pieces were always surer in their touch with the top halves. It is the cabriole front legs which disappoint; they are too curvaceous, too wavy to provide the 'Queen Anne' solidity and proportion that one seeks. The three deep drawers could have done with a fielded effect also, to relate them to the top.
1900-1920   *£500-£700*

549 An oak dresser in a style which derives from court cupboards of the early 17th century and later influences. The top half in its way is impressive, even if the downward-going turned knobs do conflict with the upward-going turned pillars with their bulbous bases. The lower half is less sure, as the turned legs are thinner and the stretcher arrangement an eyesore. Inconsistency has triumphed by putting applied split balusters on the end stiles but a split bobbin turning at the centre. The asymmetric arrangement of a cupboard with two doors occupying one side and two drawers the other is purely 20th century.
1900-1920 *£500-£700*

550 An oak dresser in the 'William and Mary' style, incorporating a central top cupboard with a Hollandish arch and fielded door panel. The base has inverted-cup turning to the legs and a pot-board stretcher. The shaping of the friezes is consistent with the style, but the flat-capped top moulding is typically Edwardian.
1900-1910 *£550-£750*

551 An oak 'Jacobean' dresser with much twist turning to the legs, stretchers and tier shelf supports. The central and top aprons are shaped with stylistically consistent forms, but the two side cupboards, while doubtless useful, are borrowed from the 18th century sideboard. Geometric applied mouldings to drawer and cupboard doors complete the Jacobean effect. A bold and decorative piece.
1910-1920 *£500-£700*

552 Another oak 'Jacobean' dresser sporting art nouveau handles to the drawers which are set beside a pair of cupboard doors in an asymmetric arrangement. Twist turned legs, stretchers and top supports and a rather more expensively panelled back than the usual vertical planking.
1910-1920 *£350-£450*

553 Although in oak, this dresser exhibits the typical bas-relief machined carving in panels also to be found on walnut and mahogany furniture of this period. The weakest point of the design is the use of the prissy cabriole front legs and scrolled bottom apron. If these are ignored, the base and top half are quite a bold, well-proportioned construction.
1900-1920   *£550-£750*

554 An oak dresser with twist-turned front legs and inlaid boxwood and ebony stringing lines to the panels on the very deep drawers. Borrowing a bit from the Jacobean in design and a bit from the Arts and Crafts Movement.
1900-1920   *£700-£900*

555 An open oak dresser by the same maker as the previous example, but without the smashable glazed centre door disapproved of by Percy Wells (see 558). The use of ebony and boxwood diagonally-banded stringing lines and inlays seems to have originated with Arts and Crafts Movement designers and remained popular in the 1910-1925 period.
1910-1925   *£500-£650*

556 An oak dresser on 'Queen Anne' cabriole front legs and plain construction but with a centre cupboard to the top shelf with a glazed door showing a stained glass tulip motif as decoration. Quite an Arts and Crafts addition to a commercial mass-produced piece.
1900-1920   *£275-£375*

558 This traditional dresser, taken from a book written by the cabinet-maker lecturer Percy Wells, c.1920, shows how little dresser design changed over a very long period. It was intended to be made from whitewood and stained light brown. The intention was to put it in new cottage dwellings. Wells was obsessed with simplicity and the avoidance of surplus on which dust could settle; he also disapproved of the upper glass doors featured on many 19th and 20th century dressers. These reactions to what were undoubtedly over-fussy mass-produced cabinets used as sideboards are interesting because Wells clearly intended this dresser to stand in the dining room, not the kitchen. The ageless dresser was back in the public rooms again, although the new cottages might have a kitchen-dining room combined.
c.1920   *£200-£350*

557 An oak dresser of plain construction sporting a set of art nouveau hinges to the doors, otherwise unremarkable.
1900-1920   *£150-£200*

Colour Plate 35. A low bow-back Notting-hamshire Windsor probably made of ash, with an elm seat. The stretchers are not crinoline and the splat is much simpler than 261, which is by Isaac Allsop of Worksop. This chair is of a design nearer to Whitworth of Gamston, or possibly Frederick Walker of Rockley, intended for more economic production than 260 and 261 but with, nevertheless, commendable turning to the arm supports.
1840-1850   *£450-£650*

Colour Plate 36. Lancashire or Yorkshire bow-back Windsor with double ring turning, tulip feet and single 'H' stretcher. In the lower half of the chair the smoker's bow design can clearly be discerned — not all these chairs carried the centre splat down below the arm-bow; they often had turned arm-bow supports all the way round like the previous examples and confined the splat to the top half. The pierced and shaped centre splat is highly decorative, especially when made in yew like this example. Note the collar reinforcement to the cut arm-bow. These chairs are also found with double 'H' and crinoline stretchers. Despite the Lancashire and Yorkshire nomenclature, these chairs were made in quantity in the North Midlands and in the Thames Valley at High Wycombe, where the catalogue of Glenister and Gibbons (1865-79) shows variants of the chair. A chair of this exact design is shown on the trade card of I. Allsop of Worksop 1871-87 described as a 'Smoking High' chair.
c.1850 onwards   *£1,200-£1,800*

Colour Plate 37. A slightly later variant on the smoker's bow chair in which the turning of the arm supports has become more exaggerated and the flat, cut arm-bow in two parts can clearly be seen, with the reinforcing collar above providing an important stylistic element to the chair. A double 'H' stretcher unites the turned legs. A chair to be seen in public houses, offices, institutions and homes throughout Britain from the time of its mass manufacture and still popular today.
c.1860-present day   *£250-£350*

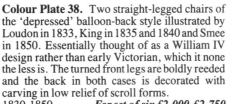

Colour Plate 38. Two straight-legged chairs of the 'depressed' balloon-back style illustrated by Loudon in 1833, King in 1835 and 1840 and Smee in 1850. Essentially thought of as a William IV design rather than early Victorian, which it none the less is. The turned front legs are boldly reeded and the back in both cases is decorated with carving in low relief of scroll forms.
1830-1850   *For set of six £2,000-£2,750*

Colour Plate 39. Chairs and table made of papier-mâché, japanned black and much inlaid with mother-of-pearl or, strictly, pearl-shell decoration as well as painted flowers. The chairs are spoon-backs (centre and right) with a prie-dieu chair (left) all showing the cabriole leg of the 1850s to the fore. Caned seats appear to be the most commonplace in this type of chair, much associated with Jennens & Bettridge of Birmingham, who are said to have obtained a patent for pearl-shell inlaying in 1825.
1850-1870
Chairs £800-£1,500

Colour Plate 40. A very handsome ivory lacquer and parcel gilt 'prie-dieu' chair by Jennens and Bettridge of Birmingham, who were associated with papier-mâché (q.v.) furniture. In this case the T-shaped back has been developed from the top arm-rest, used while kneeling at prayer on the seat, into something slightly more occasional and decorative rather than devotional — the chairs were useful for ladies with crinoline and extensive skirts. The chair has scrolled cabriole legs as befits the rococo and the needlepoint upholstery is foliate and naturalistic. Perhaps a bit flashy for traditional English taste.
1845-1865
£750-£1,000

Colour Plate 41. A button-back closed armchair with bargello fabric covering (which is new). The broad sweep of the back and the naturalistic carving to the cabriole legs are characteristic.
1850-1870
£1,000-£1,400

Colour Plate 42. The severe, early Regency form of davenport. Subsequently made in almost every variant of Victorian style, this rosewood, brass-galleried version with its flat classical columns gives little hint of the events to come.
1820-1840   *£4,000-£6,000*

Colour Plate 43. A burr walnut 'piano-top' davenport shown fully open. The very top section has a hinged letter rack operating on a spring mechanism released by a button inside an inner drawer. The shaped lid (like a piano) is shown lifted to reveal two inner drawers and the pull-out writing slide. Note that the curvaceous 'cabriole' scroll supports of the rococo period have been replaced, here, by two 'Louis XV' turned columns. Shoolbred, 1876, shows a very similar desk.
1860-1880   *£3,000-£5,000*

Colour Plate 44. A slightly more severe 'piano-top' davenport with similar characteristics to the previous example but omitting the column supports in favour of scrolled top and bottom brackets. The 'pop-up' section released by a spring has fretted envelope/writing paper sections but vertical pigeon holes in favour of further writing paper dividers.
1860-1880   *£3,000-£4,000*

Colour Plate 45. A walnut kidney-shaped writing desk by Gillows of Lancaster, c.1860, the red leather top embossed with stylised basketweave. The vertical pedestals have locking flaps to secure the drawers and tulipwood is used to outline the frame and panels. This is a very high quality piece; the panelled back is also crossbanded with tulipwood. Kidney-shaped desks, mostly inspired by Sheraton, became very popular in the 1860s and continued to be so well into the Edwardian period but with stylistic variants.
1860-1870 *£10,000-£15,000*

Colour Plate 46. An Edwardian satinwood kidney-shaped writing desk by Maples of London, c.1900, with silverplated handles. The leather top is crossbanded with satinwood inside boxand-ebony stringing lines which are repeated in the sides.
1890-1910 *£4,000-£6,000*

Colour Plate 47. A mahogany kidney-shaped desk with satinwood inlay and marquetry, of a type more unrestrainedly Edwardian Sheraton than the previous example. The side panels are banded and exuberantly inlaid; even the top is banded with inlaid mahogany round the green leather writing surface.
1890-1910 *£5,000-£7,000*

Colour Plate 48. A satin-birch pedestal desk with painted decoration and a brass gallery round the top. An interesting version of the 'Sheraton' to be associated with the late 19th/early 20th century.
1890-1910   *£4,000-£6,000*

Colour Plate 49. A burr walnut pedestal 'partners' desk of generous proportions, at which two workers — one each side — can work. There are drawers in the pedestals on the reverse side and the piece is designed to stand centrally in the room or library.
1850-1870   *£4,000-£5,000*

Colour Plate 50. A kneehole desk or, strictly-speaking, dressing table, in mahogany and harewood with marquetry inlay. It has one long shallow drawer across the top which is fitted inside with writing surfaces and compartments. The central door inside the well is crossbanded with satinwood and inlaid with an oval decoration. Stamped 'Maple & Co.'
1890-1910   *£3,000-£4,500*

Colour Plate 51. This small gilt circular mirror or girandole is approximately 2ft. (60cm) in diameter. Of a type illustrated in furniture catalogues such as Shoolbred's in the 1870s and 1880s, it shows an earlier rococo treatment in the scroll and leaf decoration surmounted by a pierced naturalistic ring or wreath with a finial above.
1870-1890   *£500-£650*

Colour Plate 52. A pine kneehole dressing table which has had leather panelled into the top surface to convert it into a writing desk. In this case the pedestals have simple square-panelled cupboard doors and hence the piece is not as desirable as one with drawers down the pedestals like that shown in the Maddox 1882 catalogue page (No. 600).
1870-1900   *£800-£1,200*

Colour Plate 53. A good quality towel horse which shows early 19th century baluster and ring turning under the hooped top support and bobbin-turned bases with square joints. From prices measured in shillings in the 1970s these useful antiques have appreciated considerably.
1830-1880   *£80-£140*

Colour Plate 54. This slightly more countrified approach to the towel horse still retains the decorative turning under the hooped ends at the top, but has gone for a more sledge-like (and perhaps more stable) design to the feet which is simpler to execute. In later years towel horses acquired 'Edwardian' broken pediments and bas-relief carving, but this simple form was long lasting.
1830-1880   *£80-£140*

Colour Plate 55. A pine wardrobe of a type illustrated in catalogues of the 1880s and 1890s when a more multi-purpose approach seems to have crept in. Here one has a hanging space on the left-hand, mirrored side; a cupboard above the right-hand side, perhaps for hats; a small, mirrored, dressing surface with drawers below; and a deep, long drawer across the entire base for bulkier items, blankets, etc. A very useful piece, enlivened by the new, brass, 18th century style handles which replace the original wooden or china knobs.
1880-1910   *£450-£650*

Colour Plate 56. A hazel pine washstand with marble top surface and cheerful tiled back above a pot shelf with a central cupboard intended to house jug, basin, etc. Shoolbred illustrated this type in 1876.
1870-1900   *£350-£500*

179

Colour Plate 57. Simple pine dresser with three graduated shelves and panelled back above a base with two drawers and plain panelled doors on an apron base. A type made for cottage and mass housing throughout the 19th century.
1830-1890

£600-£900

MIRRORS

The Victorian approach to mirrors was not very original. In the 1840s it had a sub-Empire classicism but the rococo fashion led to a happy return to reproductions or versions of Chippendale's varieties of rococo including Chinese. Mass-produced mirrors, like those shown by Shoolbred, exhibit a fussy frivolity which eventually sobered down to more restrained versions of the Georgian Revival.

The Victorians were rather fond of somewhat florid mirrors and overmantels, mostly made by building up gesso or plaster on a wood frame and subsequently gilding the surface. Some carved wood mirrors were made as well and these are, obviously, the most expensive type. Overmantels of the very large variety are difficult to place, since they require extensive walls with high ceilings, but the oval and circular wall mirrors, or girandoles, are being re-appreciated now that it is possible to touch up the faded or discoloured gilding with one of the many proprietary types of gold waxes and paints available for the purpose.

MIRRORS
wall and pier, including girandoles

570 18th century mirrors were not simple things. This page of mid-18th century mirrors from the design book of Thomas Johnson shows the rococo elaboration which the Victorian era was only too happy to copy. By the end of the 18th century, however, Hepplewhite and Sheraton were promoting a formality which, although relative in modern terms, had reduced the fragile wispiness of the rococo style. The Victorians enjoyed copying most of these designs.

571 Later Hepplewhite designs reproduced in the 19th century.

572 Small gilt circular mirror or girandole. See Colour Plate 51.

573 A 19th century reproduction of one of the 18th century's most popular numbers — the Chinese rococo, with its scroll, leaf, branch and ornithological decoration — birds have always been popular. If this mirror were gilded on to a carved wood frame it would be very, very expensive but the highest probability is that it is of gesso or plaster, moulded on to a simple frame. If in good condition it will still not be cheap.
1860-1890   *£2,000-£3,000*

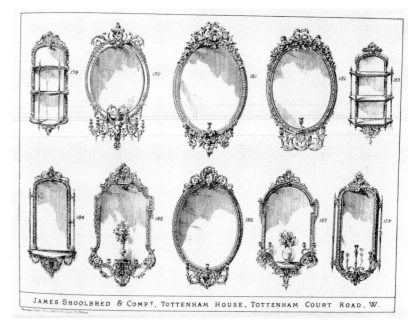

575 'Girandoles' from Shoolbred's catalogue of 1876. The decoration is made of plaster, subsequently treated with gesso and gilded. Until comparatively recently these ornate pieces were considered somewhat vulgar but prices have been mounting steadily in the last few years.
1876   *£250-£1,000*

574 Another Chinese rococo mirror which is a reproduction of an 18th century form. The style has enduringly proved synonymous with elegance and exoticism.
1860-1900   *£1,750-£2,500*

576   An oval gilt mirror of the gesso and plaster type with 18th century rococo styling. Mirrors of this type appear to have been popular in the later 19th century, when many reproductions of 18th century types were featured in furnishers' catalogues.
1870-1890   *£650-£850*

577   A really ornate rococo mirror with great depth to the frame which is surmounted by a cherub figure of Cupid, holding a bow. The depth is remarkable and the shape of the oval mirror is elegant.
1900-1920   *Carved wood £3,500-£4,500*
                                      Gesso £1,000-£1,700

578   A rococo oval wall mirror in emulation of mid-18th century carved mirrors incorporating similar birds and decoration. Made of giltwood and plaster. Very decorative and of good quality.
1900-1925   *£1,250-£1,750*

579 A carved rococo mirror, with scroll and leaf forms, which is again an imitation of an 18th century style.
Early 20th century   *£900-£1,200*

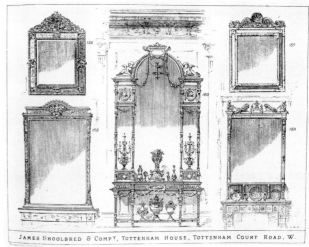

580 An oval gilded mirror of 'Empire' design with seated griffins on either side of a classical urn with Olympic torch as a decorative cresting. The solid frame to the bevelled mirror has gilded edges and gilded classical motifs on a painted background.
1910-1920   *£400-£500*

582 These 'ornamental glasses' from Shoolbred's catalogue of 1870 languished for many years due to the lack of space in modern houses. The top left and top right examples, however, with their bevelled panels in imitation of 18th century types, are now extremely desirable.
1870-1890
£1,200-£1,600

JAMES SHOOLBRED & COMP.Y, TOTTENHAM HOUSE, TOTTENHAM COURT ROAD, W.

581 A carved oval mahogany mirror frame with bevelled-edge mirror. The scrolled carving is slightly coarse and the shape a little too elongated for elegance. It is a Victorian or Edwardian oval, not an 18th century one.
c.1910   *£350-£450*

583 Not all overmantels are overpoweringly large and made of crumbling plaster on which the gilt is flaking. This Georgian Revival satinwood and rosewood overmantel has kingwood banding and is delicately inlaid with marquetry. It is important that it should have its original glass.
1870-1890   *£1,750-£2,500*

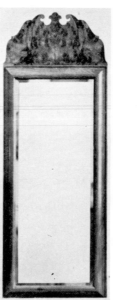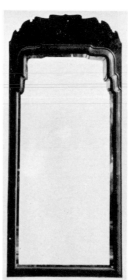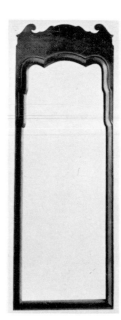

584 A straightforward 'picture frame' mirror in which a mirror has been fitted into a moulded gesso picture frame with a gilded finish. It is now very popular to fit mirrors into pine frames, obtained by stripping the gesso off frames such as this.
1900-modern day   *Pine £90-£140*

586 Walnut wall mirrors, of early 18th century design, from a manufacturer's catalogue of the 1920s. They have bevelled plate mirrors but not the gilded inner moulding to the frame which is an adjunct to value.
1910-1930   *£225-£300*

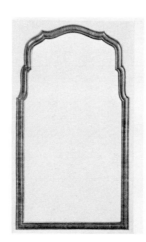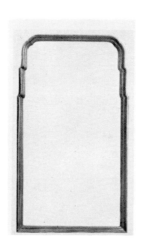

585 A reproduction of a Georgian mahogany wall mirror with carved gilded cresting rail with a gilded bird. A good imitation of an 18th century piece.
Early 20th century   *£350-£450*

587 Reproductions of early 18th and late 17th century wall mirrors. The bottom two mirrors are walnut-framed versions of simple Queen Anne styles, whilst the top two, with their deep 'cushion' moulded surfaces around the mirror and shaped cresting boards, are more sophisticated reproductions of walnut-veneered and moulded 'cushion' mirrors of the 1680-1720 period.
Early 20th century
Two above £250-£350
Two below £90-£110

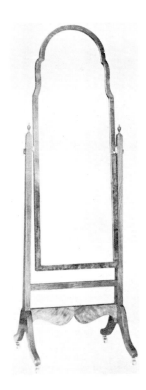

588 A satinwood cheval glass in the highest 'Edwardian Sheraton' manner, with its accompanying dressing table and (separate) dressing mirrors. The decoration is painted and gilded with classical motifs in the French Empire manner, and the whole effect is one of great elegance.
1900-1920   *£900-£1,200*

589 A walnut 'cheval' mirror in the 'Queen Anne' style. Actually cheval mirrors date back to the start of the 18th century, but to find an original one like this would be a very rare event. Mirrors of this type can be safely recognised as reproductions.
1910-1930   *£400-£500*

590 A mahogany cheval glass of the Georgian Revival, with inlaid Adam motifs.
1870-1890   *£600-£900*

591 A mahogany oval cheval mirror in the Edwardian Sheraton style, inlaid with floral decoration. The scrolled broken pediment has a vase-shaped finial above a cavetto-moulded cornice.
1890-1910   *£600-£900*

592 A circular dressing mirror on a segmented pumpkin-style base. Similar designs occur in Smee's catalogue of 1850 and as far back as King's of 1830.
1840-1865   *£225-£300*

593 A typical mahogany dressing mirror of a design made from 1845 until the 1880s. The scrolled supports and rather heavy flat base with semi-circular plinths at each end are characteristic.
1850-1890   *£60-£90*

594 Three typical early 19th century designs of dressing mirrors made in the early 20th century. The central mirror is a shield-shaped 'Hepplewhite' design which has been much reproduced; it has three small drawers in the serpentine-fronted base.
1910-1930
Central mirror £140-£180
Others £60-£90

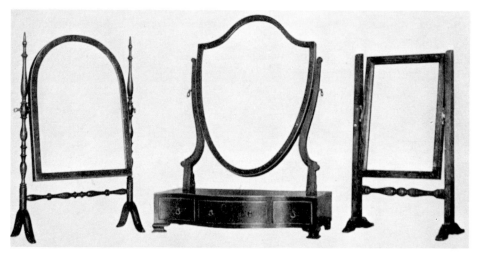

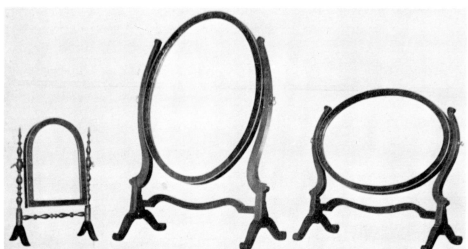

595 Three more reproduction mirrors, copying early 19th century designs, of a very popular type.
1910-1930   *£40-£65*

PINE

To devote a separate section to a particular variety of wood may seem inconsistent but the popularity of pine furniture over the last decade, especially for kitchen furniture, has given it a special status. In 19th century catalogues of furniture manufacturers and retailers such as Shoolbred, pine or rather 'deal' furniture is shown separately, usually for bedroom items such as chests, kneehole dressing tables, washstands, wardrobes, pot cupboards and towel rails. These items form much of the stock-in-trade of many of today's pine dealers along with kitchen dressers, tables, desks, bureaux, shelves, hanging cupboards, settles and so on. In short, one does not find High Art in pine furniture although the Gothic style is to be treasured in pine since it confers higher value on the piece.

Generally speaking, two varieties of pine were used in English furniture making. Scots fir *(Pinus sylvestris)* provided much native timber and was known as deal, particularly when cut. Pine from America, known as yellow pine *(Pinus strobus)* was used for carcase work in mahogany and other furniture, being generally regarded as superior to deal. A sub-variety of yellow pine is pitch-pine *(Pinus palustris)*, known as southern yellow pine since much of it came from Louisiana. Pitch-pine is dense, resinous and distinctively darker yellow with a close grain almost like yew. It is the wood of some church pews, school furniture and certain engineering or structural applications due to its hard, enduring character.

Much 'period' pine furniture is now reproduced extensively and is sold as new. This has affected the price of some pine furniture since, clearly, a relationship must be maintained between the premium worth paying for a genuine period piece and the price for which it can be freshly made.

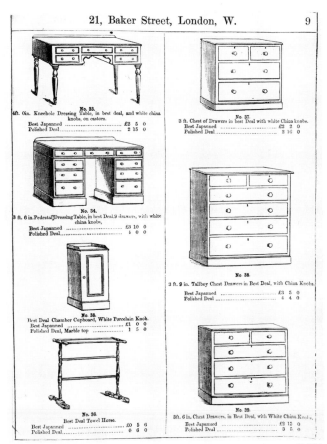

21, Baker Street, London, W.   9

No. 33.
4ft. 0in. Kneehole Dressing Table, in best deal, and white china knobs, on castors.
Best Japanned £2 5 0
Polished Deal.................. 2 15 0

No. 34.
3 ft. 6 in. Pedestal Dressing Table, in best Deal, 9 drawers, with white china knobs,
Best Japanned £3 10 0
Polished Deal.................. 4 0 0

No. 35.
Best Deal Chamber Cupboard, White Porcelain Knob.
Best Japanned £1 0 0
Polished Deal, Marble top 1 5 0

No. 36.
Best Deal Towel Horse.
Best Japanned £0 5 6
Polished Deal.................. 0 6 0

No. 37.
3 ft. Chest of Drawers in best Deal with white China knobs.
Best Japanned £2 2 0
Polished Deal.................. 2 16 0

No. 38.
3 ft. 9 in. Tallboy Chest Drawers in Best Deal with China Knobs.
Best Japanned £3 5 0
Polished Deal 4 4 0

No. 39.
3ft. 6 in. Chest Drawers, in Best Deal, with White China Knobs.
Best Japanned £2 15 0
Polished Deal 3 5 0

600 A selection of deal furniture from G. Maddox's catalogue of 1882. Deal was particularly used for kitchen and bedroom furniture. Most of these items were furnished with white china knobs. The two dressing tables (upper left) would now be adapted for bedroom or for writing use.

Much furniture made from deal was painted or stained to suit the kitchen or bedroom decor, although the top, working surface was scrubbed white by the conscientious housewife where kitchen tables and dressers were concerned. The present fashion has been to strip the paint from such pieces and polish the wood to its natural colour.

PINE - bedroom furniture

The use of pine for bedroom furniture in the Victorian and Edwardian periods was extensive and covered the following variety of pieces:

Chests of drawers and dressing tables
Cupboards
Tables, dressing and occasional
Wardrobes
Night cupboards (euphemistically, commodes) or chamber pot holders
Towel horses
Washstands

and other innovative items. Since the furniture in question was not on public view, pine was considered quite sufficient for the purpose, painted or polished, especially where children's or servants' quarters were concerned. It follows that an enormous amount of this pine bedroom furniture was made, most of it simple and without a particular style, over the whole period. Towards the end of the 19th century the Aesthetic Movement and the broken pediment with bas-relief machine carving had their influence on better pine pieces but on the whole a simple solidity prevailed, continuing much further into the 20th century than is generally realised.

Almost all this pine bedroom furniture is nowadays sold in a stripped or cleaned-down condition and polished, except for decoratively-painted items which usually have been completely re-painted, with floral patterns and so on, as a specific feature. Pine coffers have been popular for the storage of extra bed linen, pillows and duvets. The demand has continued strongly enough for a large industry to produce reproductions of the most popular pine bedroom furniture brand new and if anything the balance has shifted towards the major part of availability being in newly-produced items, thus following the 'Georgian' mahogany furniture demand, where reproductions obviously far outnumber period items.

187

601 Straightforward pine chests of drawers of a type made in huge numbers, particularly in the 1870s and 1880s. That on the right has its original white china knobs, whereas the left-hand example has been prettified with modern reproduction brass plates of 18th century design.
1860-1900   *£175-£250*

602 A Wellington chest and a rather tall chest with sunken 'military' handles. The Wellington chest is not made of pine but of 'satin walnut', which has been stripped, bleached and waxed to a pale yellow colour. This wood is more correctly described as 'hazel pine' and is, in fact, American Red Gum, which was used for better quality work. The other chest on the right is pine and has the unusual feature of a single handle for the top drawer, whereas all the rest have the normal two.
1840-1880   *Wellington chest £400-£600*
                            Other chest £150-£250

603 This standard form of five-drawer chest is of the type illustrated by Maddox in 1882 except that the base is shaped and the knobs are of turned wood, not china. Suitably polished and clean, such chests have become a standard furnishing piece a century after their creation.
1870-1890 *£350-£450*

604 A low four-drawer chest on turned feet with a shaped gallery around the top intended to house washing accoutrements. The piece would probably have been painted and the top protected by linoleum or washcloth of some sort.
1820-1870 *£350-£450*

605 A plainer gallery surrounds the top of this satin finish chest, possibly of an oriental wood, on a classical apron base.
1850-1890 *£375-£475*

606 A satin finish tiled back washstand-chest with towel rail. The green tiles incorporate an Art Nouveau motif and there is a broken pediment to the cresting rail.
1890-1910 *£400-£500*

607 A pine dressing chest and all-purpose bedroom piece with its cupboard for chamber pot or jug and basin, its tiled washstand incorporated above a marble slab, a tilting mirror, and drawers.
1870-1900 *£250-£350*

608 Another dressing chest of multi-purpose type but this time without the incorporated pot cupboard. There is still a washstand with tiled back and a tilting dressing mirror.
1870-1900 *£250-£400*

609 A pleasant pine bedroom chest with a tiled back, used for dressing/washing purposes.
1870-1900 *£300-£400*

610 A pitch-pine dressing chest in which the influence of the Aesthetic Movement (q.v.) can be detected in the turned, spindled galleries around the mirrors. The durability and colour of pitch-pine have given it a premium above ordinary pine or deal grades.
1870-1890 *£400-£600*

611 A straightforward pine dressing chest with two small flanking drawers to the mirror section and turned wooden knobs to the four drawers.
1870-1900 *£350-£500*

612 A pine bureau of a type originating early in the 19th century and remaining on manufacturers' catalogues almost to the end of it. Very often originally sold in stained or painted finish; now inevitably stripped and waxed.
1820-1885 *£450-£550*

614 A grander satin finish dressing chest with broken pediment, incised carving and shaped apron to form 'bracket' feet. 1880-1900
£550-£700

613 Two pine dressing chests of a type very popular around the turn of the century. Many have had the mirrors removed to leave useful low chests but there seems to be a recognition lately that the mirrors really are quite useful. 1890-1920
£300-£400

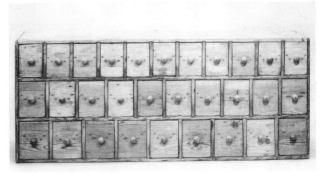

617 A pine veterinary medicine chest marked 'Restorine Remedies' of small — 24in. (61cm) — width. 1880-1900
£150-£200

615 A pine mule chest of a type made from the 18th century onwards and in this case fitted with brass swan-neck handles. These useful storage pieces are now used for a wide variety of purposes. 1800-1850
£250-£350

618 Popular for bedroom or kitchen use are pine apothecaries' drawers or shop fittings of this type, which can be used for a variety of storage purposes from spices to sewing materials. Very often painted and requiring extensive stripping if they are to be incorporated in a natural wood decor. 1840-1890
£400-£500

616 A plain pine coffer with iron hinges to the lid, illustrating the most basic form of storage box available. 1800-1900
£150-£250

PINE - bedroom furniture: *dressing tables*

The kneehole dressing table was an 18th century innovation which dates back to the walnut period and which was popular during the whole of the mahogany one. In Victorian times this successful pedestal type, with drawers to each side, was made in pine as well as more expensive woods (see Tables, Dressing). It was undoubtedly intended as a piece of bedroom furniture but has been much used for writing in later periods, especially recently, when leather panels are inserted into the top surface.

The low gallery surrounding the sides and the back of the top surface of the kneehole dressing table, intended to retain the washbasin or other bedroom articles placed on it, tends, in modern times, to be regarded with disfavour and removed, so as to provide a more desk-like appearance. Traces of this back can often be detected from filled screw or dowel holes.

Other forms of pine dressing table are the long central mirror type, with drawer pedestals to either side, and a variety of tables on turned legs, usually with a drawer or drawers in the frieze, and with an upper structure including a tilting mirror and small drawers or shelves. These were made in pine and birch or beech as well as the more expensive woods.

619 A pine kneehole dressing table converted into a writing desk. See Colour Plate 52.

620 A pine kneehole dressing table on turned feet. The centre door has an arched panel and the stained knobs are possibly original. Intended as a piece of bedroom furniture but now used as a pedestal desk.
1840-1880 *£500-£600*

621 Another pine kneehole dressing table with its back still in place, not yet adapted to become a writing desk, although the brass scutcheons and handles have been added to give a more 'antique' appearance than the original knobs.
1840-1890 *£500-£700*

622 More obviously a kneehole dressing table, this shaped-back version has its honest china knobs still in place. This view shows the affinity of such pieces with the dressing chests (q.v.) with similar tops.
1865-1885 *£600-£750*

623 A mirrored pedestal dressing table with four drawers to each pedestal and a long central arched mirror which can be tilted. It provides an interesting comparison with the rosewood version shown in the main section, No. 943.
1870-1900 *£350-£500*

624 A heavy side or dressing table in pine with turned finials below the top corners and thick turned end supports. A design which was used for many years.
1840-1880   *£100-£150*

625 A pine dressing table with spindled gallery above the mirror and incised lines to the drawers in a style much featured in 1870s catalogues. Original handles. The turned double column end supports are joined by a shelf or possibly footrest to tie the construction together.
1870-1890
£600-£750

626 A simpler dressing table on turned legs with two drawers to a table section which could perhaps be used for a variety of table applications. The upper structure fixed to the table looks later in concept — incised lines, ogee curves and a pediment to the finialled mirror — but it could just be that the maker used a long proven table design with pre-1850s turning to the legs when producing the top some time after 1870.
1860-1890   *£250-£325*

627 This dressing table has 'sunburst' bas-relief carving and the later 19th century version of a broken pediment to the mirror which followed the change in fashion back to 18th century forms. The lower part, with its pierced brackets, is a bit finicky and the turned legs and stretcher are a bit thin.
1880-1900   *£250-£350*

628 A pine pot cupboard which is shelved inside for more convenient storage and which also doubles, nowadays, as a bedside cabinet. The solid plinth base is typical of the mid-Victorian period.
1840-1890   *£100-£160*

629 A small night table or pot cupboard with a shelf below. The universal form of chamber pot holder and bedside table made in large quantities in the early 19th century, but emulating an 18th century form — most late 19th century pot cupboards tend to be a solid pedestal with a single door all the way down.
1790-1840   *£150-£250*

PINE - bedroom furniture: *towel horses*

631 A good quality towel horse. See Colour Plate 53.

632 A slightly more countrified towel horse. See Colour Plate 54.

630 A pine towel rail or clothes horse (or, sometimes, towel horse) with baluster-turned double uprights linked at the bottom by turned stretchers and at the top by moulded hoops or U-bends. The towel horse and clothes horse were used in both bedrooms and kitchens in the 19th century for the drying of towels and clothes. The form originated in the mid-18th century but types like this and the one in Maddox's selection of deal bedroom furniture of 1882 were little changed from the original shape. More fashion-conscious Aesthetic and 'Queen Anne' versions are not uncommon, however.
1870-1890   *£100-£125*

The wardrobe (q.v.) was made in a range of designs from simple to ingenious. Clothes were hung or stored on shelves or sliding racks, with drawers used for smaller items. Fashion affected even the pine wardrobe although the arched panels of the late 1830s and 1840s can be seen in catalogues of the 1880s such as Maddox's and C. and R. Light. There has been a revival of interest in the pine wardrobe which for many years was junked along with other wardrobes or converted for a different purpose.

633 A pine wardrobe of three doors with the arched panels which came into fashion in the 1830s and continued to be used into the 1880s. The left-hand door is opened to show lower drawers and upper sliding trays for haberdashery.
1840-1880   ***£600-£800***

634 A smaller pine wardrobe with a mirrored central door flanked by two smaller doors, the left-hand one open to show a pegged hanging space above a deep bottom drawer contained within the doors.
1860-1890   ***£300-£450***

635 A plain double-door pine wardrobe with pleasant moulded panelling of a form which was used throughout the century, not only on wardrobes but on cupboards, doors and similar applications.
1860-1890   ***£600-£800***

636 A small double-door wardrobe with the arched panels and leaf scrolls of Loudon's 'Grecian' style of the late 1830s onwards. The single deep drawer below has turned wooden knobs and the piece stands on turned feet.
1835-1850   ***£300-£500***

637 A mid-period plain double-door wardrobe with simple panelled doors. The shaping of the base is possibly a later 'improvement'.
1850-1880   *£550-£750*

638 A wardrobe on which the diagonal planking associated both with Reformed Gothic (q.v.) and Eastlake (q.v.) furniture, along with their concomitant bevelled edges, is rather too abundantly evident. What is more, that precision which the designers and reformers so earnestly sought in their, usually oak, pieces is not so evident here since the angle of the lower left panel of planking is out of true with its opposite top right panel and its neighbouring bottom right reflection. Something has gone wrong with this lower left panel in some way.
1870-1890   *£300-£400*

639 A pitch-pine wardrobe which also owes something to the Reformed Gothic movement in its use of bevelled edge mouldings, incised lines and arcaded cavetto under the top moulding.
1870-1890   *£450-£650*

640 A pine wardrobe with a more multi-purpose approach. See Colour Plate 55.

641 The use of hazel pine (often misnamed satin walnut) was quite frequent in wardrobes of the later period such as this, with its bas-relief carved panel in the left-hand door, long mirror to the right, and drawer under. The pediment above is also typical of the post-1890 period.
1890-1910   *£350-£500*

642 A more elaborate hazel pine wardrobe with panels of East Indian satinwood and a broken pediment above the arrangement of mirrored end doors, five drawers and central panelled doors.
1890-1910   *£1,400-£1,800*

643 A hazel pine washstand with marble top surface and tiled back. See Colour Plate 56.

644 A simpler tiled-back washstand with marble top on turned legs joined by a pot shelf. The shaped cresting above the tiles is embellished with incised carving. There are similar designs in Wyman's 1877 catalogue.
1870-1890   *£250-£325*

645 A pine washstand on turned double-column end supports linked by a pine shelf. The marble top is backed by a tiled gallery with spindle turning and incised lines above following the influence of the Aesthetic Movement.
1870-1900   *£300-£400*

646 A hazel pine marble top washstand on turned legs joined by a pot shelf and with a central cupboard below the two drawers. The brass swan-neck handles are not original.
1870-1900   *£250-£350*

647 A pine washstand on turned legs, of a type seen in catalogues from the 1840s to the 1880s. Very often the top surface was cut with a circular opening in which to fit a wash basin and sometimes a drawer was fitted under the lower pot shelf. The shaping of the frieze under the top is possibly later.
1850-1870   *£200-£275*

648 This piece combines the duties of washstand with night table or pot holder, having an uncompromising marble top and back with shelf on which all the materials for ablutions could be placed. The simple moulded door and the drawer below the top are fitted with brass knobs, probably replacing the original china or wooden ones. In common with much modern pine practice, a new base with 'bracket' feet and ogee curving to the apron has been added later.
1850-1890   *£150-£250*

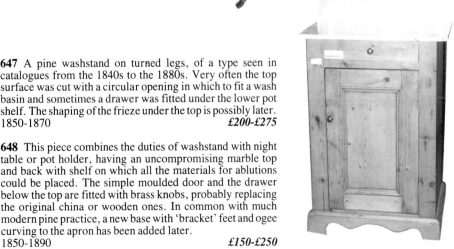

PINE - cabinets, cupboards and chiffoniers

The section of this book dealing with cabinets (q.v.) is one of the largest but pine, traditionally used for carcase work and under veneers, was not considered suitable for display purposes. It is, however, ideal for utilitarian cabinets and for storage cupboards, which may have been painted or simply varnished and polished. Many attractive kitchen and bedroom cupboards were made of pine. Although it was not popular for display, bookcases made of pine, which may originally have been painted, occur frequently. Pine chiffoniers were almost certainly mostly painted in their original form and some may have been intended for japanning or black lacquer work not in the end carried out. This section therefore has a miscellany of examples, some of them clearly 'marriages' of bases and tops not originally joined together.

649 A highly desirable pine corner cupboard with arched inset shelf space to the upper half and two doors to the cupboard below. Much appreciated for the display of pottery.
1800-1900   *£800-£1,200*

651 A large pine glazed cupboard or display cabinet with two pairs of glazed doors above two pairs of panelled doors. Presumably intended for the storage of kitchen china, implements and/or linen.
1840-1890   *£1,800-£2,800*

650 (Left) A pine cupboard which could be used as a dresser or bookcase, with diagonal planking to the lower doors as approved by Talbert, Eastlake and other Gothic reformers. The two drawers below the glazed upper doors lead one to believe that the piece was equally at home in the kitchen as in the library.
c.1880   *£900-£1,300*

652 A bookcase or display cabinet with a deep and complex top moulding or architrave and glazed doors, which has been placed on a chest with two serpentine-moulded top drawers above two deep single drawers. The use of such serpentine-moulded drawers is commonplace on chiffoniers (q.v.) and sideboards (q.v.) of the 1840s — examples in mahogany may be seen in both sections — but could also be of Continental origin. An odd marriage.
1840-1860 *£600-£750*

653 Another display cabinet or bookcase in which the serpentine moulding of the drawer fronts of the base is evident. This time there are cupboards below and the glazing arrangement of the (married) top is more in keeping with the period.
1840-1880 *£800-£1,000*

654 A pine bookcase with glazed doors perched on a shaped apron bracket foot base. It has a very deep, emphasised top moulding with the air of belonging somewhat higher up than this arrangement allows it — such mouldings were not made to be looked down on or even to be seen at eye level. This bookcase belongs on a more substantial base.
1850-1880 *£400-£550*

655 A low glazed display cabinet of deep dimensions which argue that there might have been a top structure — more shelves or cupboards — intended to be above it at its inception. Plain panelled doors on such pieces are often replaced by glazing like this. The bracket feet are probably a later substitute for a plain apron.
1850-1880 *£200-£300*

656 A pine double-door corner cupboard with moulded arched panels and a small drawer below.
1830-1850   *£500-£750*

657 A small pine chiffonier of the late Regency and early Victorian period, with pillars and a shelf above.
1820-1840   *£350-£450*

658 A mid-Victorian pine chiffonier/sideboard with drawers and cupboards below a shaped and carved upper structure incorporating two small drawers.
1850-1870   *£350-£550*

659 A pine side cabinet decorated with sunflowers and Aesthetic Movement motifs which has possibly escaped from, or been relieved of, the ebonising usually applied to such pieces.
1870-1890   *£350-£500*

660 An interesting pine Welsh dresser with a central panelled cupboard door inset below a drawer and flanked by three drawers each side. The sides of the lower half are panelled and the top displays the pendant turned knobs seen on early North Wales dressers of the 18th century.
Late 18th/early 19th century   *£2,500-£3,500*

PINE - dressers

In the dresser section of this book the point is made that dresser designs remained unchanged over a long period and that regional varieties persisted decades after their introduction. This was as true of the pine dresser as of its oak counterpart and makes dating extremely difficult.

The popularity of the pine dresser in modern kitchens has given rise to a huge reproduction industry without which the demand could never be satisfied. There are thus some antique pine dressers, some old dressers, some brand new dressers and a substantial quantity of made-up, half-new, half-old dressers currently available on the market. The purchaser of an 'antique' or old pine dresser must reconcile himself or herself to the likelihood that the base and the plate rack very rarely started life together and whether, in this case, it matters anyway; most pine dressers are bought for decorative and utilitarian reasons, not as an investment.

662 A pine 'dog kennel' dresser with a shaped arch to the dog's central space and simple panelled doors to the flanking cupboards.
1840-1880   *£1,750-£2,500*

661 A fairly simple pine dresser with a central cupboard door with arched panel flanked by three drawers on each side.
1840-1880   *£1,200-£1,800*

663 (Right) A late 19th century pine dresser of two cupboard doors and two drawers below a pair of glazed cupboard doors to the upper half.
1870-1900   *£750-£1,250*

664 (Left) A simple pine dresser of the late 19th century with a single cupboard and three drawers below a shelved top with the back boarded in uniform pine planking.
1860-1890   *£650-£900*

666 A simple pine dresser. See Colour Plate 57.

667 Another simple pine dresser. See Colour Plate 58.

668 Pine 'dresser base', probably a shop fitting. See Colour Plate 59.

665 A pine dresser with two glazed side cupboards above a base with three drawers and panelled cupboard doors embellished with shaped arching.
1840-1880   *£1,500-£2,500*

669 A pine base of the 1840-1850 period on turned feet, showing the arched doors associated with that era, with three long central drawers flanked by cupboards, on to which a plate-rack has been added later.
1840-50 onwards   *£1,000-£1,600*

670 An example of a very plain cupboard base to which a glazed break-front plate rack or display cabinet has been added. The two lower cupboard doors, which require opening space, are considered less desirable than a combination of drawers and smaller cupboards.
Combined dating   *£600-£850*

671 A combination of drawers and cupboards to the lower half of this pine dresser makes it more desirable than the previous example. Additionally, the base is pitch-pine (more desirable still) but the top isn't; the plate rack of plain pine has been added later.
1880-1900   **£550-£700**

672 A bold, rather commercial-looking North Country dresser base on turned feet with three wide drawers to each side and an inset cupboard door with shaped panel below the smaller central drawer. There is a short gallery back to the top and the brass handles are not original.
1850-1880   **£650-£850**

673 A rather square dresser base with central cupboard door surrounded by graduated drawers with cock beading, on turned feet.
1830-1860   **£400-£600**

674 A pine serpentine-front Yorkshire dresser base with scrolled 'chiffonier' style back capped by a leaf carving. The elaborate shaping and aggressively Victorian appearance are often modified by reconstruction and the substitution of the original wooden knobs by brass 'period' plates — see the next example.
1850-1880   **£1,400-£1,900**

675 A pine serpentine-front Yorkshire dresser base to which a plate rack has been added above in substitution of the original back, leaving the spice drawers in place. Wooden knobs have been replaced by brass 'period' plates and handles. The piece should be compared with the previous example to see the original form.
1850-1880   **£1,100-£1,600**

676 A 'Lancashire' pine dresser base with panelled door and three drawers. The original wooden knobs are in place. Small pieces such as this, almost of chiffonier form with back and shelf above, could fit into cramped conditions in industrial terraced housing.
1840-1880   *£350-£450*

677 A 'Lancashire' pine dresser base with panelled door and three drawers below the top, with its shaped back and shelf. 18th century style brass handles with back plates have been substituted for original knobs.
1840-1880

678 A large dresser with diagonal planking to the doors in the lower half as approved by Talbert, Eastlake, etc. The bevelling and square joints of the shelves and centre upright in the top half also reveal Reformed Gothic influence.
1870-1890   *£3,000-£4,000*

679 A large pine dresser-cum-display cabinet with pillared supports to the top half, which is much more imposing than the very mundane bottom half. Would the man who turned out such an elegant double-pillared top with a break-front and deep cornice really have put it on so ordinary a base with such lamely-framed doors? And no bottom moulding or plinth to balance the top? Surely not.
1890, perhaps   *£2,000-£2,750*

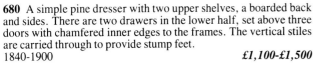

680 A simple pine dresser with two upper shelves, a boarded back and sides. There are two drawers in the lower half, set above three doors with chamfered inner edges to the frames. The vertical stiles are carried through to provide stump feet.
1840-1900 *£1,100-£1,500*

681 A Pembrokeshire 'dog kennel' dresser so called because of the space under the centre drawer. A very popular type made originally to fit into the small houses of this poorer part of Wales. Normally quite simply made (notice the simple boarded side, no panelling and the plain frieze). A type which is now much reproduced.
c.1830-1860 *£1,500-£2,000*

682 A slightly later development of the 'dog kennel'. It is better made than the previous example with panelled sides and bracket feet. By breaking the upper structure into a central shelved area flanked by two deeper sections, often enclosed by glazed doors, the design is more interesting and the emphasised arch above the central well or 'dog kennel' adds to its sophistication. Also reproduced.
1840-1880 *£2,500-£3,000*

Having been fairly abusive on the subject of settles (q.v.) in the relevant major section of this book it may seem wayward to show warmer feelings towards the pine settle and bench, which continued to be a standard country-made item for cottages, farms and pubs over the whole period. These settles were not, however, consciously trendy attempts to avoid modern manufactured comfort; they were genuinely rural, rather uncomfortable pieces of utilitarian furniture made by honest country craftsmen using traditional methods. In their jointing, panelling, turning, where relevant, and mouldings they illustrate a long-term connection with much earlier forms and vernacular practices.

683 Settle or bench with turned legs and supports. See Colour Plate 60.

684 A charming pine settle with an unusual lattice back design produced from laths. See Colour Plate 61.

686 Bacon settles, as this pine type is traditionally called, usually have drawers beneath the box seat like this, while the back is boxed in with panelled doors to form a cupboard in which bacon was said to be hung for curing. These pieces, starting in the 18th century, are found in ash, oak, elm and pine, the last being the least expensive. The turned knobs to the drawers and doors look original.
1840-1890 *£1,000-£1,750*

685 A pine settle of a simple type made from the late 18th century well into the mid-Victorian period in country districts and of a type advocated by Loudon in 1832 although his design has a 'Gothic' back to it, and drawers in the space below the seat, which would add greatly to present-day value.
1780-1850   *£250-£350*

PINE - tables

The pine table for eating purposes is inevitably associated with the kitchen, whether of farm or town dwelling. Any table with pretensions to a presence in a dining room would, in the 19th century, be made of a more expensive wood than pine. Pine tables were for working surfaces and practical, unostentatious eating, but they are now fashionable and appreciated for their solid qualities.

Gateleg tables are not as common in pine as they are in oak and other hardwoods but cheap gateleg pine tables were used for incidental purposes throughout the 19th century. The turning of the legs can be an indication of date but care must be exercised because certain forms of baluster were used, especially by country makers, for a long period.

687 A pine three-legged 'cricket' table with turned legs, of a type used extensively in pubs and places of refreshment in the country, particularly where floors were uneven. The turning on this example is of early 19th century form and would be changed to local and regional taste as the century progressed.
1820-1880   *£150-£250*

688 A large pine farmhouse table, 3ft. wide x 5ft. 6in. long (91cm x 168cm) of the classic 19th century type with the heavy emphasised bulbous turning associated with the second half of the century. Extremely solid, very useful and now much appreciated since large period dining tables have become very expensive.
1850-1880   *£450-£600*

689 Simple pine kitchen table on four turned legs shown with two typical spindle scroll-back chairs.
1840-1900   *£180-£250*

690 A reproduction pine refectory table on four solid turned legs with heavy connecting stretchers. The top is made of three heavy thick planks and has a 'bread board' end locking the planks together.
20th century   *£800-£1,200*

691 Pine kitchen tables of late 19th/early 20th century manufacture. That on the left is of Pembroke type with flaps supported by 'butterfly' gates underneath. The table on the right is more solid and of more traditional kitchen design. Both have a drawer in the end for cutlery. 1890-1910   *£120-£160*

692 A pine gateleg table with only one flap and gate, shown open. This type of kitchen table, intended to be placed along a wall, is very useful for use as a side table with extra surface available from the flap. 1840-1890   *£120-£180*

POT CUPBOARDS

The pot cupboard, sometimes euphemistically and erroneously referred to as a commode, had been an item of bedroom furniture throughout the 18th century and remained so during the 19th despite the gradual introduction of the water closet and other hygienic arrangements. Even the upper end of society lived in houses which frequently only had one lavatory upstairs and that at the end of a cold and gloomy corridor. The bedroom chamber pot remained in use until well into the 20th century as far as night-time arrangements were concerned. To house it, a variety of ingenious or utilarian small cupboards, designed in the latest taste or style, were used. In modern times some of these have been deemed desirable collector's items for a variety of fashionable purposes, although their fortunes seem to fluctuate.

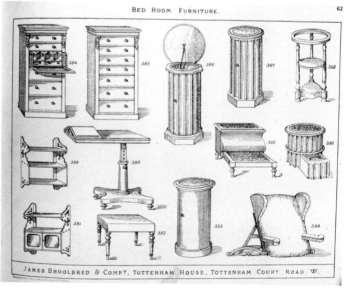

700 This page of bedroom furniture from Shoolbred's 1876 catalogue shows three or four variants on the pot cupboard theme amongst its Wellington chests, washstand, shelves, stool and reading table-tray for the bedridden, etc., etc. The cylindrical pot cupboard has been adapted for a variety of purposes in modern times and the scalloped version has had an enthusiastic following for use as a pedestal or occasional table.

701 Two pot cupboards of a design to be found in Smee's catalogue of 1850 and still, again, in Shoolbred's of 1876. Suitable for conversion to all kinds of uses.
1850-1880
Round £350-£450
Square £300-£400

702 A typical bedside cabinet design current from 1850 to 1880. This version is in walnut.
1850-1880
£200-£275

703 Walnut bedside table-cum-pot holder with a marble top. Cleverly scalloped design on octagonal base.
c.1870
£700-£900

704 Two satinwood bedside cabinets/pot holders of Edwardian taste stimulated by 'Sheraton' trends of the time.
c.1900
£275-£350

SCREENS

The screen on a pole or stand was intended to shield the heat of the fire in a room from the face of anyone seated or working near it. Generally an embroidery decoration was used, with floral designs which sometimes included birds and heraldic animals. In the 18th century both tripod poles and square or rectangular frames, sometimes equipped for reading or writing on the cool side, made their appearance.

The cheval screen (from the French 'cheval', meaning a horse, so that this is a fire-horse as against a clothes-horse) seems to be a more 19th century phenomenon and was intended to hide the remains of a fire as yet not cleaned or made-up or, during the summer months, empty fireplaces and grates.

711 The rococo character of the frame on this cheval screen marks it as a type emulating the French rococo which became popular in the mid-1830s and illustrated in T. King's design book of 1835. This is a more Anglicised version, elaborately carved in walnut, with a pierced inner frame or mount fretted in scrolls and a romanticised needlework scene of fishermen's children on a sea shore. The condition of the carving and fretting, as well as the embroidery, is a vital determinant of price since it is expensive to repair such pieces.
1840-1860   *£900-£1,400*

710 Pole screens from Loudon in 1833 showing the triform base and round base used. Loudon believed that the pole screen was exclusively British due to the British habit of heating rooms only by an open fire until the early 19th century. The screen could be of silk, but also was frequently covered with 'odd prints, portraits of men, animals, plants etc., and even with select passages from newspapers, conundrums, riddles, enigmas and charades'. He went on to extol the use of screens for the education of the young, for by putting 'instruments of education such as globes, maps, chronological tables, tables of the heights of mountains, lengths of rivers etc.' such information could be 'insensibly, and without effort' impressed on the mind.

712 A rosewood cheval or fire screen in an elaborately carved frame with scroll and leaf forms. These forms and the turning of the uprights, ending in finials, are to be seen on screens illustrated by Henry Wood in 1846 but originated earlier, at the end of the William IV period.
1840-1855   *£600-£900*

713 A walnut cheval firescreen of more 'naturalistic' design with an elaborate wool tapestry screen of heraldic design. The frame is carved with leaf and floral forms. The cabriole type feet end in scrolls and the whole effect is altogether simpler and freer than that of the previous example, which retains a certain formality in the restraint of the turned uprights but which has come only halfway towards the freedom of this one.
1845-1865   *£600-£800*

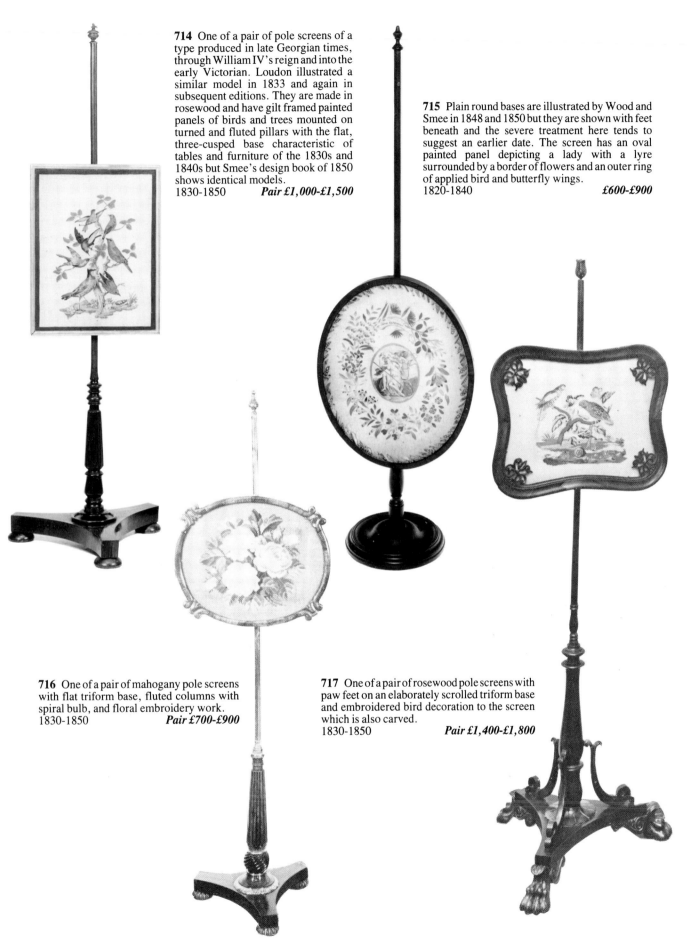

714 One of a pair of pole screens of a type produced in late Georgian times, through William IV's reign and into the early Victorian. Loudon illustrated a similar model in 1833 and again in subsequent editions. They are made in rosewood and have gilt framed painted panels of birds and trees mounted on turned and fluted pillars with the flat, three-cusped base characteristic of tables and furniture of the 1830s and 1840s but Smee's design book of 1850 shows identical models.
1830-1850   *Pair £1,000-£1,500*

715 Plain round bases are illustrated by Wood and Smee in 1848 and 1850 but they are shown with feet beneath and the severe treatment here tends to suggest an earlier date. The screen has an oval painted panel depicting a lady with a lyre surrounded by a border of flowers and an outer ring of applied bird and butterfly wings.
1820-1840   *£600-£900*

716 One of a pair of mahogany pole screens with flat triform base, fluted columns with spiral bulb, and floral embroidery work.
1830-1850   *Pair £700-£900*

717 One of a pair of rosewood pole screens with paw feet on an elaborately scrolled triform base and embroidered bird decoration to the screen which is also carved.
1830-1850   *Pair £1,400-£1,800*

211

718 One of a pair of mahogany pole screens, this one featuring Leda, in Victorian dress, being rather delicately eyed by the swan. On triform base with turned column and additional scroll supports.
1840-1860   *Pair £800-£1,200*

719 An ill-fitting rather banner-like pole screen with an elaborately twisted mahogany column and tripod base with scroll feet.
1850-1860   *Each £200-£300*

720 A pair of mahogany pole screens with floral needlework panels in carved naturalistic frames and scrolled pierced carved bases. This variant on the tripod base tends to be of a later date, illustrated by Yapp in 1879 and Wyman in 1877.
1860-1880   *£800-£1,200*

721 A three-fold embroidered screen by William Morris & Co. which exhibits residual aestheticism in its turned uprights and pierced lower lattice, but an element of rococo in the scrolled carved upper rail of the frames. It holds embroidery possibly designed by May Morris.
1870-1890   *£3,000-£5,000*

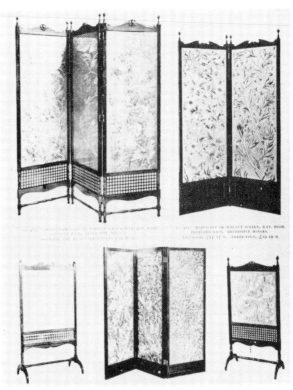

722 Cheval and folding screens from Norman & Stacey's catalogue of c.1910, entitled 'screens for mounting embroideries'. Not far removed from the William Morris example, including the lower lattice.
1900-1910   *Folding £800-£1,200*
                                                                      Cheval £300-£500

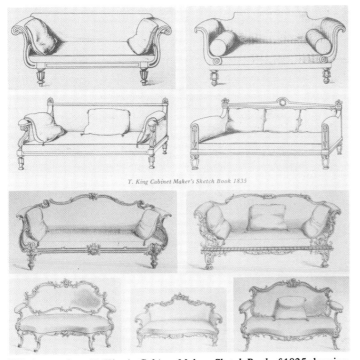

T. King Cabinet Maker's Sketch Book 1835

730 Settees from T. King's *Cabinet Makers Sketch Book* of 1835 showing, above, the essentially unaltered sub-classicism of late Regency types and, below, 'Elizabethan' and 'Louis XIV' styles which exhibit the rococo scrolling which was to become so popular during the 1840s and 1850s.

SETTEES,
CHAISES-LONGUES AND SOFAS

At the opening of Victoria's reign the design of the two-ended settee had changed little from the Regency. A heavy sub-classicism still permeated generally and the settee of the 1830s, whether shown by Loudon, King, or other catalogues of current taste, was a hefty affair.

During the 1840s, however, the scrolls of the rococo reaction were beginning to wave their way across these rather severe frames as the 'Elizabethan' or 'Louis XIV' styles took their effect. By 1850 the wavy mid-Victorian settee was well established even though the earlier fashion was quite a long time a-dying, as the catalogue of Taylor, in 1850, shows. During the 1860s the French 18th century settee had a revival and in various forms was reproduced quite well as an elegant item of drawing room furniture in competition with the single-ended chaise-longue, arm and single chair plus set of six occasional chairs — popular at the time.

The development of the Chesterfield sofa from the fully-upholstered two-ended settee of the 1850s probably occurred in the 1870s, when the form becomes prominent in catalogues.

731 A double-ended mahogany sofa of the type illustrated by T. King in 1835 with the reeded scrolling to the back, combined with bas-relief carved naturalism, which is seen on bookcase and chiffonier backs of the period.
1830-1850   *£2,000-£3,000*

732 Another double-ended settee of more Victorian characteristics — acanthus leaf carving, ponderous ends and back, fat baluster legs unrelieved by reeding, in which elegance has been discarded in favour of impression.
1840-1880   *£1,000-£1,600*

734 A double-ended settee in which the shield-panel separate end upholstery is joined by a long padded back frame supported on twist-turned uprights. A combination of rococo and 'Elizabethan' styles of the 1840s and 1850s.
1840-1860   *£1,400-£1,800*

733 A walnut sofa and armchair from a classic Victorian rococo suite. See Colour Plate 62.

735 (Right) An example of a single-ended chaise-longue which is part of a suite in a combination of scrolled rococo and shield-panelled styles. This somewhat open-carved approach to the chaise-longue makes for elegance perhaps, but not for comfort.
1840-1855   *£1,300-£1,700*

736 (Left) A form of two-ended settee which was well established by the 1850s. The cabriole-legged ends and the scrolled central carved back frame are to be found in many design books of the period.
1845-1880   *£1,800-£2,400*

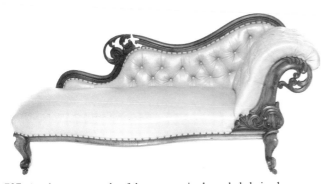

737 An elegant example of the rococo single-ended chaise-longue, on which the scroll and leaf carving has been extended into pierced flourishes on the back and end supports.
1850-1865   *£1,200-£1,800*

738 A rather inelegant design in which the flowing curve of the back is contradicted by the straight turned legs at one end and the front, i.e. three of them, and a 'thrown-back' fourth leg on the right to brace the frame. This is a rather unhappy combination of single and two-ended settees which does not really come off.
1855-1870   *£1,400-£1,800*

739 A rather enclosed two-ended settee with high central buttoned back of a type favoured in catalogues such as Blackie's of 1859. Made of rosewood with buttoned velvet covering.
1850-1870   *£1,500-£2,000*

740 The inlaid decoration and 'Sheraton' approach to the square legs of this settee might lead to an Edwardian attribution as far as dating is concerned. Catalogues of the 1880s such as Heal's had already adopted the overall design in a revived Louis XVI manner and it only remained to add the 'Adam' decoration of the Georgian Revival to achieve the piece above, which is probably of 1890s production. Since the wood used is rosewood and the upholstery has been restored to excellent condition, this is a relatively expensive piece.
1880-1900   *£1,800-£2,400*

741 A Victorian rococo single-ended settee or chaise-longue in the style so popular in the 1850s and made on to the 1880s. The buttoned upholstery gives it a luxurious appearance and the walnut cabriole legs are suitably over-scrolled to impress.
1850-1880   *£1,750-£2,500*

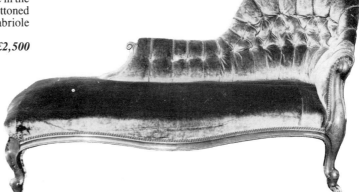

742 A more developed settee, again in walnut, with buttoned back upholstery and rococo curves which are so exuberant as almost to parody themselves. The legs and arm supports are carved with doubly-accentuated scrolls and with leaves. Like much Victorian rococo furniture, it is designed more for effect than for heavy wear, but one cannot help admiring the sheer confidence of the maker.
1850-1880 *£2,000-£3,000*

743 (Below) Typical chaise-longue, with matching chairs, of a type made from the 1880s onwards, with turned legs, solid construction and turned-spindle gallery along the back. Covered in an imitation leather.
1880-1910 *Chaise-longue £400-£650*
Suite of chaise-longue, two easy and six single chairs
£1,400-£1,800

744 A slightly later suite with spindled galleries to chaise-longue and armchair.
1890-1900 *Chaise-longue only*
£200-£400
Suite of nine pieces
£900-£1,200

745 A chaise-longue, tub easy chair and single chair of a type made from c.1890 onwards. The curvy legs are a forerunner of the 'Louis' style popular in the early 1900s.
1890-1910 *Chaise-longue only £300-£350*
Suite of nine pieces £900-£1,400

216

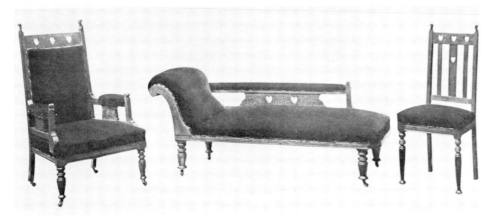

746 A commercial 'art nouveau' chaise-longue and easy chair, with single chair of a suite. The 'art nouveau' bit is from the cut-through heart shapes but, since the legs remain rotundly turned throughout (and not square section as normally done with art nouveau), it is a commercial gesture rather than a genuine design.
1890-1910 *Chaise-longue only £200-£250*
Suite of nine pieces £800-£950

747 A fully upholstered chaise-longue and easy chair with attendant 'arty' chair. The upholstery is of c.1910 velvet in a contemporary design.
1900-1910 *Chaise-longue only £250-£300*

SETTEES - chesterfields

748 Fully upholstered settees appear prominently in manufacturers' catalogues of the 1850s onwards. The chesterfield sofa is one of the enduring types but possibly appeared later. By the 1870s fully buttoned chesterfields are visible in the catalogues of Shoolbred and others. The examples shown here are from later catalogues, but that on the right is a typical example of the breed.
£1,400-£1,800

749 A selection of six chesterfields from 1900 to 1930 showing variations in coverings over the period.
1900-1930 *£1,000-£1,800*

SETTEES - Art Nouveau

750 An 'art nouveau' settee-settle inlaid with stylised flowers. The bowed sides are slatted above the upholstered arms and the square feet have castors inset.
c.1900 *£2,250-£2,000*

751 A mahogany corner settee with an arm rest with turned column supports at one end. An odd 'art nouveau' piece designed for some special corner.
c.1900 *£450-£650*

SETTEES - drop arm

752 The drop-arm settee appears to have lost favour recently. There was a time when the pull of a lever could transform a settee into a piece of reclining furniture. Three versions are shown here, two of chesterfield type and one shaped one on square tapering legs.
1900-1920   *£350-£500*

SETTEES - 'reproduction' styles, 1890-1930

753 (Left) An Edwardian settee very much in the 'Sheraton' style, with Regency striped covering. It is of mahogany, with inlaid stringing and a touch of marquetry to the back rail centre panel as well as a satinwood band inlaid round the back.
1900-1910   *£800-£1,200*

754 (Right) A rather splendidly-covered 'French' style settee with gilded frame with gesso decoration.
1860-1890   *£1,750-£2,500*

755 An ebonised sofa with an inlaid panel in the back. The piece is made in a style derivative of French and dimmer traditions, with a hint of the Prince of Wales' feathers thrown in in this part of the suite of drawing room furniture. The overall effect is rather flimsy.
c.1890   *£650-£900*

756 A 19th century English reproduction of a French sofa, made with considerable skill and expertise. One of the great difficulties with the classic French designs from Louis XIV to Louis XVI is the fact that they have been so much reproduced and so accurately. Even now, Italian and Spanish workshops, as well as the French, are turning out Louis XV chairs on a grand production scale.
1860-1890   *£2,500-£3,500*

757 (Left) An 'Edwardian Sheraton' settee with a buttoned back and turned front legs. There is a characteristic inlay in boxwood and ivory in the centre of the top back seat rail, and inlaid boxwood stringing lines in the mahogany frame.
1890-1900   *£550-£700*

758 (Above right and right) A settee and a day bed in walnut with much twist turning to meet the demand for 'medieval' furniture. The styles are, in fact, more attuned to Restoration furniture than the 'Elizabethan' taste they were intended to satisfy.
1900-1920
Settee £275-£350
Day bed £250-£300

SETTLES (see also Pine Furniture)

There was a revival of the settle by the Gothic reformers. After all, it was sufficiently medieval-bucolic in origin, 'honest' in construction and laudably uncomfortable to sit on; no one idles for long on a settle. What is more, no man in a cold, sober condition would sit on a settle unless he expected shortly to get either very warm or very drunk. Its sentimental association with insanitary hovels, inns and farmhouses characterises British attitudes fostered by Victorian art and literature and made it a sure-fire winner with Morris and similar designers initially intent on a reaction to bourgeois Victorian comfort.

To be fair, some settles were designed to go into the inglenooks revived by Norman Shaw and other domestic architects but by the 1920s the settle seems to have become a piece of hall furniture with a seat that lifted as a lid to give access to a coffer-like compartment under it — to house boots? slippers? bottles? — and no one was expected to sit waiting in the hall for long.

770 (Above left) The full treatment — a William Morris settle with profuse painted decoration. Note the detail of the coved top shown above.
1885-1895   *£18,000+*

771 An oak and beaten copper settle in the 'art nouveau' manner, using the copper plaques with tulip forms associated with Arts and Crafts furniture of what is now thought of as English art nouveau. The hinged seat lifts to give access to the coffer-like interior.
1900-1910   *£450-£600*

772 The classic reproducer's version of the oak settle, not very much removed from the original 17th century piece except that the panelling is symmetrical, modern in construction and rather austere. The seat lid lifts up to give access to the storage space in the lower half. The price is affected by the now very high price of the original period version.
1900-1915   *£250-£350*

773 An oak settle or 'monk's bench' which is, in fact a chair-table, since the back of the seat tilts over to form a table top at an inconvenient height. There is a hinged lid in the seat, giving access to the storage space. The front is panelled with a shaped apron. Not now very desirable — the storage space was intended for rugs, presumably used when travelling.
1900-1915   *£100-£140*

774 An oak seat or settle from Percy Wells, 1920. An object which seems to have taken a long time dying and which was used as a 'hall seat', although Wells claimed it could be used just as well in a living room, with the addition of cushions to make it comfortable. Not a cheap piece and an interesting example of the survival of older forms of furniture, modified slightly in design, well into the 20th century. Wells pointed out the lack of 'meretricious ornament' which dignified the piece and the simple strap carving.
1920   *£150-£200*

SIDEBOARDS

The sideboard followed the evolution of styles in much the same way as other Victorian furniture, with a few slight differences. From its original, Adam form, it became a heavier, end-pedimented piece made in sub-classical, usually Grecian, style with a heavy, drawered top connecting the two end pediments. Sometimes there was a gap between the two pediments, under the top, like a large 'kneehole'; sometimes this area was cupboarded in. The latter type, with cupboards, has been much preferred by the antique trade and is more expensive. Rococo forms of sideboard exist, but rococo seems to have been more used for the chiffonier or side cabinet intended for the drawing room. The dining room furniture was far more serious, heavier stuff, more suited to the grave atmosphere to be associated with eating. Chairs followed a similar pattern.

Commercial production continued to supply these heavy dining room sideboards and even carved oak versions in emulation of the famous 'Chevy Chase' piece, smothered with carved fauna, fruit and vegetables, until the end of the century. In the 1870s the return to 18th century reproductions saw the re-introduction of the Adam form and the 'Sheraton' or late 18th/early 19th century versions of it. In Edwardian times some satinwood reproductions were made — even the William Morris Company produced them — which were quite good versions of the originals, with the possible exception that inlaid or painted decoration in the Adam style tended to be overdone. These pieces are elegant, however, and are now quite highly priced.

The Gothic reformers, the 'art furniture' boys, Godwin, the Arts and Crafts Movement, the Cotswold crafties and the 'garden city socialists' in their various turns, despised 'commercial' sideboards almost more than any other form of furniture. To them the Victorian sideboard epitomised the vulgarity, the parvenu tastelessness, the crass greed and the ostentation of the rising middle class Philistine. They reacted to it in their various ways and the commercial manufacturers copied them all. Talbert produced his 'Pet' sideboard in Reformed Gothic. Godwin, with William Watt, produced his celebrated Anglo-Japanese versions, one of which is in the Victoria and Albert Museum. The art furniture boys laid the ebonising on thick, spindled the galleries, coved the tops and painted some of the panels in startling colours which contrasted with the

continued

Sideboard by R. Adam.

780 Above — the sideboard as Adam saw it in 1760. A pair of pedestals flank a centre section with drawers, cupboards and space below. No. 808 in this section reproduces the form.
Below — a sideboard, plate and wine cooler by Adam. The formal table has on it a pair of cutlery boxes surmounted by plates.

781 The sideboard as seen by Shearer in 1788. Shearer was a contemporary of Sheraton and Hepplewhite; his designs are similar to theirs. Note that the pedestals, with their vase-shaped urns, are becoming more incorporated into the whole piece. The other alternatives, for smaller sideboards, are nearer the Sheraton type.

223

ebonising. The Arts and Crafts Movement went in for plain oak surfaces, flat-capped tapering columns, art nouveau beaten copper hinges with heart shapes and fretted holes in weepy shapes. The Cotswold crafties and the garden city socialists really didn't like to get involved with sideboards at all. They preferred dressers, since dressers are more in the medieval tradition, more 'country' than the wealthily-inspired sideboard. The sideboards they produced are often really a form of dresser base or an adaptation of a simple dresser form or, in the case of Gordon Russell, a universal pedestal desk/dressing table principle used for sideboards.

By the 1900s the medieval oak taste had set in with a vengeance as well as the desire for 18th century reproduction. From about 1900 onwards the sideboard became subject to an extremely varied number of styles, some of them employed all on one piece. But the 'Jacobethan' mass-production of post-1918 was probably the major feature and sideboards were produced to go with the bulbous-legged 'refectory' or draw-tables of cheap stained oak.

782 Where the sideboard had got to by the time of Loudon in 1833. There were also Gothic and Elizabethan versions of these pieces in varying degrees of elaboration but the form had essentially got down to a pair of cupboards flanking an open space under the actual sideboard. Upper superstructure gradually developed as the century wore on. The antique trade has always preferred the open space to be cupboarded in, since doing so makes more use of the area occupied by the piece.

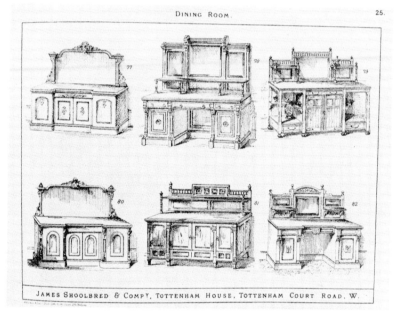

783 Sideboards from Shoolbred's 1876 catalogue. The heavy cupboard base of the 1830s and 1840s has been retained but a superstructure, either mirrored or shelved, has been added. Panels exhibit the arched design of the 1840s or a square, fielded or planked surface in accordance with the fashion followed. Spindled galleries or bas-relief carving embellish the upper shelves. These commercial versions of Reformed Gothic (planks), Aesthetic (spindles) and other styles represent a catch-all page covering forty years of Victorian sideboard design.

784 A sideboard of the 'Chevy Chase' variety. See Colour Plate 63.

785 A small mahogany sideboard with Gothic panelled doors. See Colour Plate 64.

786 A sideboard in mahogany with the low-arched panels which came into fashion in the 1840s and which continued to be made until the 1880s. This is a very simple version with serpentine shaping to the drawer fronts.
1840-1880   *£600-£750*

787 Another mahogany sideboard with classical pillars and cheap leaf-and-scroll carving around the mirror back. It is a type which, with dismemberment and reassembly, can be turned into a 'Regency' chiffonier by the adept converter.
1840-1860   *£650-£850*

788 The characteristic early Victorian chiffonier-sideboard made from the 1840s onwards. Panelled doors with the flattened arch and 'feather' mahogany figures; ogee moulded drawer fronts; acanthus leaf carving; solid plinth and carved curvy back. Cheaply made and mass produced; hated by all 'progressive' designers.
1840-1880   *£700-£900*

789 A walnut sideboard in the severer lines of the 1860s with a galleried top incorporating turned spindles and finials. The inconsistent use of oval mirrors in conjunction with rectangular ones is disconcerting. The burr walnut veneer is inlaid with boxwood and ivory stringing lines and formalised marquetry and there is a white marble top.
1860-1880   *£700-£950*

790 A carved oak sideboard of a design inspired by the 'Chevy Chase' type exhibited prominently in the mid-Victorian period. Carved oak (or mahogany) sideboards with large quantities of unfortunate fauna and flora suitable for gastronomy carved upon them became quite popular, even if expensive. It was a taste that continued despite the disapproving scowls of the Gothic reformers and subsequent progressives.
1850-1880   *£8,000-£10,000*

791 A Bruce Talbert 'Pet' sideboard made by Gillows in oak with characteristic carving of foliage, use of spindles in galleries and a quotation above.
c.1873   *£17,000+*

792 An oak sideboard designed by Charles Eastlake (see *Hints on Household Taste,* Plate XI) showing the restrained version of Reformed Gothic with angled planking and incised mouldings so characteristic of the type. There is a carved quotation in Latin across the top.
1870-1880   *£9,000+*

Photo: Courtesy Jeremy Cooper

793 Another oak sideboard showing a wealth of angled tongued-and-grooved planking and a carved panel of birds as well as painted panels in the Aesthetic Movement manner.
1870-1880   *£3,500-£5,000*

794 A simpler Reformed Gothic sideboard with tongued-and-grooved planking but with a pierced gallery above with four carved seated lions.
c.1880   *£1,000-£1,500*

795 An oak sideboard, or more properly buffet, in the manner of Bruce Talbert but with overtones of Eastlake in the tongued-and-grooved planking, having a castellated top moulding. Note the black inlaid lines, chamfered edges and general emphasis on the construction so dear to Reformed Gothic design.
1875-1885 *£1,500-£2,500*

796 An ebonised Anglo-Japanese sideboard designed by E.W. Godwin (q.v.) of a type now exhibited in the Victoria and Albert Museum. Godwin's use of Japanese design is discussed on page 33. What is important from a value point of view is that the piece exhibits a design trend towards the Modern Movement in its vertical and horizontal lines. It is thus, as a milestone in furniture history, that its value to suitable museums is extremely high.
c.1877 *£80,000+*

797 Another ebonised Anglo-Japanese sideboard by E.W. Godwin. A buyer paid nearly £7,000 for this piece at Sotheby's Belgravia in 1978. Why so much less than the previous example? A telling point this — because it does not so clearly exhibit the horizontal and vertical lines which point the way to the designs of the Modern Movement. It is thus of less interest to museums as a furniture history milestone, even though it has great value as a piece by Godwin.
c.1877 *£30,000+*

798 A characteristic Aesthetic Movement sideboard of ebonised and mahogany construction with a coved top with spindled gallery. The bevelled-edged mirrors, panelled construction and turning are all typical.
c.1880 *£1,200-£1,600*

227

799 A rosewood inlaid sideboard which shows how, at the end of the century, the return to 18th century styles had affected commercial production. Indeed, this piece shows traces of the 'Victorian Queen Anne' style or 'bracket-and-overmantel' style in the broken pediment and design of the upper half, but it still has traces of a spindle-turned gallery and 'pot-board' bottom shelf of the Aesthetic Movement. Yet the inlaid decoration is 'Adam' or 'Sheraton' and the piece would now be sold as 'Edwardian Sheraton'. It is not quite as late as the Edwardian styles shown in later pages of sideboards, as the reader may note, however.
1890-1900   £1,200-£1,800

800 An odd oak sideboard of slightly progressive-cum-quaint associations in design. (The wavy-line pierced gallery is the 'quaint' part.) The photograph gives it a slightly asymmetric look, which is misleading. Probably by Liberty's.
1890-1900   £800-£750

SIDEBOARDS
Art Nouveau and Progressive, 1890-1915

We have explained elsewhere how art nouveau is a term now used to describe furniture which many of its English original designers would have hotly refuted. The Scottish school and the Century Guild are another matter, since their sinuous designs are much more akin to Continental art nouveau.

In this section we show sideboards from blatantly art nouveau originals to commercially watered-down versions and one or two other 'progressive' designs. There are many side cabinets which might have been included here but we have preferred to retain them in the Cabinet section out of a sense of technically philological purity.

801 A sideboard-cum-side cabinet of interesting art nouveau decoration on serpentine bracket feet. Included here because surely the lower half, with its three central drawers and flanking cupboards, dictates that it was intended as a sideboard. The piece has rather astonishing inlaid 'tulip' decoration with whip-lash curves and the two high side cabinets on the top half flank a much more conventional glazed cabinet of shorter dimensions. The glazing bars have an additional curved bar each side of the central panel, as though the designer was tired of the verticality of the construction and wanted to relate something to the sinuous inlays. Note the interesting use of diagonally-chequered stringing lines which give an Arts and Crafts touch.
1890-1900   £2,250-£3,000

802 A mahogany sideboard of interesting design which combines a traditional English form with the use of inlays of 'whip-lash' art nouveau floral decoration. The canted glazed side-cupboards are a design associated with Liberty's, who espoused art nouveau and quaint furniture enthusiastically.
c.1900 *£750-£1,000*

803 An almost aggressively art nouveau oak sideboard, more on the Continental lines of the style than the British. The sides of the lower half, with their protruding tapering stiles in the 'Eastlake' manner, are broken by the sinuous curves of carved floral decoration. The bronze hinges, handles and applied tulips are over-decorative and there is a good deal of ostentation about the amount of carving used all over. Notice the flat capped finials along the top — a feature used by Voysey but emulated in a way he disliked intensely.
1900-1910 *£1,500-£2,250*

804 Liberty's oak dresser-sideboard. See Colour Plate 65.

805 An art nouveau sideboard in oak with inlaid decoration, smaller and more restrained than No. 803 but with similar characteristics, i.e. bronze hinges ending in heart shapes, flat-capped finials, pierced heart shapes and sinuous motifs.
1900-1910 *£600-£900*

806 A nice small oak sideboard which shows how the principles of the Arts and Crafts movement could be applied to a piece with restraint. The bronze panel let in to the back with its typical spade shapes and the carved 'trees' in the door panels relieve the almost altar-like severity of the pointed uprights.
1880-1910   *£750-£950*

807 Commercial adaptations of the 'art nouveau' style in sideboards, from the use of leaded-light cupboards (an English favourite, this) to the simple, rather bankrupt embellishment of heart-shaped frets and added fretted curves on (e). Notice the tapering upward columns on the sides of the top of (b), ending in flat caps — a feature of Voysey's designs for several pieces of furniture.
1890-1914   *a, b, c, d £400-£600*
                                                        e £200-£325

a

b

c

d

e

The revival of 18th century designs in the 1880s saw the return of the traditional 'Georgian' mahogany sideboard which has persisted as a favourite ever since. Conceived by the Adam brothers around 1760 as a rather extended range of table and pedestals, the form has been modified until very suitable for most dining rooms. The traditional pillared dining table, mahogany chairs and sideboard are such a deeply-ingrained English form that even now the industry producing modern reproductions must account for a large proportion of all dining furniture sold in the British Isles.

808 The sideboard almost as Adam originally saw it in 1760. Two pedestals flanking a table with a wine cooler under it. The pedestals have urn-shaped vases lined to take iced water for drinking and hot water for washing silver. The pedestals could be used as plate warmers and wine storage (cellaret) if required. The central table has a high brass rail behind it. This is a faithful Edwardian reproduction — they were good at making these. The pedestals and urns are now the most valuable part for their decorative qualities.
1900-1920   *without cellaret £5,000-£7,000*

809 The next stage on from the Adam design. The end pedestals have been integrated with the table. The urn-shaped vases (or is it vase-shaped urns?) remain. The brass gallery is more decorative. A reproduction of a 1780-1800 design.
1900-1910   *£3,500-£4,500*

810 Now comes a third stage. The pedestals have been attenuated into two cupboards on square tapering legs and the central table has a deep drawer. The vase-shaped urns have gone. Almost the accepted form of Georgian sideboard so beloved of the reproducer.
1900-1910   *£1,400-£2,000*

811 An integrated half-circular version where the deep cupboards either side and the central section are now the same depth. To fill in the space, the central section has a drawer and a large space below it. A high quality version would have a tambour shutter to draw across this space.
1900-1920   *£800-£1,100*

812 A mahogany sideboard of shallower proportions without the shelf under the central section. A very faithful copy of a style popular around 1790-1820 but made a hundred years or more later. The bow front contains a central drawer and kneehole flanked by two deep cupboards. The boxwood stringing lines provide an elegant and restrained decoration appropriate to the spirit of a simple George III piece.
1900-1930   *£900-£1,300*

813 A mahogany bow-fronted sideboard now much shallower with little difference in depth between central drawer and cupboards. In this case the decoration is a little more elaborate than that of 812, but the proportion is clumsier, partly due to the thick legs and partly to the overemphasis on the thickness of the top.
1900-1930   *£1,000-£1,500*

814 A sub-classical design following somewhat after Thomas Hope (1810) but now embellished with 'Adam' marquetry inlays and stringing lines. It is tempting to believe that this is, in fact, an early 19th century piece which has been subsequently 'improved' by inlaying, around say 1890, but the integration of the inlay with the overall design argues against it, even though the inlaying 'improvers' of the late 19th century were very clever.
1890-1900   *£2,000-£3,500*

It is not quite clear when the return to 18th century designs led to a thirst for 'Queen Anne'. Certainly the cabriole leg was used on dining chairs before the end of the century. This feature, on sideboards, seems to have been a bit later — say in the 1890s — but the design seems to have gathered popularity until its heyday in the 1930s.

The 'Queen Anne' style, exemplified by the use of the cabriole leg, should not be confused with 'Victorian Queen Anne' which was a more Palladian, William Kent-ish architectural style with triangular or broken pediments popular around the 1870s and 1880s for cabinets. The Queen Anne of Edwardian times is nearer the real thing, using cabriole legs and fiddle-shaped splats for chairs. It is not a pure style, however, and is distinct from exact reproductions of Queen Anne pieces.

815 An oak sideboard (also made available in mahogany at the time) whose only real claim to Queen Anne pretensions lies in its thin, weakly-designed cabriole legs. There is the high back of Victorian taste and the large central mirror. The open central section was rather hopefully called a cellaret by the makers but the bowl placed within it in the photograph has unfortunate connotations of night-time use.
1900-1910   *£250-£350*

816 A second variety of oak sideboard where, again, the only claim to Queen Anne styling is in the weak front cabriole legs.
1900-1910   *£250-£350*

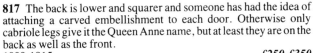

817 The back is lower and squarer and someone has had the idea of attaching a carved embellishment to each door. Otherwise only cabriole legs give it the Queen Anne name, but at least they are on the back as well as the front.
1900-1915   *£250-£350*

818 Still coming down, the back is lower and the flat-capped uprights of art nouveau contrast somewhat with the Queen Anne cabrioles. Made in mahogany; not a Queen Anne wood. The popular Edwardian semi-circular central arch has had a Queen Anne carved 'shell' put in it — very appropriate.
1900-1915   *£150-£225*

233

819 Four typical late Victorian/Edwardian sideboards of a type made in oak or walnut of the straight-grained American type. Mostly identified as to period by the bas-relief carving in panels or on pediments, and the use of a modified classical pediment so dear to the Edwardian heart. The common features to all are the large back mirrors with columns either side, drawers with cupboards under in the lower half and panelling to the cupboard doors, achieved by either fielding or mouldings.
1900-1914

£600-£800

The 'Jacobean' style was popular well before the onset of the standard 'Tudor' dining room of the 1920s and 1930s. By the 1890s the popularity of medievalism had brought out a surge of 'old oak' manufacture. Commercially produced sideboards of the period simply reflect the desire to satisfy this trend.

820 An oak sideboard of almost standard top design, except that the prevailing columns on either side of the mirror are twist turned. The drawer fronts are moulded and the door panels are fielded. The piece has a pot-board stretcher beneath and bulbous turned front legs in imitation of Elizabethan types.
1900-1910   *£600-£800*

821 Again a variation of standard design at the top but this time the cupboard doors are on either side of three central drawers and have geometric mouldings on them. Twist-turned legs, with square section stretchers, end in bun feet.
1900-1910   *£450-£650*

822 A lower back without mirror — the start of the move towards lighter furniture for lower ceilings, perhaps. Actually a piece designed in emulation of a court cupboard, with a dominating, overhanging top moulding with a big, turned finial suspended under each end. Doors and panels are geometrically moulded and, in the cases of the two end doors, fielded as well.
1900-1915   *£400-£600*

823 A very interesting oak sideboard in an amalgam of 'Olde English' styles with inlays in boxwood (or holly) and a darker wood, perhaps ebony. The geometrically moulded drawer fronts and back panels are 'Jacobean' in design, emulating oak chests of the 1670-1690 period and the bobbin-turned double-column front legs and stretchers are taken from lighter furniture of the 1680-1700 period, such as gatelegs and side tables. The inlays, with the Prince of Wales' feathers motifs, are quite 19th century in inspiration and the checked boxwood-and-ebony stringing lines are of the type favoured by designers of the 1890s to 1920s, such as Waals and the Barnsleys, although such lines were used in the 18th century also. The occasional square sections in the bobbin turning of the stretchers are an erroneous diversion, since such square sections, in the original period, were only used at the joints, not left stranded in mid-section such as these. The thumb-nail moulding round the serving top and its lower moulding outlines are quite authentic to the 17th century but the top to the back incorporates a dentillated moulding which is mid-18th century in design. It is not clear whether the piece is meant to be stained in any way when finished, but the implication is not, since it was the fashion, 1880-1910, for such 'back-to-Elizabeth I' designers to leave the natural wood unstained and simply to wax polish it.
1900-1910   *£600-£800*

824 The 'lower' move continued. This time the back has been cut down to a simple one with the central arch characteristic of Edwardian furniture. Geometric mouldings and applied split balusters decorate the surfaces. Large turned bulbous feet/legs in Elizabethan style.
1900-1915   *£300-£400*

825 (Above right) An oak sideboard in the 'Jacobean' manner, incorporating moulded drawer fronts, twist-turned legs and stretchers, scrolled pierced carving in Restoration style and a low arched back as favoured by Edwardian fashion, but getting ever lower.
1900-1920   *£300-£400*

826 The back has almost gone, preparing the way for the simple Jacobean styles of the late 1920s and 1930s. Otherwise similar decoration to previous examples.
1900-1925   *£150-£200*

236

Colour Plate 59. This pine 'dresser base' is probably a shop fitting rather than a genuine dog kennel style of dresser base. Such fittings, originally painted to blend with shop or kitchen decoration, are now usually stripped and polished to provide kitchen or bedroom furniture.
1850-1900   *£700-£950*

Colour Plate 60. Settles and benches with turned legs and supports were popular throughout the 19th century, although the baluster shaping of both legs, arms and back turning of this example indicate an earlier 19th century form. With suitable cushioning to relieve the hardness of the seating provided, this would be a very pleasant and decorative, as well as useful piece.
1830-1850   *£450-£650*

Colour Plate 61. A charming pine settle with an unusual lattice back design produced from laths. The form is essentially 18th century and this example would almost certainly be sold as such but it is, again, one which would be made by traditional country methods for a long period.
1800-1880   *£600-£800*

Colour Plate 62. A walnut sofa and armchair from a classic Victorian rococo suite, covered in velvet, with scrolled cabriole legs and naturalistic carving to the spoon-shaped back.
1850-1880 *Sofa £2,500-£3,500*
Chair £1,000-£1,400

Colour Plate 63. A sideboard of the 'Chevy Chase' variety, in this case one of a pair. Embellished with carvings of fowl (storks or herons, pheasants etc.) and flesh (a rabbit) as well as grapes, surmounted by a carved cornice including leaves and flowers but culminating in a shell. The blank back panels were intended as a background to the display of vases, plates, cups etc. placed on the shelf.
1840-1870 *£4,000-£6,000*

Colour Plate 64. A small mahogany sideboard, c.1840, with Gothic panelled doors to which carved fruit and foliage have been liberally applied. The right-hand door is missing its bottom carved moulding.
c.1840   *£2,000-£2,750*

Colour Plate 65. Liberty's oak dresser-sideboard in which the influence of C.F.A. Voysey is clearly discernible. Uprights ending in flat caps and hinges ending in heart shapes were almost a Voysey trademark, and the arched recess emulates another Voysey original. Beaten bronze became popular for hinges and handles. The upper doors, however, are inset with bottle-glass panes which add a 'quaint' element of which Voysey would not have approved. The piece has a massive, unadorned tradition in which the handling of proportion appears deceptively simple: it is in fact sophisticatedly designed. The clock, pewter trays and tea set (in the lower arched space) are all originals in the 'art nouveau' manner.
1890-1910   *£2,000-£3,000*

Colour Plate 67. Needlework footstool with gilt-gesso base decorated with moulded naturalistic forms. In this example the needlework is enriched with beadwork to heighten both colour and effect. Low footstools of square and circular form, but more generally square, are to be found in catalogues of the 1800-1835 period. The circular form is more general in later catalogues such as C.and R. Light, 1881.
1850-1870 *£250-£350*

Colour Plate 68. Needlework footstool with mahogany base enlivened by an inlaid band of satinwood. The floral needlework decoration, on red ground, is lively and its moulded surround suggests a lid, not unusual for such stools, which then have a small storage space beneath. A type very similar to those illustrated by C. and R. Light in 1881 and already influenced, in the banded mahogany, by the Georgian Revival.
1880-1900 *£200-£300*

Colour Plate 66. A rosewood folio stand by Gillows of Lancaster, c.1835, showing the rococo scrolling and acanthus leaf decoration associated with early Victorian furniture of this style. The upper frame is hinged to allow folios to be opened in the usual way.
c.1835 *£2,500-£3,250*

Colour Plate 69. A rosewood and marquetry circular breakfast table on which the top is segmentally veneered and inlaid with floral sprays. The central turned column is gadrooned and supported on three scrolled legs with carved leaf and flower decoration.
1850-1870 *£4,500-£6,000*

Colour Plate 70. A papier-mâché breakfast table, c.1850, possibly of Birmingham manufacture. The tip-up top is painted with flowers, inlaid with mother-of-pearl and decorated with gilt foliage, which is also used on the base. The flat circular base below the central baluster support has three dolphin's-head feet.
c.1850 *£8,000-£12,000*

Colour Plate 71. An oak centre pedestal table with a tip-up top which is of Puginesque design, although probably not by him. The use of the grotesque carved animals' heads and the heavily-pillared centre column, more like stonework than wood, is typical of the use of Gothic design. Note the carved edge of the table top, with its Gothic-Islamic motif. Possibly intended as a library table and of the mid-Victorian Gothic style transitional between fanciful Regency 'Gothic' and the severer Reformed Gothic of the 1860s.
c.1850 *£1,750-£2,250*

Colour Plate 72. Centre and library tables with double-column end supports and outswept feet ending in scrolls, connected by a turned stretcher, are fairly commonplace in design books of the 1850s to the 1880s. What distinguishes one table from another is the use of fine veneers, marquetry, inlays, and brass mounts. In this case the inlaid bandings and the mounts indicate a fine quality piece.
1850-1880 *£4,500-£6,000*

Colour Plate 73. A marquetry centre table, c.1860, of the type associated with Holland & Sons, in a style influenced by French neo-classicism but with 'Elizabethan' headings on the octagonal fluted tapering legs. The quality of the marquetry is of the highest order and the ebonised mouldings emphasise the richness of the inlays and their designs.
1850-1870 *£9,000-£12,000*

Colour Plate 74. This double-drawered frieze version of a Carlton House writing table is nearer to Gillows' than that of Shearer, who showed one in his *Prices of Cabinet Work* in 1797 with only single frieze drawers. The type has been made in satinwood, mahogany and marquetry and has given rise to a whole range of similar tables in descending order of sophistication.
1870-1900 *£6,000-£10,000*

243

Colour Plate 75. Another variant on the Carlton House writing table, this time in mahogany with satinwood crossbanding. Nearer in design to Shearer's (1797) illustration but the late 19th century's desire to liven things up a bit has over-emphasised the bandings and the oval panel in the concave corner doors.
1890-1900   *£5,000-£7,000*

Colour Plate 76.
A large mahogany break-front wardrobe incorporating a set of drawers in the centre sections and hanging cupboards to each side. The central doors above the drawers enclose a series of slides in the same way as the Georgian clothes press. A design common from 1850 into the 1880s but in this case the simplified upper moulding indicates a later date.
1880-1900
£1,000-£1,500

830 A hall stand which was produced in oak or mahogany, incorporating a broken pediment, finials and two cupboards either side of the umbrella stand. More 18th century in conception but typically Edwardian in its use of the bas-relief carved panels and, indeed, in that particular form of broken pediment, which was used on so many pieces of larger furniture.
1900-1915 *£175-£250*

STANDS

The hall stand is an interesting piece of furniture for sociological reasons as much as stylistic ones. What did the first hall stand look like? Are there 18th century hall stands? There are boot racks and planks full of pegs or nails from the 18th century but the hall stand in its form shown on these pages appears to be a 19th century development, something which grew along with the increase in halls in houses. For the 18th century cottage, there was rarely a hall. One simply fell down the front step into the living room, hitting one's head on the beams. For the wealthier gentry, external clothes and hats would be taken away by a servant. No, it must have been the same, well-worn old Rise of the Self-Sufficient Middle Class, with its entrance hall or passage, where coats, hats, boots and umbrellas were parked, which gave rise to the need for this piece of furniture. Now the hall stand is gradually dying, too wasteful of space to compete with pegs on the wall, too profligate in providing for far too many umbrellas and walking-sticks made redundant by the motor car. The hall itself is under attack, shrinking and shrinking so as to provide more space allocation to the living areas within a house.

And yet one retains an affection for the old hall stand. Its ability to tear a sleeve if passed by in a hurry; its mirror, uselessly hidden behind coats hanging upon it; its metal umbrella trays, full of cigarette ash; its cunningly-designed centre of gravity, so sure to allow it, when the last heavy coat was hung upon it, to tip forward and crush one beneath it; these are the things that one misses. And the sheer exposure of leaving a good coat or umbrella open to view on the hall stand of a populous family house; the certainty that it or they would be missing when needed.

What really makes the hall stand a thing of the past is the modern desire for neatness and order. A hall stand covered in coats, mackintoshes, umbrellas and galoshes or wellies is a muddlesome, unlovely sight. The clothes closet, with its hangers and the vacuum cleaner, has supplanted it. There has been a recent vogue in America to use wardrobes (q.v.) in place of a stand, thus hiding the offensive paraphernalia away and causing yet another container shipping boom, this time from the old wardrobe market. The Habitat brigade have gone in for bright red bentwood stands. The hall stand of eighty years ago is having a job to avoid the hatchet; mark this progression of them before they disappear, leaving only the odd survivor in the museums.

831 A combination hall stand incorporating a broken pediment and a cupboard on bulbous carved 'Elizabethan' legs. A piece to meet the prevailing fashion for carved oak furniture, with lion masks, scrolled dolphin-like objects and acanthus leaves all proclaiming the maker's open-minded attitude to the use of motifs from widely different periods. The temptation to break this piece up for use as various bits of other pieces of furniture would be strong to the modern producer.
1900-1915 *£175-£250*

832 The influence of art furniture upon hall stands. A mahogany or walnut model with a gallery of turned spindles above the mirror and a tiled panel above the glove box. Alas, however, a broken pediment surmounts the whole, reverting to a classicism Collcutt and Godwin would not have liked.
1900-1915 *£50-£75*

833 A slight genuflection towards the progressive movement here. Look at the flat top with its deep-set moulding; the hooped umbrella rail; the tapering frontal leg under the brush drawer. Art nouveau has had a look in. The round bevelled mirror, though practical, is out of keeping with the shapes preferred by the art nouveau designers, however.
1900-1915   *£35-£60*

834 A bamboo hall stand in which the maker, confronted with a surplus of material, has joyfully cross-strutted the framing and added fanciful chinoiserie grilles around the mirror.
1900-1915   *£50-£80*

835 A hall stand, available in oak, mahogany or American walnut, of slightly more developed form. The bevelled mirror has beaten metal panels over and above it and the front legs are turned.
1900-1915   *£35-£55*

836 An oak hall stand with an oval mirror and a brush box, surmounted by a broken pediment on top. It is 6ft.9ins. (205cm) high and the top pegs ensure that only the master of the house or a particularly lanky offspring can reach the hats parked up there. A wise precaution: many a Homburg has been smashed due to juvenile collisions with the hall stand.
1900-1915   *£30-£40*

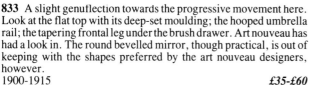

837 A simple hall stand with a narrow mirror, a glove box and two umbrella holders, with metal trays. The fretted corner brackets are decorative, an attempt to disguise its appearance as a guillotine frame.
1900-1915   *£20-£35*
                          (No, not a penny more)

838 An oak hall stand for umbrellas, with a glove box or drawer. The carving is typical of late 19th/early 20th century 'oakiness' with a lion mask and scroll-and-leaf forms. Now something of an anachronism and ripe for conversion into a console table of some sort.
1900-1915   *£60-£90*

STANDS - music, folio or portfolio

Music stands, along with music Canterburies (q.v.), were more important than modern thought may imagine simply because music was an everyday entertainment in the Victorian home. Some of the stands were versatile and could be folded down to form a small table.

Folio or portfolio stands were considered useful for the library or drawing room. Some could be locked up so that large prints or folders could not be stolen.

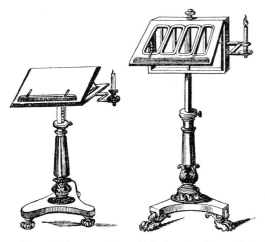

839 Music stands from Loudon, 1833, showing the candle holder.

841 A rosewood folio stand by Gillow of Lancaster. See Colour Plate 66.

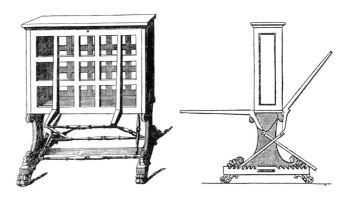

840 Portfolio stand from Loudon, 1833, showing, in section, the mechanism which allowed the sides to be opened to any convenient angle or folded level to act as a print table.

842 A rosewood folio stand of considerable quality, with scroll and leaf carving embellishing the base and feet. The arched arcaded supports are repeated in the folio holder which can be adjusted by the arms and clamp knobs. The inside of the body is divided like a Canterbury (q.v.) to contain reserve folios or documents.
1830-1845   *£3,000-£4,500*

843 A folio stand in walnut with fretted decoration, of a type which can be opened wide by the use of the rack below and the leverage of the supports.
1845-1855   *£1,200-£1,800*

Nos. 846-853 show a selection of perennially favourite stands for plants, busts and other ornament requiring elevation, from a manufacturer's catalogue of 1900-1910.

844 A burr walnut 'jardinière' or pot holder in the French rococo manner. With typical ormolu mounts on the 'knees' of the cabriole legs and a brass gallery rail around the top.
1860-1880   *£1,500-£2,000*

845 An Edwardian 'art nouveau' pot stand in oak, flimsily made but with typically-shaped gallery or railing in the lower half. Ideal for Art pottery display.
1900-1915   *£120-£180*

846 An oak palm stand on four long legs with shelf stretcher.
£120-£180

847 An inlaid oak jardinière of a type often made with decoration of hanging chains.
£300-£400

851 A more conventional ebonised fluted pedestal of 18th century classical design.   *£400-£500*

852 A mahogany palm stand similar to 846 but inlaid with 'Sheraton' stringing and decoration.   *£150-£200*

853 Another palm stand based on a jardinière design. *£250-£325*

848 An ebonised turned pedestal suitable for a bust of Mr. Gladstone.   *£300-£400*

849 A mahogany palm stand on a tripod base in mid-18th century style.   *£300-£400*

850 Ebonised turned pedestal of heavy dimensions and of distinctly 19th century design.   *£350-£450*

854 An oak reading stand with a hinged pierced slope on the upper surface, here shown folded flat. There are turned spindles and inlaid sunflower or perhaps sunburst motifs, which has led to an attribution to the Arts and Craft Movement, but the piece is a cross between that and Aesthetic in its appearance. The panel on the front has a quotation from Milton: 'To know that which before us lies in Daily Life is the prime Wisdom', an observation of Milton's not included in the *Concise Oxford Dictionary of Quotations* for reasons upon which we can only speculate.
1870-1880   *£200-£300*

855 A Boulle jardinière with ormolu mounts in the French rococo manner. Similar to No. 844 but more expensive because of the Boulle (q.v.) treatment.
1860-1880   *£1,800-£2,500*

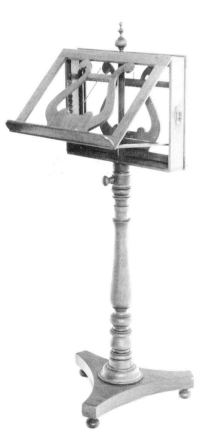

856 A mahogany duet stand on a flat triangular cusped base on turned knob feet. The panels have lyre-shaped frets and are mounted on a frame which in turn is on a brass rod with clamp to adjust for height. The angle of the panels can be adjusted on a ratchet seen here open on the near side.
1840-1860   *£700-£900*

857 A walnut musical duet stand on tripod base with scrolled feet. The pierced scroll and leaf carved panels are mounted on a ratchet to adjust for angle and a brass pole to adjust for height.
1850-1870   *£850-£1,150*

858 An unusual umbrella stand made in similar fashion to a washstand, with six turned spindle supports and brass base tray and brass mounts for decoration. Carved lion masks decorate the capitals
1840-1880   *£350-£450*

860 The universally-recognised Victorian piano stool on rococo tripod base with scrolled decoration. The seat has been re-covered and the buttoning is not as deep as the original would have been.
1850-1875   *£500-£700*

861 A similar but higher quality base adds value to this square stool with needlework seat.
1850-1875   *£750-£1,000*

862 A scrolled rosewood stool with a woolwork covering. The 'X' supports at each end are connected by a turned stretcher with baluster shaping.
1850-1870   *£600-£800*

864 An oak reproduction 'joint' stool with a top which is hinged like a lid to allow access to a storage space under, concealed by the frieze, which is carved with an arched pattern. The column-turned legs and square stretchers are correct copies of a 17th century type. Joint stools were much reproduced from about 1900 onwards and still are. To an oak fancier they provide the only means of having a low occasional table, suitable for coffee-cum-armchair use, which is in period with oak furnishings. Due to the high price of originals, these are pretty expensive too.
1900-present day   *£200-£250*

863 A Victorian 'Queen Anne' stool of reproduction style in walnut. The cabriole legs are good imitations of the original, with shell carving on the knees and ball-and-claw feet.
1890-1900   *£600-£800*

867 The French craze of the early Victorian period is here exemplified by one of a pair of giltwood stools on scrolled feet of slender cabriole form with hipping at the top. The stools are covered in satin buttoned upholstery.
1840-1860   *Pair £1,200-£1,800*

868 Needlework footstool with gilt-gesso base. See Colour Plate 67.

869 Needlework footstool with maho-gany base. See Colour Plate 68.

865 A leather-covered and buttoned stool on four scrolled and fluted legs.
1835-1845   *£550-£750*

866 An interesting duet stool on turned legs of a type which are derived from Regency designs.
1840-1860   *£600-£900*

TABLES

Along with chairs, cabinets, desks and sideboards, the table section represents the fifth major section of this book. The Victorian and Edwardian cabinet maker expressed himself and the fashions of the time as much in this article of furniture as he did in the other four, tables providing the place for the principal daytime activities of life — eating, working and, occasionally, playing games. Naturally there was some overlap in the application of tables to particular functions — a side table might be used for writing and a games table might have a sewing box below it — so that not all definitions can be rigidly applied.

Many varieties of the principal styles were used. Commercially produced tables varied in quality from extremely fine to dreadfully flimsy. If there was a 'Victorian' genre of table not found in other periods it was probably the oval, burr walnut veneered 'loo' table used for occasional purposes and for light refreshments. The Victorians created their own form of gate-leg in the Sutherland table. For dining, they had serious, solid, four-square tables that did not tip or tilt. Occasional tables came in a wide variety of invention. Nowadays the centre pedestal table — circular or oval — and four-legged extending table are the most popular form of Victorian dining table, but library tables and occasional tables for all sorts of purposes are keenly collected.

880 It is interesting to compare these two tables, the one on the left paw-footed and hence 'William IV', the one on the right equipped with turned and carved 'half buns' and so, traditionally, described as early Victorian. In fact both could be found in design books of the 1830s, 1840s and even 1850s. They are similar in conception and design, if not in execution. A folding top sits on a frame which in turn is supported by a centre column; this frame acts as a support when the folding top is swivelled through ninety degrees and opened to provide the card-playing surface. The table on the left is slimmer and its column has leaf petal carved collars and an acanthus carved bowl; the quatreform base is raised on paw feet with brass castors. The table on the right has a thicker, strongly fluted column with acanthus carving and the base has 'melon panel' feet. Whereas the left-hand table has a frieze with carved rosettes and scrolls, the right has a frieze with a baton pilaster with scroll end. You pays your money . . .
1830-1850   *Left £700-£1,000*
Right £600-£900

TABLES - card and games

Given the lack of radio and television entertainment during the period, it is not surprising that cards and board games occupied a good deal of leisure time. For this reason there were a lot of special tables for entertainment purposes and they were sometimes ingeniously made.

Compared with tables which can be used for dining purposes, these card tables, especially the folding, baize-lined type, have not attracted a wide following. They are nowadays used as occasional tables for decoration, side tables for lamps, and so on. Unless of exceptional quality and interest, inlaid with marquetry or of special provenance, values have not risen on the same scale as tables which can be used for eating and entertaining.

881 This rosewood folding table with pumpkin-like octagonal centre column and circular podium base on paw feet is a type associated with the late Regency or William IV, but appeared in catalogues from King's of 1835 to Smee in 1850. Note the scrolls on the frieze, with its carved central rosette.
1835-1855   *£700-£900*

882 A variant on the previous example in which the giveaway scrolling under the front apron has taken over at the base, where four abundantly scrolled Victorian legs have replaced the flat circular podium on four paw feet.
1840-1855   *£600-£900*

883 The next stage on the journey — the octagonal, flat-faceted pumpkin of a centre column has been replaced by a naturalistically-reeded bulbous baluster and the scrolling under the front apron has grown in confidence, abundance and skill of execution.
1840-1860   *£800-£1,200*

884 A pair of walnut card tables in which the rococo is unabashed. The bases exhibit the central column as four scrolled cabriole legs with floral carving and the tops wave in scroll-scalloped edging, the lower in each case carved in egg-and-ribbon banding.
1840-1860   *Pair £3,500-£4,500*

885 This four-scroll support design for a table may also be seen in the centre pedestal and occasional table section, where the upwardly-spiked finial is also a feature of the breed. In this case the scrolled supports have been cranked in a manner which can only be described as quirky and the piece, which is in walnut, would be bought for its novelty and eccentricity rather than its elegance.
1840-1880   *£900-£1,300*

886 An ebonised card table decorated with inlaid boxwood stringing and marquetry. The canted edges of the folding top are banded with burr walnut. The four-pillar support and curved feet with arched cross-stretchered design topped by a vase-shaped finial is typical of mid-Victorian popular designs dating from 1860 onwards to the 1880s. C. and R. Light (1881) and Wyman (1877) show similar tables. The stylistic origins are French-classical and had a considerable vogue but ebonised furniture is not now a widespread taste. The inside top surface is baize lined.
1860-1880   *£500-£700*

887 An octagonal walnut card table with folding top, of similar date to 886. This time the base has more scroll decoration, leaning towards rococo stylistic ornament. Again a popular mid-Victorian style but more acceptable to modern taste due to the presence of walnut rather than ebonising, so a higher price to be expected.
1860-1880   *£750-£1,000*

888 A burr walnut card table with a rectangular top inlaid with ebony stringing lines and boxwood marquetry. This table has again got four turned columns supporting it but the base has been designed in end-standard or trestle fashion instead of a central platform. There is, again, the popular mid-Victorian turned finial, echoed in reverse below, between the end columns and the base is quite crisply carved with classical elaboration.
1860-1880   *£1,000-£1,500*

890 An inlaid marquetry card table in the French 18th century manner with metal mounts. As we have shown in the Bureaux — bonheurs-du-jour section, there was a considerable vogue for these high quality French pieces in the 1860-1880 period and considerable skills were involved in their production.
1860-1885
£2,000-£3,000

889 A figured walnut card table in a 'semi-Gothic' style, in which the maker has used the same principle as the previous example for construction — i.e. a double-pillar-and-stretcher base — but adapted cleverly to Gothic reformed styling in treatment with addition of some ideas of his own in the carving. A quite high quality piece probably made by a 'commercial' firm.
1860s   *£1,000-£1,500*

891 A mahogany side table in the Adam manner, with serpentine top veneered in segments and fluted frieze and legs. There is a central drawer in the frieze with a panel carved with a vase motif. Another example of the return to Adam classical designs which occurred in the 1880s. A rather difficult piece to place for the average collector and more likely to find an interior decorator's approval.
1880-1900   *£550-£700*

892 A satinwood table with folding top incorporating a shell inlay in the Sheraton manner. Useful as an occasional or games table with tray below and a superior example of a whole range of occasional tables with stretchers, trays or ledges below, made very popular in the Edwardian period.
1900-1910   *£500-£700*

893 A satinwood and marquetry card table in the 'High Sheraton' or Adam manner, inlaid with ribbon-tied swags of flowers on the top and frieze. The square tapering legs, ending in block feet, are also inlaid. It is a classic example of the return, in Edwardian times, to late 18th century inlaid furniture and is a high quality reproduction, only erring in its probable tendency to over-elaboration. The Edwardians often felt that they could out-perform the original inlayers and this results in an over-profuse marquetry that betrays the reproduction from the original.
1900-1910   *£2,500-£3,500*

894 A mahogany card table of half-round type (*'demi- lune'*), opening to a circular top, in the 'Sheraton' manner. The top and frieze are inlaid with marquetry showing swags of husks. The square tapering legs end in castors. Again a good example of the return to late 18th century Sheraton taste of classical type in the Edwardian period with a fairly faithful reproduction of the original 18th century type.
1900-1910   *£2,000-£3,000*

895 A reproduction 'Chippendale' folding card table in mahogany, on square legs with gadrooned edges. The serpentine shaping of the top is authentic but the carving on the frieze would give rise to a query from someone seeking the 18th century original. The ribbon and carving around the top edges is also perhaps a little too bold for the original article. A high quality piece nevertheless.
1900-1910   *£800-£1,100*

896 A mahogany reproduction 'Chippendale' card table in the 18th century rococo manner, on cabriole legs ending in ball-and-claw feet. The scrolled carving on the knees of the legs is crisply executed and so are the carved edges to the top. Just a little weakness at the ankles to identify the reproduction from the original, although colour and patina would be important indications.
1910-1920   *£900-£1,300*

897 An Edwardian rosewood 'envelope' type card table which is expanded by opening the four diagonal flaps which constitute the top when closed and rotating the open, baize-lined square through ninety degrees for support. The inlaid stringing lines and marquetry on top add to value.
1900-1910   *£800-£1,200*

898 An interesting high quality inlaid envelope table with Edwardian 'Adam' inlaid marquetry to the top and stringing to the drawer and frieze. The legs are turned and spiral fluted and united by turned stretchers which support a circular undertray.
1900-1910   *£1,200-£1,600*

899 A simpler, mahogany 'envelope' top card table with satinwood crossbanding round the drawer and the top and without the centre, stretcher-supported undertray of the previous examples.
1900-1910   *£600-£800*

TABLES - centre pedestal

The Victorian centre pedestal table is now popular for dining on but not all such tables were intended for that purpose. The true Victorian dining table (q.v.) was on four or more legs. Most centre pedestal tables were for occasional use, in a parlour or sitting room where they served a general purpose even though light refreshments could be taken from them.

The use of burr walnut veneers on circular or oval tables, often combined with inlays or marquetry, has made these decorative tables very sought after. They are often known as 'loo' tables, even though the original loo table was a circular card table on a pillar, designed specifically for a card game known as lanterloo, and illustrated by George Smith in 1836. They exemplify the mid-Victorian rococo style admirably. Earlier tables on flat bases with three or four small feet tend to be thought of as 'William IV' and are graver, usually in plain mahogany or rosewood, but many are in fact early Victorian.

900 A rosewood and marquetry circular breakfast table. See Colour Plate 69.

901 A papier-mâché breakfast table. See Colour Plate 70.

902 An oak centre pedestal table with a tip-up top. See Colour Plate 71.

903 This kind of rosewood centre table or breakfast table, now used for dining, is of a style generally associated with William IV rather than Victoria. While it is perfectly true that such tables appear in Loudon's 1833 *Encyclopedia*, they are also to be seen in Smee (1850) and C. and R. Light (1881) even in such detail as the paw feet so much identified with the reign of the Sailor King. The design is very similar to George Smith's 1836 'Loo Table'.
1830-1880   £2,500-£3,500

904 Like the previous example, this pumpkin-like rosewood table is generally associated with William IV, but could have been produced in the 1840s. The photograph has the table in a rather collapsed, off-centre condition which indicates the problems in support which the design can exhibit.
1835-1850   £1,000-£1,500

905 This mahogany extending table by Johnstone, Jubb & Co. of New Bond Street was undoubtedly intended for dining. The circular top is in eight sectors which open on a brass spiral mechanism to allow for the insertion of extra numbered leaves (two sets) to increase the diameter from 60ins. to 72ins. (152cm to 183cm).
1835-1845   £8,000-£12,000

906 Another early Victorian extendable dining table shown both open and closed. It is unusual for a centre pedestal table to extend very far due to the risk of instability but the illustration clearly shows how extra leaves (or no leaves at all) can be inserted.
1835-1845   £6,000-£9,000

907 A later circular extending dining table in which the problem of the centre pedestal has been solved by enlarging it to include four bulbous, scoop-faceted legs united by a shaped undertray on ponderous scroll feet. The eight segments of the top may be wound out on a spiral mechanism (iron this time) like the Johnstone, Jubb table to accept eight numbered leaves, to extend the diameter from 62ins. to 82ins. (157cm to 208cm).
1870-1880   *£10,000-£12,000*

908 The traditional form of burr walnut Victorian 'loo' table on a turned and carved central pillar supported by four cabriole scrolled legs with floral carving on the 'knees', ending in scrolled feet. A popular classic of its type, in this case with the top quarter veneered without any inlaid stringing, banding or other decoration.
1840-1880   *£2,000-£3,000*

909 A variant on the previous table which shows the bas-relief carving and 'Regency Knee' to be found on slightly later and lesser quality examples of this type. Still made in walnut with quarter-veneered burr top but a base of much lesser refinement to which machinery has been applied.
1850-1880   *£1,750-£2,500*

910 An oval walnut centre table on a centre turned support and four carved scrolled supports on an X-shaped platform on four scrolled feet. This elaborate base is of a type popular in the 1850s and 1860s.
1850-1880   *£2,500-£3,250*

911 A circular walnut centre table on a gadrooned baluster column and three scrolled rococo legs. The top is veneered in sections of burr walnut whereas the base is solid. A design popular in the 1850s but still offered by various manufacturers in modified form to later dates.
1860-1870   *£2,000-£3,000*

912 A walnut centre table on four scrolled supports which are themselves on four scrolled cabriole legs. A very popular design in the 1850s. Now perhaps regarded as a high-point of Victorian rococo, whose exuberance and frivolity snap their fingers at the stolid, classical dourness of the other prevailing styles.
1850-1870   *£3,000-£4,000*

913 An example of fine marquetry inlays in a good circular table. This banded decoration, echoed in the complex centre medallion, adds to value in a way which overcomes any reservations which may be incurred if, say, the base is not of equal quality.
1850-1870 **£3,500-£4,500**

914 A highly inlaid walnut oval table with gadrooned edge. Again, the floral marquetry in four asymmetric panels — technically 'cartouches' — adds enormously to value. The oval centre panel is veneered in a dense burr, possibly walnut or amboyna.
1850-1870 **£3,500-£4,500**

915 An oval walnut table on a four-column base with four scrolled feet and a finialled circular central section. The top is inlaid with boxwood stringing and stylised foliage marquetry. Stylistically derived from the 1850s and 1860s but more likely to have been made twenty years later when this four-column version of the base was very prevalent in commercial catalogues such as C. and R. Light.
1865-1885 **£1,300-£1,800**

916 A walnut oval breakfast table inlaid with stringing lines and a centre marquetry panel. The designer has adopted a belt-and-braces approach in using both a centre column and four smaller supporting columns rising from the curved legs. Similar designs occur in catalogues of the 1860s to the 1880s.
1860-1885 **£1,000-£1,400**

258

917 A typical Reformed Gothic octagonal centre table using 'revealed' construction and an architectural structure to the base, following Pugin's example. The top is inlaid and the joints are pegged, with ebony 'dowels' to mark them, reiterated in the decoration of the frieze. Note also the carefully-designed handles. C. and R. Light's catalogue of 1881 shows this version.
1860-1885   *£3,500-£5,000*

918 Another very popular design of octagonal table in which the Reformed Gothic style is marked by the heavy crossed stretchers on the base on which the four turned column supports stand. These crossed stretchers curve downwards to form feet and, in this case, have a further stretcher between them at the base of each column.
c.1865   *£2,500-£3,500*

920 Put here for contrast and instruction, this octagonal pitch-pine table is still 'Gothic' in style but is probably ecclesiastical in origin and taken from a chapel or a church. The base looks a little out of proportion with the top.
1870-1880
£700-£1,000

919 An octagonal walnut centre table on four column supports and a structural stretchered base ending in shaped feet. The piece has all the hallmarks of Reformed Gothic design: turned collars on the columns, ebonised for emphasis; moulded stretchers connecting the heavy central crossed base with its chamfered edges; incised Gothic trefoil motifs.
1865-1870   *£1,400-£1,700*

TABLES - dining

The Victorian dining table was a solid piece of furniture, usually in mahogany, which could be extended by the addition of extra leaves if required. The turned legs, at the beginning of the period, were fairly straight in emulation of late Georgian fashion, but usually reeded or fluted. They became more bulbous and balustered as the reign wore on. For a long time such tables were not highly regarded or priced, but their use for business purposes and the obvious value inherent in them has caused a fairly rapid climb in price. The design of the legs — elegant tapering rather than bloated bulbous — affects the value although a good big table is a good big table if you need one.

921 This type of extending mahogany dining table on four turned and arcade-fluted legs is usually classified as of William IV period but in fact such tables appear in catalogues of the 1840s and 1850s. The choice of leg design offered was always wide.
1835-1855   *£2,000-£3,000*

922 A six-legged mahogany extending dining table which will take up to five extra leaves and is therefore ideal for the boardroom of a prosperous company. The reeded legs are of a restrained tapering shape introduced in the early 19th century and hence more desirable than later types although the table could have been made at any time during a period of twenty to thirty years.
1830-1855 £3,500-£5,000

923 An expanding mahogany table with turned and fluted pumpkin-like legs at the four corners and an extra support leg in the centre for expansion purposes. A very similar design appears in Smee's catalogue of 1850 but without the centre leg.
1840-1860 £2,500-£3,500

924 The reason for a centre leg in addition to the principal four is illustrated in the table shown open here, which is a rounded-end variety with one large central leaf inserted.
1840-1880 £2,500-£3,500

925 A mahogany expanding dining table of a type often thought of as mid- or even late-Victorian but whose legs belie the later dates. Although the constructional form was used later, it originated in the 1830s and 1840s. These legs are of a bulbous-and-baluster turning with collars, more popular initially in the 1840s than in the 1880s and later, where one might be tempted to place this piece. The examples of 1880-1910 incorporate the top bulb but the lower turning is straighter or tapering, less of baluster form. The piece does highlight the diffi-culty of dating Victorian furniture, however, since the use of this form of baluster at a later date is always possible.
1840-1890 £1,750-£2,250

926 Another large expanding Victorian mahogany dining table, this time with semi-circular ends which can open to receive up to four flaps. The tapering reeded legs are of a design popular in the 1830s, featured by Smee in 1850 and still used in variant form in the 1880s.
1835-1885   *£2,500-£3,500*

927 (Right) An example of the previous type of table, adapted in style to be more 'Sheraton' in appearance, with square tapering legs and inlaid stringing lines. Available originally in a size 7ft. long by 4ft. wide (213cm by 122cm).
1890-1915   *£1,400-£1,800*

928 Four examples of the leg styles available in the late Victorian and Edwardian era. From 'almost-art-nouveau' through 'oak' to 'Queen Anne'.
1890-1915   *£140-£180*

929 A mahogany extending dining table which, with its three leaves inserted, is 2ft.6ins. wide by 10ft. (76cm by 305cm) long. The top, shown here without leaves, is slightly serpentine in shape and has an edge decorated with a blind fret. The tapering rectangular legs have paterae at the top and carved husk decoration. An example of 18th century Georgian designs used on a modern table.
1900-1925   *£1,400-£1,800*

930 An Edwardian version of a typical late 18th century extending table composed of two 'D' ends with hinged gate legs and a centre table also with hinged gates so that the four leaves or flaps which add to the centre section can be supported. Much valued in its original 18th century form but not highly regarded as a reproduction.
1900-1910   *£2,000-£3,000*

TABLES
dining: *oak reproductions*

The vogue for the medieval led to a tremendous rise in demand for oak furniture of suitably aged appearance from the 1880s onwards. 'Old oak' refectory and dining tables might be made up from old pieces (just as 'coffers' might be made from three-panel carved bed-heads) or simply reproduced new and 'aged' by various processes. It was not always the intention to deceive, nor is it so now.

We show a small selection here to show how close some versions came to the original and to advise the reader to be warned: old reproductions of good quality are worth about half the value of the originals.

931 A really heavy oak reproduction refectory table with primitive lion-mask carving, on six enormous carved bulbous legs. The sheer quantity of oak involved would make such a table enormously expensive to produce today, let alone the question of the carved decoration.
1890-1920   *£3,000-£5,000*

932 A simpler oak 'draw-leaf' table on four bulbous carved legs. The stretchers have been jacked up off the ground by the addition of four square 'feet' at a later stage. The top has been panelled across the length which is considered a less attractive proposition by the trade.
c.1900 *£1,750-£2,500*

933 A rather unattractive oak 'refectory' table which looks as though it has been 'made-up' from old pieces but the legs have turning which is plain and rather modern. No attempt has been made to 'age' the stretchers by wearing down the edges.
c.1920 *£1,200-£1,800*

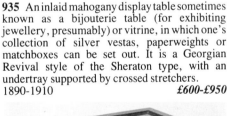

TABLES - display

The Victorians always had something to display, whether it was an expensive collection of porcelain, botanical or zoological specimens, or mementoes of dead relatives, all of which provided useful subjects of conversation.

In addition to their numerous display cabinets (q.v.) they used small tables of the type shown here, which would enable a few choice examples to be placed at a strategic point.

---

935 An inlaid mahogany display table sometimes known as a bijouterie table (for exhibiting jewellery, presumably) or vitrine, in which one's collection of silver vestas, paperweights or matchboxes can be set out. It is a Georgian Revival style of the Sheraton type, with an undertray supported by crossed stretchers.
1890-1910 *£600-£950*

934 A tripod-based small display table on a faceted turned column. The top has a shaped edge to the glazed lid, which lifts for access to the shallow, lined area beneath. This particular table had inside it a bouquet of dried flowers, tied with a ribbon bearing the dates 1814-1894.
1860-1890 *£350-£500*

936 An Edwardian display table in a sub-Queen Anne style with cabriole legs. The glass top is hinged to give access to the display area — the front drawer is false.
1900-1910 *£250-£350*

TABLES - dressing

The most successful form of dressing table seems to have been one with drawers in pedestals on either side. Indeed, the walnut reproduction desk shown in the Desk section (No. 513) is, in fact, a copy of a kneehole dressing table of c.1700. The simpler the design, very often, the more successful it was. Apart from the pedestal type — which has been much converted into desks — the 'lowboy', with its two deep drawers and one central shallow one, on cabriole legs, is the very other popular form.

The advent of built-in bedroom units has meant the demise of many large pedestal dressing tables but the smaller, prettier ones have survived as whimsical occasional tables, even in the bedroom. These smaller tables tend to be the more highly valued.

937 A dressing table of a type made by Holland & Co. in satin ash with ebony stringing lines and brass gallery rails above the upper drawers. Perhaps made en suite with the 'Wellington' chest No. 446. A high quality piece of furniture in a simple pleasing style.
1850-1880   *£1,200-£1,800*

938 A dressing table designed by Owen Jones for Eynsham Hall, Oxon, in 1873. In fact, Shoolbred's catalogue of 1876 shows examples very similar in design. This piece is in a pleasant, light wood and the stringing lines and neat black knobs contribute to an easy formality of design which is wholly missing from much furniture of the period. Unfortunately many dressing tables of this sort have had the top section removed to cater for the enormous trade in pedestal desks.
1870-1880 (for unattributable piece)   *£1,500-£2,000*

939 A rather more 'Victorian' mahogany version of the preceding examples, with scrolled carved supports to the shaped mirror. The pedestals are bow-fronted and the descent from simple clean lines to something less tasteful is clearly illustrated.
1850-1880   *£700-£1,000*

940 A mahogany dressing table which exhibits the transitional signs of the 1830s to the 1840s — William IV heaviness is yielding to the scrolls and leaves of Victorian rococo. The rectangular mirror is supported by two blatantly scrolled uprights which sweep outwards in a flourish. The top with its two drawers is again supported on curved members embellished with scroll-and-leaf carving. The flat base is on feet which would have been hairy paws under the Regency and early William IV period but are now of naturalistic form.
1835-1845   *£700-£900*

941 A classic mid-Victorian dressing table in satin birch which might have come straight out of Shoolbred's catalogue and which is not far removed from a sideboard design, except that the mirror can be tilted (the sideboard's would be fixed) and the top structure has little drawers in it whereas sideboards left these minor shelf constructions open. The reeded pillars and black 'keyed' mouldings to emphasise door panels and drawers are similar to those used on display cabinets of the period.
1850-1870   *£1,800-£2,500*

942 Bird's eye maple and marquetry make this dressing table extremely flamboyant. It has floral and naturalistic motifs but is solidly pedimented with a flat apron base. The matching mirror is supported on turned uprights with baluster shapes terminating in finials and has three drawers under. Because it is so deep there is a set of drawers in the side, at the back.
1845-1865   *£3,000-£5,000*

943 The dressing table with full-length tipping centre mirror had become established by the 1880s but this rosewood version with satinwood crossbanding to the curved drawer fronts and side panels is probably later — c. 1900. The form was already established in C. and R. Light's 1881 catalogue in sub-classical form and it is but a short step from there to this version. Part of a suite.
1890-1910   *£1,000-£1,400*

944 A dressing table from an Arts and Crafts bedroom suite in oak, showing the rather elongated form and 'plain' approach of the late 19th century, rather self-conscious designer. Not in the slightest bit art nouveau yet often confused with it.
1890-1900   *£900-£1,200*

945 Down further we go, into semi-rococo ugliness. The oval mirror is all right but the rest is fairly unpleasant and extremely wasteful of space. Apart from the central drawer the frieze is totally unused and probably 'false' while as for the legs and bottom shelf . . . !
1850-1880   *£300-£450*

946 An oak dressing table and mirror to match with revealed construction in the manner approved by the Gothic reformers. The arcaded painted decoration is in keeping.
c.1870   *for table and mirror £450-£600*

947 A painted dressing table which has borrowed something from the art furniture brigade in its design and perhaps something from Regency 'bamboo'.
1890-1900   *£350-£500*

948 An inlaid mahogany dressing table in the Sheraton manner, owing something to the Carlton House writing table in the curving design of the centre section which leads, in the upper storey, to two drawers. The inlays incorporate shell and swag motifs.
1900-1910   *£600-£800*

949 An inlaid mahogany kidney-shaped dressing table in the 'Sheraton' manner, depending on a late 18th or early 19th century original design but somewhat over-decorated by the Edwardians.
c.1900   *£4,500-£6,500*

950 A Liberty's dressing table in the 'art nouveau' style in its more straight-line English variety. Usually made *en suite* with an accompanying washstand (see No. 1062).
c.1900   *£300-£450*

951 A mahogany dressing table of 'art nouveau' design with inlaid decoration and square tapering legs ending in round feet.
c.1900   *£275-£350*

952 A dressing table of quartered satinwood veneer arranged in chevron style of a type favoured by the William Morris company around 1900. Based on Sheraton design but with a curved adaptation of the mirror which is not very true to the spirit of the original.
1900-1910   *£900-£1,400*

953 The Edwardian conception of Sheraton satinwood with shield-shaped mirrors à la Hepplewhite. Again the drawers are quartered in chevron style but this time the legs are turned and fluted and united by stretchers. Inlaid stringing lines are used to emphasise drawer and side panels. An ebony inlaid pattern embellishes the low back beneath the mirrors.
1900-1910   *£800-£1,100*

954 A fully-kitted-out dressing table in mahogany of the Georgian Revival period, based on Sheraton-type dressing tables of novelty conception — things slide out and in, hinge up and down, pop up on springs etc., etc. The idea is based on a rather optimistic view of human neatness and order. The figured panels under the lid open to reveal a mirror. The whole folds down to an 18th century style mahogany side table in appearance.
1890-1900   *£1,200-£1,800*

TABLES - gateleg

The gateleg table was a great favourite of the 17th and 18th centuries. It did not die out in the 19th century but continued in other forms, like the Sutherland (q.v.) table.
During the last quarter of the 19th century, however, it was back to the Good Old Days for gatelegs, as with so many other forms of furniture. The oak gateleg was back in its late 17th century form, to meet the prevailing demand aroused by the medieval and 'Olde Englishe' taste.

955 Two oak gateleg dining tables of good reproduction of styles of 1670-1720. The above example has the column turned legs — here slightly balustered — which were put on many conventional tables of this sort at the end of the 18th century. The right-hand table features spiral or twist turning to the legs (but not the stretchers, which are left square) which met 'Elizabethan' taste, but which in fact dates back to 1670-1690. Both tables have a give-away feature for those anxious to identify period. Both have a deep 'thumb-nail' or ovolo moulding around the top. This is not a feature generally to be seen on period tables and was much used by reproducers from 1900 onwards.
1900-1920   *above £250-£350*
                                                  right £300-£400

956 A fine quality centre table with inlay and brass mounts. See Colour Plate 72.

957 A marquetry centre table c.1860 of the type associated with Holland & Sons. See Colour Plate 73.

959 A walnut centre table with the classic four-scroll and platform approach to the support structure shown in other centre pedestal types. This wavy-line system, with its central finial spiked upwards on the low platform supported by four scrolled legs, is a variant on the four-column approach shown in the centre pedestal section. Tables of this sort were obviously considered elegant and are to be found in catalogues from the 1840s to the 1880s, although their popularity must have waned in the later years.

1840-1880   *£1,750-£2,500*

958 A scrolled two-end support table with a linking turned stretcher. The top is veneered in two matched panels of burr walnut. Such occasional tables, used centrally or at the side of Victorian rooms, were used extensively and made in large numbers.

1845-1880   *£1,200-£1,600*

960 This example follows on from the previous one with a later, more rigidly 'Louis XVI' approach but in which the same principle of support, including the centre finial, is used in conjunction with turned and fluted columns with ebonising and gilding to provide emphasis. The top is burr veneered in amboyna and the edge moulding is ebonised. The use of ebonising, extensively on the base, reduces value in these cases.

1850-1875   *£1,000-£1,500*

961 An uncompromising central column supports this wavy-edged (serpentine) walnut centre table with plain, rather unadorned top surface. The four legs are carved with scrolls and acanthus leaves.
1850-1860   *£1,000-£2,000*

963 A coromandel and thuya banded centre table which shows the shift in style from the curvaceous rococo to the rectilinear styles to which the Victorians returned after 1860. The top has a broad band with anthemion and drapery motifs surrounding it and there are satinwood and inlays to the frieze, which has no drawers. The square tapering legs are fluted and the quality of the piece, plus the rare woods used, give it a high value.
1865-1885   *£5,000-£7,500*

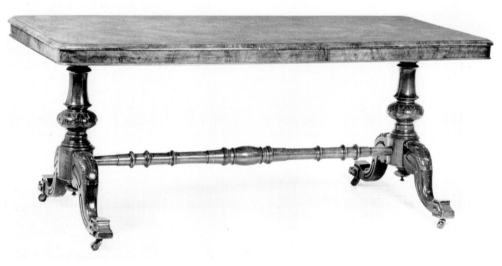

962 A walnut or centre table with baluster end supports which is perhaps a bit long for domestic rooms but typical of mid-Victorian furniture in its use of figured walnut, scrolled carved legs and turned centre stretcher between the turned and carved end supports.
1850-1870   *£1,200-£1,800*

964 A walnut centre table inlaid with a marquetry panel and with ormolu mounts. Very similar to the writing table 1009 and, again, made in a French Louis XV style of perennial popularity. Not as high quality as 1009 but nevertheless still a well-made and very decorative piece.
1860-1890   *£1,750-£2,500*

965 A centre table of Reformed Gothic character from Blackmoor House, c.1872 (see *British Furniture, 1880-1915* by Pauline Agius, p.74, pl.81). Possibly designed by the Manchester architect, Alfred Waterhouse, a friend of Norman Shaw. Waterhouse designed for Blackmoor, starting in 1869, and imitated Shaw's 'Old English' style as used at Leyswood, which still had Gothic features such as the gate tower. The table is interesting in its construction of Reformed Gothic style and structure but incorporating half- and full suns of Japanese character and the spindled gallery. The move from Gothic to Anglo-Japanese can be perceived.
c.1870   *£3,000-£4,000*

966 An interesting ebonised centre table with a turned spindled gallery connecting the end supports which are pierced and carved with stylised flowers and leaves. Of Reformed Gothic character but with later developments in the carving.
1880-1890   *£3,000-£4,000*

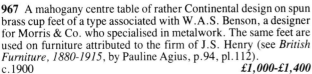

967 A mahogany centre table of rather Continental design on spun brass cup feet of a type associated with W.A.S. Benson, a designer for Morris & Co. who specialised in metalwork. The same feet are used on furniture attributed to the firm of J.S. Henry (see *British Furniture, 1880-1915*, by Pauline Agius, p.94, pl.112).
c.1900   *£1,000-£1,400*

968 An occasional centre table of octagonal shape, in rosewood, with eight turned legs and a centre column joined by stretchers radiating from the centre. An arcaded apron also joins the legs. Possibly by Collinson & Lock.
c.1880   *£1,500-£2,000*

969 Another spider-like centre table with a moulded top edge, by Morris & Co. Made in mahogany. The firm produced several similar designs, available in mahogany or fumed oak.
c.1900   *£1,500-£2,000*

970 A six-legged mahogany centre table by a commercial firm of general furnishers. Clearly the type was popular up to 1914. Also available with only four legs.
c.1910   *£350-£450*

971 (Left) A shaped, fretted and turned mahogany table in the 'Louis' style to be seen on cabinets at the turn of the century. Four ball and column supports are mounted on cabriole legs to support a wavy-edged top. To this basic structure are added cross stretchers with fretwork angles which in turn support a shaped central undertray or platform. Other curves and angled scrolls have then been put in to clutter the overall effect.
1890-1900   *£500-£650*

972 (Above) An oval 'Sheraton' style centre table on four tapering square section legs ending in castors and connected by curved stretchers emanating from a central finial. The top is inlaid and crossbanded; there is satinwood banding and boxwood stringing around all the normally approved edges.
1890-1900   *£1,100-£1,500*

973 A marquetry version of the 'Sheraton' occasional table, made in rosewood with ivory, box and satinwood inlays. The deep top has drawers set in it and the piece is on castors, perhaps for use as a work or sewing table of some sort.
1890-1900   *£1,200-£1,600*

974 A popular revival of a 'Sheraton' type of occasional centre table, known as an etagère, with a tray fitted on the top. This example is circular but many were oval. Considered very useful for light refreshments — the tray bearing them could be placed on top and the goodies unloaded on to the surface below.
1890-1910   *£1,000-£1,500*

TABLES - Sutherland

975 (Above) A walnut drop-leaf gateleg table of a type known in the trade as a Sutherland table (for some obscure reason). Made in mahogany or walnut (i.e. veneered in figured or burr walnut), these tables can be supported on a single turned column at each end, as shown above, or on a double column with spiral or other turning. There is an extra, thin, turned leg on a gate at each side which swings out to support the flap when open. They can be seen clearly above. The Victorians do not seem to have minded this rather unhappy lack of cohesion in leg design; the gatelegs often look like a pair of poles or walking sticks that someone has leant in random fashion against the frame under the flaps. The merit of the design is, of course, that the table, when folded, is very slim in end elevation and the whole is mounted on castors so that it can be tucked away neatly. The spiral grooving turned into the legs of the above example is often found on these tables.
1860-1890   *£900-£1,200*

976 (Above right) A similar design of Sutherland table in mahogany, with the same form of end columns and mounted on white castors.
1860-1890   *£650-£950*

977 (Right) An ebonised Sutherland table which shows very clearly how undesirable ebonised furniture looks when dusty and in poor condition.
c.1890   *£175-£250*

978 A rectangular Sutherland table with spirally-turned double end supports on a simple arched foot design. The thumb-nail top edge moulding appears on almost all the tables at the time. 1870-1890 *£400-£600*

979 An interesting Sutherland table in walnut with pierced, moulded and carved end supports connected by a turned stretcher. The top is veneered in highly-figured walnut and shaped in a semi-scalloped manner, known as serpentined. 1850-1880 *£900-£1,200*

TABLES - tripod

The tripod table is an 18th century invention probably developed from the turned candlestands of the start of that century. It has proved enduringly popular and was made throughout the Victorian era in rococo and other varieties, until the Georgian Revival took it firmly back to the 18th century again.

980 A papier-mâché tripod table with ogee-moulded top edge and mother-of-pearl floral inlays. The turned centre column ends on a scalloped base supported by three scrolled feet. 1840-1870 *£500-£750*

981 Not quite a tripod — this circular form of base, on three turned bun feet of flat cheese shape is found in design books of the 1830s to the 1860s below turned pillars of the sort illustrated by this papier-mâché table. The decoration this time is floral painting and gilt festoons. 1840-1860 *£500-£750*

982 The Victorians could always add to basic designs and here the tripod table has been developed into a walnut reading table, with a revolving candle sconce and a revolving undertier with spindle turned galleries to support books. The top is inlaid and there are gilt-metal mounts on the fluted centre column and the 'knee' of each tripod leg. There is also a brass or gilt-metal beaded edge to the top. One spindle gallery (on the right) is broken.
1850-1870   *£700-£900*

983 The Victorians were fond of spiral or 'barley-sugar' turning and used much of it on so-called 'Elizabethan' style furniture. This twist-turned tripod column is fitted above scrolled tripod legs and supports a top veneered in radiating sections of alternating woods with a central circular panel and crossbanding to the edge.
1850-1880   *£800-£1,100*

984 A Victorian version of the tripod table, in walnut, with a scalloped edge in emulation of the 18th century 'pie crust' edge. The shaping of the column is unmistakably mid-19th century and the use of the finial below the column is also characteristic of mid- to late Victorian furniture. The shaping of the legs is also not that associated with Georgian tripods.
1860-1880   *£150-£225*

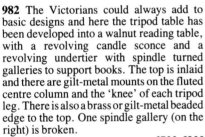

985 A rather grand tripod table with an extensively carved base exhibiting scroll and acanthus leaf work of an extremely crisp finish.
1850-1880   *£900-£1,400*

986 A rather misleading occasional tripod table with scrolled rococo legs and base in walnut, but the top of satinwood with marquetry inlay of high sophistication. For this reason, an expensive piece.
1860-1880   *£3,000-£4,000*

987 A mahogany tripod table with a brass gallery rail around the circular top and decorative scrolled supports in addition to the centre column.
1900-1920 *£350-£500*

988 Mahogany tripod tables with moulded rims, fluted columns, reeded vases — spiral above, straight below — and elegant legs carved with acanthus leaf decoration. Essentially straight reproductions of 18th century tripod tables but looking shorter in proportion and the tops of a greater diameter than the period originals would probably have had. Good quality pieces, though.
1900-1920 *£250-£350*

TABLES - work and games

989 Small work tables, with flaps, on four turned legs of this type are illustrated in design books from Loudon in 1833 to C. and R. Light in 1881. It was evidently a standard format, with two 'real' drawers in one end and false ones at the other. The Pembroke-style flaps made it a usefully compact unit which could be extended for use.
1830-1880 *£700-£1,000*

990 A burr walnut work table on four turned legs with reeding at the top and bottom. The intricate arrangement of drawers and the silk bag beneath indicate a use for sewing, but there is a writing slope as well, so it is a multi-purpose and decorative piece.
1840-1860 *£1,000-£1,500*

991 A rosewood work table which can be used for games as well as sewing. The folding top is inlaid with velvet and there is a drawer and silk work bag. Note the open scrolls of the end supports and the scroll feet.
1840-1860 *£600-£900*

992 A walnut combined work and writing table on turned end-column supports with scrolled feet connected by a turned stretcher. Under the hinged top there is an adjustable reading and writing flap covered with tooled leather, and stationery compartments on each side of this flap. The drawer pulls out to provide a fitted interior and the wooden work bag below can also be pulled out for access. The figured walnut top surface, drawer and bag are inlaid with stringing lines and marquetry. The whole piece is very similar to one illustrated in the design book of C. and R. Light in 1881 but such pieces were popular throughout the mid-Victorian period.
1850-1885 *£1,400-£1,800*

993 A walnut work and games table with inlaid chequerboard and backgammon board, on a twin-column end support stand with connecting turned stretcher. A type illustrated in manufacturers' catalogues up to 1885.
1860-1885 *£1,400-£1,800*

994 A walnut combined games and work table with double end cupboards on splayed feet. The top is inlaid with satinwood stringing and the fold-over top has a backgammon and chess-board inlay but more seriously the frieze drawer has compartments for sewing materials (or games counters) above the lined well.
1850-1880 *£1,400-£1,800*

995 A walnut work table shown open, revealing a lined well, compartmented drawer, leather writing surface, pen trays and stationery compartments.
1850-1880 *£900-£1,200*

996 A papier-mâché work table inlaid with ivory and mother-of-pearl in floral patterns and scrolls. The design is not unlike those of the 1830-1840 period with a baluster central column and a flat base with four scrolled feet.
c.1860 *£1,200-£1,600*

997 A black lacquer and painted work table decorated with gilt and pearl-shell inlay, with a slate top painted with floral panels.
1840-1860   *£700-£1,000*

998 A handsome yew work table on centre pedestal of the Irish school associated with Muckross Abbey, inlaid with ivory and marquetry, including the characteristic harp.
c.1860   *£1,200-£1,800*

999 A walnut work table of a type which was introduced in the late 1850s as an urn shape, but which had settled to this funnel or trumpet variety by the 1870s. This example is inlaid with floral marquetry and stands on rather cocked-knee cabrioles with scrolled feet. The top has been inset with leather: this almost certainly means that the original marquetry top has been damaged and, to save expense, a new leather top has been fitted. Damage to the top surfaces is frequent with these tables; the veneer was very thin and was easily lifted by heat or spillage of liquids.
1860-1880   *marquetry £700-£900*
walnut £500-£700
mahogany £400-£600

1000 (Above left) Another octagonal work table, this time of papier-mâché decorated with gilt chinoiserie and mother-of-pearl inlays and with a pierced 'keyhole' frieze under the top. This piece appears to be in excellent condition.
1860-1880   *£800-£1,200*

1001 (Above right) A rosewood chess-top work table inlaid with marquetry, on pierced trestle-type supports with a turned stretcher ending in characteristic finials.
1840-1880   *£1,000-£1,500*

1002 (Right) A late 19th century work table very much in the Sheraton manner (Sheraton was fond of multi-purpose furniture). There are three slides for working surfaces, a fitted writing drawer with a baize surface, a fabric work bag, a cusped undertray uniting the four tapering legs with inlaid stringing lines and — wait for it — a vertical sliding screen so that the piece can be used near the fire, thus qualifying it for an additional entry under Screens.
1890-1910   *£2,500-£3,500*

1003 A circular walnut games top table on a single turned column with four-legged base. The simplest form of inlaid chess-board table; many tripod-based tables of this type were produced.
1850-1870   *£400-£600*

1004 An altogether different edition — this marble-topped and gilt-gesso games table has an Italian top inlaid with a chess-board specimen marble inset within a floral scroll border on a white marble ground. Marble tops to centre pedestal tables, whether the bases are turned, columned, legged, wood or iron, are expensive.
1850-1870   *£3,500-£4,500*

TABLES - writing

The borderline between a writing table and a desk or bureau is sometimes hard to define. On the whole a writing table remains a table, on four legs with some drawers in the frieze, but the Carlton House version is almost a desk or bureau due to the upper structure. Here we have followed accepted practice and show the simpler pieces of furniture, with a separate section on Carlton House types.

1005 A mahogany writing table of the type usually associated with the late Regency period but found in design books up to 1850. Sometimes with a stretcher and made in rosewood.
1830-1850   *£7,000-£9,000*

1006 A walnut writing table with twist-turned end supports on scroll feet and a brass gallery round the back and sides. This variant on many side, centre and occasional tables of similar design required only very little adaption — a brass gallery to prevent papers from falling off — to be classified as a writing table.
1850-1880   *£800-£1,200*

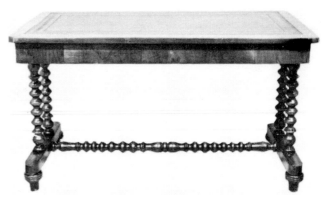

1008 A bobbin turned version of a type more often seen in the design books as spiral turned. It produces decoration for less original cost than the previous example.
1840-1880 *£900-£1,200*

1007 Fussy it may be, but the parquetry top in exotic woods with bold corner finials goes well with the equally bold fretted base and stretcher to make a good solid ornate writing table. Rather hard to date with assurance because, looking through the *Pictorial Dictionary of British 19th Century Furniture Design*, one sees that the variations were being offered in the 1840-60 period.
1840-1860 *£3,500-£4,500*

1009 The French revival brought some excellent English copies of the Louis XV style into manufacture — bonheurs-du-jour provide another example. This walnut writing table has ormolu mounts and is veneered in that diagonal, V-shaped manner characteristic of smaller Louis XV pieces.
1850-1880
£2,000-£3,000

1010 An inlaid satinwood writing table in the French Louis XV style on cabriole legs with ormolu mounts. The top surface has an inset leather area, crossbanded around it with additional inlay. The top edge has an ormolu moulding surround.
1860-1880 *£3,500-£4,500*

TABLES - writing - *Carlton House and similar*

The Carlton House writing table, or desk, was one of the Georgian Revival pieces taken to with enthusiasm in the late Victorian period. The name probably derived from a table made by Gillows, who show one in their cost books for 1796, made for the Prince of Wales, whose residence was Carlton House.

1011 A mid-Victorian 'Louis XV' walnut writing table with gilt-metal mounts and a pierced brass gallery. The form is one found in many later 19th century writing tables but usually with English straight legs. Here the moulded cabrioles end in metal sabots and castors. The back structure has six drawers and a fall-front centre panel with pigeonholes behind.
1860-1880 *£3,000-£4,000*

1012 A Louis XVI writing table in walnut, thuya and marquetry with brass mounts. A type associated with Gillows and of a form which is squarer, much more rectilinear, than the curvaceous rococo of the previous example. Again the form — upper structure of two sets of three drawers flanking a central panel, mirror, or similar feature — is one which, as a variant on the Carlton House type, was to become very popular. The stage is set for the Georgian Revival.
1860-1880   *£3,500-£4,500*

1013 Double-drawered frieze version of a Carlton House table. See Colour Plate 74.

1014 Another variant on the Carlton House writing table, in mahogany with satinwood crossbanding. See Colour Plate 75.

1015 A satinwood 'Carlton House' writing table with oval panels in the upper doors. The type appears in Gillows' cost books for 1796 and is also illustrated in Shearer's *Cabinet Maker's London Book of Prices* of 1788. Gillows simply describe the piece as 'A Ladies Drawing and Writing Table'. We tend to associate square tapering legs with Sheraton, but this type of table had a considerable revival in about 1870 and is still being made to the present day. (Harrods usually stock one or two.) There are marquetry ones, satinwood ones, plain mahogany ones and there are even painted ones. Variations in the design are very frequent in lesser Edwardian pieces. See also Colour Plate 74.
1870-present day   *marquetry/satinwood £6,000-£8,000*
satinwood as above £5,500-£7,000
painted/inlaid satinwood £5,500-£8,500
mahogany, little decoration £2,750-£3,750
satinwood, little decoration £3,000-£4,500

1016 The next step down from the full Carlton House writing table. A mahogany writing table which uses figured mahogany veneers and variegated crossbanding to good decorative effect. The number of side drawers flanking the centre well has increased but the back has been simplified and concave surfaces reduced to the oval-panelled hinged upper compartment lids.
1890-1910   *£2,500-£3,500*

1017 An even simpler form of the Carlton House writing table in mahogany, which retains a similar upper structure to the previous example but now has two simple drawers under the writing surface.
1890-1910   *£1,100-£1,500*

1018 A Shoolbred & Co. rosewood writing table in the Carlton House manner but with variations — Adam inlays and shield-shaped mirrors for decoration. High quality and fine proportion.
1890-1900   *£1,800-£2,500*

1019 A Georgian Revival mahogany writing table of a type which might easily double as a sideboard or even a dressing table (except that the fixed mirror is too low for a dressing table and has to do with the provision/reflection of light rather than self-viewing). The drawers are crossbanded with satinwood and stringing lines are inlaid into them and the legs. The top has an inset panel of leather, crossbanded in mahogany, as a writing surface. Not as popular as a pedestal desk — the raising of furniture on open legs or feet was to do with a late 19th century preoccupation with disease — circulation of air was considered an essential preventative.
1880-1900   *£1,300-£1,900*

1020 (Left) An 'Edwardian Sheraton' satinwood writing table inlaid with 'Adam' marquetry decoration and ebony stringing lines. The centre drawer is painted with the portrait of an 18th century lady in a cocky, plumed riding hat. The top surface is panelled in leather with satinwood crossbanding and marquetry.
1880-1910   *£2,000-£3,000*

1021 (Left) A writing table by Gillows in mahogany with an interesting blend of 1880s incised-line panels and Aesthetic spindled galleries round undertrays, veneered in burr yew, which unite the turned legs. The drawers have inset fruitwood panels carved in bas-relief with shell and leaf decoration. The rectangular top has a tooled leather inset panel.
1870-1890   *£1,500-£2,500*

1022 (Above) An Edwards & Roberts mahogany writing table-cum-desk, inlaid with satinwood and banded with satinwood in the classic Edwardian Sheraton manner. A handsome, high quality piece by a celebrated firm.
1890-1910   *£2,500-£3,500*

1023 Three writing tables in 18th century styles, using square tapering or turned legs, brass ring handles with circular pressed plates and with drawers in the frieze. The central example has small upper drawers as well. All have an inset leather top. 1890-1920

£550-£900

WARDROBES

Although the wardrobe, with hanging space inside or shelved and drawered like a clothes press, had an important function in the Victorian bedroom, its design in Loudon's 1833 *Encyclopedia* was of a minimalist, functional character. Shoolbred's catalogue forty-three years later shows such simple wardrobes almost completely unchanged. Yet, at the same time, another page of Shoolbred confirms that bedroom furniture was subject to fashion like everything else and that Reformed Gothic and Georgian Revival entered the bedroom door equally with sub-classicism.

The period wardrobe has not much been collected except by trade breakers who need the useful material — panels, doors, mirrors, mouldings, pediments, cornices — for 'restoration' of other pieces or for outright rebuilding into more desirable 'antiques' such as large bookcases. Even now, unless a wardrobe is part of a bedroom suite deemed to be desirable *en masse* — an Edwardian Sheraton, say, or a Reformed Gothic, or Aesthetic Movement suite of particular merit — then its value tends to remain low. 19th century wardrobes, even when traced in Gothic fancy, or planked in Reformed Gothic or Arts and Crafts honesty, are often too large, too encumbering, for the modern bedroom. There is a market for them, however, and the Georgian Revival or Edwardian Sheraton versions lead this market. It would be impossible to produce these inlaid pieces now at the price at which they still tend to sell, so perhaps there is a potential for upward movement of price — if a sufficient number of large bedrooms and collectors are to be found.

An exception may be made for the pine wardobe (q.v), particularly the smaller variety with drawers, which has become a stock-in-trade item with pine dealers, but which is, very often, of Continental origin.

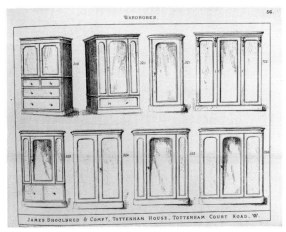
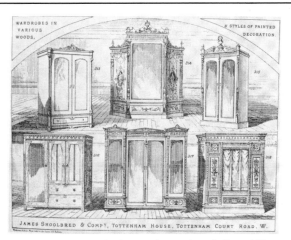

1030 An interesting contrast of wardrobe styles from Shoolbred's catalogue of 1876. The simpler versions (left) could have come from Loudon's work of the 1830s — the design has changed very little. The page (right), however, shows the influences of Reformed Gothic (lower left, planked oak) and Georgian Revival (centres and lower right, 'Adam' decoration) in the large pieces illustrated.

1031 A large mahogany breakfront wardrobe. See Colour Plate 76.

1032 Clothes press wardrobes of typical Edwardian type, based on late 18th century Georgian models. In walnut and oak.
1900-1910
£100-£140

1034 Mahogany clothes press in the 'Sheraton' style with boxwood stringing.
1900-1910
£400-£600

1033 A comprehensive wardrobe in oak. The long shallow drawers in the lower section were for trousers and were fitted with presses, a section which could be reconstructed as a folio chest.
1900-1910
£120-£150

1035 Small Edwardian wardrobe with dressing chest and washstand *en suite*. Typical of many such sets made in large numbers in the period.
1900-1910
wardrobe only £70-£90

284

1036 Large oak wardrobe *en suite* with dressing chest and washstand. Note the deep drawers under the hanging section. The inlay is of ebony and pewter.
1900-1910   *wardrobe only £100-£200*

1038 (Above) A double-door mirrored wardrobe of 'Sheraton' design with a centre breakfront section containing three deep drawers below a central door inlaid with marquetry and banded with satinwood. Satinwood banding embellishes the carcase uprights and satinwood highlights the dentil moulding under the deep top moulding. In the past the temptation to convert a piece like this into a breakfront bookcase has proved irresistible to some cabinet makers and restorers, so that not too many are left in this original condition.
1890-1900   *£700-£1,000*

1037 (Left) A veneered satinwood wardrobe suite including a shield-back Hepplewhite-style chair (solid wood) with turned legs and a bedside cabinet veneered to match the wardrobe. Note how these turned legs are painted with black stringing lines to give the impression of reeding. The floral decoration is painted and the oval medallions depicting classical figures are also probably painted although on some furniture these scenes were put on by means of a printed transfer.
1900-1920   *wardrobe only £700-£950*

Colour Plate 77. A glorious example of an oak Liberty's wardrobe in the art nouveau style with a deep top moulding above enamel insets. The asymmetric design incorporates a smaller cupboard with painted panels to the doors, set above the drawers.
1895-1910

£1,200-£1,800

1039 A mahogany wardrobe crossbanded in satinwood, with two drawers below, of a type made in large numbers.
1880-1900   *£600-£900*

1040 Inlaid mahogany and 'Sheraton' wardrobes from the catalogue of William Morris & Co. c.1900. Both owe much to late 19th century design.
1900-1910   *left, mahogany £200-£300*
                                              right, if satinwood £500-£750

1041 Further wardrobes from the William Morris & Co. catalogue of c.1900. They were all made in mahogany and their dentillated top mouldings are derived from Georgian examples but the rather self-conscious panelling is not.
1900-1910   *£100-£300*

1042 An oak Liberty's wardrobe in the art nouveau style. See Colour Plate 77.

287

WASHSTANDS

At the start of Victoria's reign the washstand was still Georgian in conception. Loudon shows two or three forms, the simpler for cottages, the more sophisticated for villas. These washstands were, however, uncompromising pieces of furniture which left no doubt as to their purpose and can not be used for much else.

The washstand-table, on which a jug and basin set could be placed, was of a more adaptable nature and the contemporary antique trade has done much to find a new role — as writing or occasional table — for these pieces, usually by removing the back.

Decorative washstands with marble tops and tiled backs, for long unsaleable, have had a revival, especially if the marble is in one piece (i.e. without a hole in it) and the tiles are from a collectable maker.

The washstand was also much produced in pine (q.v) and further examples are illustrated in that section.

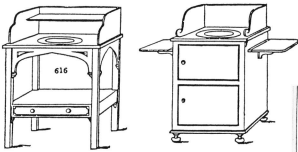

1050 Washstands for cottages from Loudon, 1833, showing, left, a 'Gothic' style, with a hole cut in the top to receive a basin and a shelf in the back board to hold a glass, trays for brushes, etc. This table could be made of oak or of deal painted and grained in imitation of that wood. The example on the right has two enclosed cupboards, one 'to hold the ewer, and the other a night-vase'. There are two hinged shelves supported by fly-brackets, so that they could be folded down when not in use.

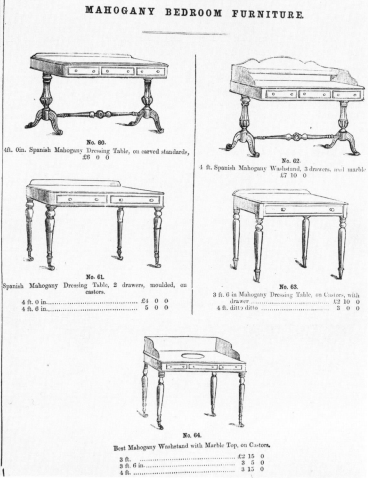

MAHOGANY BEDROOM FURNITURE.

No. 60.
4ft. 0in. Spanish Mahogany Dressing Table, on carved standards, £6 0 0

No. 62.
4 ft. Spanish Mahogany Washstand, 3 drawers, and marble £7 10 0

No. 61.
Spanish Mahogany Dressing Table, 2 drawers, moulded, on castors.
4 ft. 0 in. £4 0 0
4 ft. 6 in. 5 0 0

No. 63.
3 ft. 6 in Mahogany Dressing Table, on Castors, with drawer £2 10 0
4 ft. ditto ditto 3 0 0

No. 64.
Best Mahogany Washstand with Marble Top, on Castors.
3 ft. £2 15 0
3 ft. 6 in. 3 5 0
4 ft. 3 15 0

1051 An enclosed wash-hand stand for a villa, from Loudon, 1833, to be 'placed commonly in a library closet, or in a gentleman's study or business room. There is a slip of wood on the underside of the top, which drops down in front and completes the panel, thus shutting the whole up close.' The glass is on a rack and the cupboards may be 'fitted up with any convenience that is desired'.

1052 Mahogany bedroom furniture from Maddox's catalogue of 1882 showing, top right and bottom, washstands which had hardly changed design since, in the bottom case, the 1830s. They had marble tops, which is what distinguishes them from 'dressing' tables shown on the same page. Many of these have been scrapped but those which survive have been adapted for writing purposes.

1053 The mahogany washstand as it was in the late Georgian and early Victorian period. The deep back was intended to take the splashes but the leg turning and cock beading to the drawers are the same as those on side and writing tables of the late Georgian era.
1820-1840 *£500-£700*

1054 The Victorian version of the previous example. The leg turning has acquired baluster shapes and the drawers have lost their cockbeading. The piece awaits removal of the back and the insertion of a leather panel to convert it into a writing table.
1840-1880 *£400-£600*

1055 A washstand from a pitch-pine suite. See Colour Plate 78.

1056 A pine version of the previous example. See Colour Plate 79.

1057 A washstand with Reformed Gothic treatment, particularly in the double-column end supports and feet, united by a stretcher, but with an Arts and Crafts influence in the black and white inlays and tiling to the back.
1870-1885 *£2,500-£3,500*

1058 A walnut washstand from a bedroom suite in the Reformed Gothic-cum-Arts and Crafts manner. The tiles in the splashback below the mirror depict fairy tales. The 'Gothic' top is embellished with a row of fleurs-de-lis above the mirror whereas the rather solid, plinthed base is inlaid with ivory floral and quatrefoil motifs.
1870-1885 *£2,000-£3,000*

1059 Mahogany washstand with marble top and back. Inlaid stringing lines in box and ebony.
c.1900   *£120-£170*

1060 Slightly more 'artistic' washstand with marble top and green tiled back. Inlaid stringing lines in box and ebony. Note the towel rails.
c.1900   *£140-£180*

1061 Oak washstand on turned tapering legs. Green tiled back, marble top, integral wooden towel rails.
1900-1910   *£100-£160*

1062 A Liberty's oak washstand *en suite* with a toilet or dressing table (No. 950). The back is inlaid with pewter tulip heads above a canvas flap. The surface for the washbasin is of lead and there are cupboard doors below.
c.1900   *£300-£400*

Colour Plate 78. A washstand from a pitch-pine suite which combines influences from the Reformed Gothic (base) and Aesthetic Movement (tiles and side supports). Washstands of the major 'designers'' movements have a keen collector's following.
1870-1880   *£1,000-£1,500*

Colour Plate 79. A pine version of No. 1054, with simple square-section tapering legs. The basin is offset from the centre, which is sensible since it leaves a bigger surface to the right for the jug and washing paraphernalia.
1830-1880   *£250-£400*

WHATNOTS

The whatnot is essentially a set of shelves, supported by corner posts or side members and on castors to make it mobile. It seems to have appeared between 1790 and 1800 — the Gillows record books describe and illustrate examples as early as 1790 — and the piece could be of mahogany, rosewood or japanned. Designs are to be found from Smee's catalogue of 1850 to those of Yapp in 1879 and Wyman in 1886.

It was an occasional piece of furniture intended for the display of those objects with which Victorians liked to surround themselves — china, bronze, glass, stone, paper, wood etc. The presence of a drawer adds to value.

1072 A rosewood whatnot supported on four spirally turned uprights, with a drawer under the middle tier. The fretwork gallery round the top has been broken. 1830-1850 ***£450-£600***

1070 A handsome amboyna and black lacquer whatnot with brass gallery and mounts. The fluting of the turned column supports is emphasised by gilding. An example of the influence of French Louis XVI *ébénistes* on English furniture. 1850-1870 ***£600-£900***

1073 A simpler mahogany three-tier whatnot with 'Elizabethan' spiral-turned uprights capped by finials. The fronts of the tiers are gently curved and the leaf-fretted gallery round the top is intact. 1840-1865 ***£400-£600***

1071 A mahogany combined whatnot and Canterbury with spiral turned uprights ending in finials at the corners — the 'Elizabethan' style — and lyre-shaped centre supports to the middle tier. The Canterbury section has turned spindles and fretted uprights to the divisions. The base is ogee moulded with a drawer set in it, above four turned feet. 1840-1860 ***£900-£1,400***

1074 A walnut whatnot with three shaped tiers banded in kingwood and a brass gallery to the top. There is a drawer under the middle tier and ormolu mounts emphasise the edge mouldings. The turned upper supports are capped with ormolu finials and have that spiral grooving incised into them which is found on quite a few period turnings, whereas the lower supports are simply embellished with a central turned collar. 1850-1880 ***£900-£1,200***

1075 A mahogany whatnot with baluster-turned corner uprights set on turned feet with emphasised collars. The middle tier has an extra pair of scrolled side supports and the top is fitted with two scrolled carved handles to emphasise the mobile nature of the piece.
1850-1880   *£600-£900*

1076 The triangular corner whatnot is characteristic of the Victorians and this one is stepped in four receding tiers each supported by turned and finialled uprights. The top fretwork is broken. Each tier has an arcaded fret below it for decoration and the second tier has lost a couple of teeth from this embellishment.
1840-1870   *in good condition £450-£600*

BIBLIOGRAPHY

The reader who wishes to learn more about this very prolific and complex period will not be faced with all that great an availability of choice. The books listed below are some of the major one concerned directly with furniture — reading on certain architects is also recommended.

British Furniture, 1880-1915, Pauline Agius, Antique Collectors' Club, Woodbridge 1978
The Pictorial Dictionary of British 19th Century Furniture Design, Antique Collectors' Club, Woodbridge 1977
Victorian Furniture, R.W. Symonds and B.B. Whineray, London 1962
19th Century Furniture, Elizabeth Aslin, 1962
'England 1830-1901' by Charles Handley Read in *World Furniture*, ed. Helena Hayward, 1965
Victorian Furniture, Simon Jervis, 1968
Charles Rennie Mackintosh, The Complete Furniture, etc., Roger Billcliffe, 1979
The Adventure of British Furniture, 1851-1951, David Joel, London 1953
Victorian and Edwardian Furniture and Interiors, Jeremy Cooper, 1987
Gimson and the Barnsleys, Mary Comino, 1980
The Arts and Crafts Movement, Gillian Naylor, 1971
Architects' Designs for Furniture, Jill Lever, 1982
C.F.A. Voysey, Duncan Simpson, London 1979

DESIGNERS
AND CONTEMPORARY SOURCES

In the text various references are made to designers, contemporary design books and catalogues of furniture retailers in addition to the celebrated Chippendale, Hepplewhite and Sheraton of the 18th century. The dates of some of these 19th century sources can be difficult to establish since there were many re-issues of some of them, such as Thomas King. The list which follows sets out the dates of most of the important ones referred to in the text.

The reader is recommended to peruse the *Pictorial Dictionary of British 19th Century Furniture Design,* with an introduction by Edward Joy, published by the Antique Collectors' Club, for a more detailed selection of 5,000 examples, taken from contemporary sources.

Adam, Robert and James. Two of the four sons of a Scottish architect, William Adam, all of whom followed their father's profession. Robert Adam is generally acknowledged to have taken the leading part in the production of the *Works on Architecture* produced with James. Robert was born in 1728 and died in 1792. He was in Rome in the 1750s and instigated a Classical Revival based, like William Kent, on an overall concept of design covering a house and all its furnishings.

Ashbee, C.R. See page 37.

Baillie Scott, M.H. See page 37.

Barnsley, Ernest and Sidney. See page 40.

Blackie. *The Cabinet Maker's Assistant* of 1853 was a treatise cum trade manual subscribed to by 400 tradesmen all over the country, including William Smee (q.v.).

Bridgens, Richard. Published *Furniture with Candelabra and Interior Decoration* in 1838 although there was possibly an 1833 edition. Very much associated with the 'Elizabethan' style.

Burges, William. See page 30.

Charles, Richard. Designer who produced a *Cabinet Maker's Book of Designs,* c.1867.

Chippendale, Thomas. Not very well documented personally, but famous for his book of designs *The Gentleman and Cabinet Maker's Director,* first published in 1754, and for his work as a cabinet maker and carver, particularly in mahogany. The book starts with the five classical orders, but rapidly reflects the contemporary taste for Chinese, Rococo and Gothic styles. It is suggested that Lock and Copland's book *New Book of Ornaments* of 1746 was a source of Chippendale's. A very important book, Chippendale's 'Director', as it is called, is now used to describe the styles of domestic furniture illustrated therein, although some of the pieces were never made.

Clay, Henry. Originator of papier-mâché furniture, about 1772. Made by building up layers of paper with pitch and oil over an iron frame. Usually finished by painting and decorating with inlay.

Collcutt, T.E. See page 32.

Collinson & Lock. See page 32.

Eastlake, Charles. See Gothic Style, page 30.

Edwards and Roberts. A Victorian firm who specialised in 18th century reproductions.

Gillow, Robert. Gillows of Lancaster were in business in the mid-18th century − Hepplewhite was a Gillow apprentice − and continued on throughout the 19th century. Robert Gillow came from Lancaster, where the furniture for the Oxford Street branch in London was made. The firm's Cost Books from about 1790, with their designs, are now in the Westminster Public Library. The first reference to a davenport occurs in their Cost Books − 'To Captain Davenport, a desk'.

Gimson, Ernest. See page 41.

Godwin, E.W. See pages 33-34.

Heal and Son. See page 40.

Hepplewhite, George. Died in 1786, but his *Cabinet Maker and Upholsterer's Guide,* published posthumously in 1788, greatly influenced many cabinet makers. He is well known for his chairs, for the splayed curved foot, which replaced brackets on chests, and for much inlaid decoration on furniture. He used classical motifs a great deal, which were similar to those of Adam.

The shield and oval back chairs are particularly associated with Hepplewhite, as is the Prince of Wales' feathers motif, but he also published many other designs, including squarer backs of chairs, which we now associate with Sheraton. Knife boxes, cellarets, sideboards and particularly serpentine and bow-fronted commodes appear in Hepplewhite's designs; so do square chests of drawers with both bracket and splayed feet.

Holland and Sons. A celebrated 19th century firm who produced French and English 18th century reproductions.

Hope, Thomas. Scholar and architect who published *Household Furniture and Decoration* in 1807. His designs were of formalised classical type with much zoological decoration and drew on nearly all the ancient civilisations for their forms.

Jennens and Bettridge. Obtained a patent, in 1825, for decorating papier-mâché with pearl-sheen inlay, a feature used on papier-mâché furniture for some considerable years afterwards.

Johnson, Thomas. A mirror man, contemporary with Chippendale and described as a carver, c.1755, of Grafton Street, Soho, who produced a design book of very intricate rococo frames and console tables.

Jones, Owen (1809-74). Published *The Grammar of Ornament,* 1856. Designer associated with the firm of Jackson & Graham, who were taken over by Collinson & Lock. Also associated with Moorish designs following a publication on the Alhambra.

Kent, William. Architect, born in Yorkshire in 1684. Went to Rome in 1710 and returned to assert classical values upon house and furniture in a somewhat grand manner. The broken pediment, the supporting eagle, festoons of fruit, ball-and-claw feet, all on a gigantic scale, are the hallmarks of William Kent. He died in 1748, but had considerable influence in the early mahogany period of 1730-1745.

King, Thomas. An upholsterer who produced a number of pattern books between 1829 and 1840. Best known of these is *The Modern Style of Cabinet Work Exemplified* of 1829, which was reissued until 1862.

Lethaby, William. See page 37.

Liberty & Co. Much associated with art nouveau furniture. Founded in Regent Street in 1875.

Light, C. & R. Of Curtain Road, Shoreditch. Cabinet makers and looking glass manufacturers. Wholesalers who issued a catalogue in 1880.

Loudon, John C. *The Encyclopedia of Cottage, Farm and Villa Architecture and Furniture* of 1833 was reissued until 1867. A Scot who compiled publications prolifically, Loudon had stern views on the four styles which were then fashionable (Grecian, Gothic, Tudor and Louis XIV) and his book is a fund of information on the general furnishing of its time. It was highly influential and practical, since it did not concentrate on the most expensive and stylish furniture; Loudon directed himself at contemporary interiors of all kinds.

Mackintosh, Charles Rennie. See page 37.

Mackmurdo, A.H. See page 36.

Maddox, George. Maddox and Son first produced a catalogue of furniture in 1865, but the one used here is their 1882 version, particularly for bedroom pieces.

Morris, William & Co. See entries under Gothic Reformers and Arts and Crafts Style sections, pages 25 and 36.

Norman and Stacey. London firm of fashionable furnishers who published a catalogue and were prominent 1900-1910.

Pugin, A.W.N. *Gothic Furniture in the Style of the Fifteenth Century* was published in 1835. See page 25.

Shaw, Richard Norman. See page 31.

Sedding, J.D. Architect designer whose office was next door to Morris & Co. in Oxford Street in 1886. Creative force in the Arts and Crafts Movement.

Seddon, J.P. See page 28.

Shearer, Thomas. Cabinet maker and author of *Designs for Household Furniture,* 1788. A contemporary of Hepplewhite and Sheraton, but his designs are nearer to Sheraton in style.

Sheraton, Thomas. Not a cabinet maker but a publisher of designs, Thomas Sheraton produced, starting in 1791, *The Cabinet Maker's and Upholsterer's Drawing Book* using many of the same motifs as Adam and Hepplewhite. He is associated with squareness: square chair backs and tapering square section legs. Inlays and painted decoration were also used. Many quite complicated dressing, writing and Pembroke tables appear in his designs, which include the Carlton House writing table, cylinder and tambour tables, washstands, kidney-shaped, games and sofa tables. Very popular in the late 19th century.

Shoolbred, J. & Co. of Tottenham Court Road, London. A high quality furniture shop like Heals. The catalogue of 1876 is used here.

Smee, William and Sons. Wholesale and retail firm who produced *Designs for Furniture, 1850-1855.*

Smith, George. Cabinet maker and author of *A Collection of Designs for Household Furniture and Interior Decoration,* 1808.

Talbert, Bruce J. Published *Gothic Forms Applied to Furniture, Metal Work and Decoration for Domestic Purposes* in 1876. Highly influential. See page 28.

Taylor, John. An upholsterer of Covent Garden who produced his *Upholsterer's and Cabinet Maker's Pocket Assistant* c.1825.

Toms, W. Published *36 New, Original and Practical Designs for Chairs* in 1840, in which balloon-backs appear.

Voysey, C.F.A. See page 37.

Walton, George. See page 37.

Watt, William. Published a design book in 1877 entitled *Art Furniture from Designs by E.W. Godwin, with Hints and Suggestions of Domestic Furniture.* Had an art furniture warehouse in Grafton Street and had produced Anglo-Japanese furniture for some time. See pages 33-34.

Webb, Philip. See page 28.

Wells, Percy. Head of cabinet department of Shoreditch Technical Institute. Produced, with John Hooper of City & Guilds Institute, *Modern Cabinet Work* in 1909, revised editions up to 1924. The book covers both reproduction and modern designs. Concerned with eliminating dust, over-ornamentation, flashy or flimsy furniture.

Whitaker, Henry. Produced *Designs of Cabinet and Upholstery Furniture in the Most Modern Style* in 1825 and *The Practical Cabinet-Maker and Upholsterer's Treasury of Designs* in 1847 in which seven styles are set out. A distinguished designer for royalty and the aristocracy.

Wood, Henry. A general trade designer who produced pattern books between 1840 and 1850.

Wright and Mansfield. A firm of cabinet makers of the period 1860-1886 who made fine classical 18th century designs of Adam and Sheraton inspiration.

Wyburd, Leonard F. Head of design studio at Liberty's in 1883. Responsible for variants on Thebes stool and washstand/dressing tables. Retired in 1903 and became an antique dealer in Wigmore Street (see Sotheby's catalogue, Groombridge Place sale, September 1992).

Wyman and Sons. Produced periodicals as well as acting as retailers. Cabinet Makers Pattern Books started in 1877 with third edition in 1882.

Yapp, G.W. Published *Art Industry etc.* in 1879 with 1,200 illustrations. He was Assistant Commissioner at the 1851 Exhibition and his emphasis is much on exhibition pieces.

INDEX

Page numbers in bold type refer to colour illustrations